MW01095101

OUR
GLORIOUS
INHERITANCE

**DEEPER
REVELATION
BOOKS**

"Holding forth the word of life . . ." Phil. 2:16

OUR GLORIOUS INHERITANCE

Volume One . . . Hidden Treasure, Beyond the Veil

by
MIKE SHREVE

Foreword by Jamie Buckingham

An exhaustive study of the revelation of the titles of the children of God

---

• REVISED EDITION •

**DEEPER
REVELATION
BOOKS**

"Holding forth the word of life . . ." Phil. 2:16

Printed by: Faith Printing Company
4210 Locust Hill Rd.
Taylors, SC 29687-8911
(803) 895-3822

Cover art: design by Mike Shreve, art work by Tina Hardy.

ISBN: 0-942507-00-2
ISBN: 0-942507-04-5 (8-Volume Set)

1st Printing — June 1986, 2nd Printing — April 1987, 3rd Printing — March 1988, 4th Printing — March 1989

All ministry correspondence should be directed to:
  Mike Shreve
  P.O. Box 700
  Cleveland, TN 37364

All correspondence dealing with book orders, etc.:
  Deeper Revelation Books
  2427 Fifeshire Dr.
  Winter Park, FL 32792

DEDICATION

In sincere appreciation of Rev. H. Richard Hall, founder and overseer of the United Christian Church and Ministerial Association, this series is dedicated and sent forth. I thank God for the inspiration, revelation, leadership, and vision I have received over the years through this highly anointed minister of Christ.

COVER ART

The treasure chest, the menorah candelabrum and the crown represent the greatly enriching, illuminating, and royal heritage which is hidden "beyond the veil" of flesh consciousness in every child of God. This analagous comparison is the "chapter one theme" that introduces this concept of the revelation of **the titles of the children of God.**

TABLE OF CONTENTS

ACKNOWLEDGEMENTS

I am deeply indebted to certain individuals for their assistance in typing and proofreading this first volume of OUR GLORIOUS INHERITANCE. Some have invested many more hours of their lives than others, but all were generous and unselfish in using their talents to produce this finished work. I appreciate them very much. I pray God's richest blessings especially on my wife, Elizabeth; my mother, Winnie Shreve; and Cindy Godwin. What a blessing Winnie Shreve and Sara Thayer have been as well, overseeing the distribution of Deeper Revelation Books with all the resulting office work. Also deeply appreciated is Andrew Shreve whose counsel and assistance have always proven to be greatly beneficial. Furthermore, many thanks are surely to be extended to Margaret Kimpler, John and Nancy Schmelling, and Larry Labensky for their essential and generous help throughout this project.

FOREWORD

On the Sunday my father died I spent a long time kneeling beside his bed . . . remembering. After the funeral director, an old friend of the family, had left with his body, I wandered through the quiet house. My wife stayed back in the bedroom with my mother. I knew, as word spread that he had gone home, others in the community would be arriving to add comfort. But I needed those moments to be alone. Remembering.

I wandered into his study and sat at his desk. Across the years, since his retirement as a businessman, he had sat there — studying his Bible, writing checks to the many ministries he supported and prayed for, making notations in his ledger. I remembered, when I first entered the ministry, standing behind him and joking with him as he balanced his books.

"When you die the one thing I want to inherit is your order and neatness."

He turned, looked up from his chair, and with his characteristic twinkle in his eye said, "Son, you don't have to wait. I now bequeath it to you." Then, after a pause and a chuckle, he asked pointedly, "Now, what are you going to do with your inheritance?"

All that came to mind when I sat down and began reading Mike Shreve's books covering the "titles of our inheritance." The world is struggling with an identity crisis. Our national leaders are saying the war against drugs may be lost forever. Why do children, street people, businessmen fill their bodies with killer-drugs? The answer: They don't know who they are.

All around us gifted people are crashing, victims of poor self-image as they search in all the wrong places for identity. They don't know who they are.

In this series of books Mike Shreve takes the many hundreds of titles of our inheritance and explains who God says we are. As I read through these wonderful titles, and nodded in understanding as I read Mike's explanations, I realized: this is what is wrong with the world, this is what's wrong with me. We don't know who we are.

Once I realize exactly who I am in Christ I will no longer do terrible things to my body, my mind, my spirit. Once I realize who others are, I'll no longer exploit them, harm them, use them, degrade them. I have inherited God's glory. All I have to do is answer the question of my Heavenly Father as He looks at me with a twinkle in His eye: "Now, son, what are you going to do with your inheritance?"

Jamie Buckingham
Melbourne, Florida

The first volume in
an eight-volume series
on

The Revelation
of the
Titles of the Children
of God

HIDDEN TREASURE BEYOND THE VEIL

". . . the kingdom of heaven is like unto a treasure hid in a field."
(Matthew 13:44)

*"Which hope we have as an anchor of the soul, both sure and stedfast, and which entereth into that **within the veil.**"*
(Hebrews 6:19)

INTRODUCTORY CHAPTER

Hidden Treasure, Beyond the Veil

• It is of the utmost importance that every child of God search out, in the Word, the various *titles* given to those who have been born again and washed in the blood of Jesus.

There is no better way of uncovering the portions of the Word that directly pertain to us and there is no better way of discovering our potential rights of inheritance.

Even in the natural, by knowing a man's *title,* before ever meeting the man, you can assume a great deal about his possible influence and rank in society, the amount of respect due to him, and his level of material prosperity.

• *A title is a descriptive name that indicates rank, office, or privilege and is usually given as a gesture or mark of respect, recognition and honor.*

God, in His Word, has given His people a great number of *titles* and each one is a revelation of our rank in the universal plan of God, and an insight into the God-given privileges and responsibilities that belong to us . . . by virtue of being members of His kingdom.

If we do not know our *titles,* then we do not know our rights, nor the influence that we can have in this world, and the position that we will inherit in the world to come.

It is also just as certain that we cannot fully understand these *title-rights* except God pull back the *veil of flesh-consciousness* and grant us what Paul called — "the spirit of wisdom and revelation in the knowledge of God." This grace is poured forth so — "the eyes of your understanding being enlightened; that ye may know what is the hope of His calling, and what the riches of the *glory of his inheritance* in the saints." (Ephesians 1:17-18)

In fact, the Scripture reference mentioned above is the very one that provided the inspired words for the title of this book, and it is the very prayer that we pray for all who begin this thrilling and soul-fulfilling Word-journey.

OUR CROWN OF GLORY

I read in a newspaper, not long ago, of a beggar who died penniless. He was accustomed to having nothing, living in condemned buildings and always lacking sufficient food and clothing.

Loneliness and poverty were certainly his continual companions.

After his death, the local officials searched the appropriate records in order to notify the man's relatives.

Much to their surprise, they discovered that the man they thought was just a tramp was actually heir to an extremely large sum of money.

Apparently, he never knew it.

He could have had all the good things of life, but instead, he lived and died in squalor and destitution.

This certainly was an awful tragedy.

But there is a tragedy far worse that happens continually.

Children of God, ignorant of the riches of their inheritance, often live like beggars spiritually, slaves to circumstance and sin, when they should be living like kings in the abundant life that Jesus promised.

No wonder God declared, "My people are destroyed for lack of knowledge." (Hosea 4:6)

And no wonder that God said . . .

> *"Wisdom is the principal thing; therefore get wisdom: and with all thy getting, get understanding.*
>
> *Exalt her, and she shall promote thee: she shall bring thee to honour, when thou dost embrace her.*
>
> *She shall give to thine head an ornament of grace: a **crown of glory** shall she deliver to thee."*
>
> (Proverbs 4:7-9)

• Children of God cannot earnestly and sincerely search the Scriptures to discover their God-given *title-rights* without that same revelation wisdom promoting them, bringing them to honor, and *crowning them with glory and grace.*

Diligently searching into the unsearchable riches available to us in Jesus Christ must therefore be our consuming passion and our highest single goal in life.

Proverbs 25:2 declares that — "It is the glory of God to conceal a thing: but the honour of kings is to search out a matter."

There is no greater honor given to *God's royal offspring* than to be allowed entrance into the heart of God, where through the Word and by the Spirit, we explore those "matters" which are most important.

It is there that we discover our *crown of glory* and it is there that we return all the glory to Him.

HIDDEN MANNA

Isaiah the prophet declared that God is verily a God that *hideth* Himself. (Isaiah 45:15)

He cloaks Himself in secrecy. He shrouds Himself in mystery.

He purposefully makes it somewhat difficult to attain a deep intimacy with Him . . . for by doing so, He tests the depth of our love and the strength of our commitment to Him.

Passing through such a test, though, is certainly not wasted time.

For those who succeed in conquering the many carnal obstacles set before us all receive a blessed pledge from the risen Christ:

> *"To him that overcometh will I give to eat of the hidden manna."*   (Revelation 2:17)

Manna was the name given to that peculiar bread from heaven that sustained the seed of Abraham during their trek through the wilderness of Sin.

It was quite visible and easily gathered, falling with the hoar frost of heaven daily around the camp of Israel.

It became a predominant Old Testament symbol of the Word of God, the very bread of life that sustains our souls during this difficult earthly sojourn.

Much of this "spiritual kind of manna" is also easily "gathered" — for simple surface reading of the Bible imparts a great deal of necessary truth.

But for those who consecrate themselves more deeply, a deeper comprehension of the Word is imparted as well.

The reward is labeled *hidden manna* — the often concealed revelation of the deeper mysteries of God.

It is significant to see that the only manna ever *hidden* to the children of Israel was stored in a golden bowl and placed in the ark of the covenant . . . beyond the veil in the holy of holies.

Without controversy, that golden bowl represented Jesus — for the gold speaks of His divinity, and the *hidden manna,* of the secrets of the ages which He contains.

In Him we discover both the revelation of the character of God and the revelation of our potential inheritance as His many brethren.

In Him we discover the perfect manifestation of all our *title-rights* and *title-positions* . . . for He is the Forerunner, Our Elder Brother . . . our divine example in all things.

Such revelation-knowledge nourishes the inward man, causing us to grow in grace and mature in God.

Therefore the entitlement is so appropriate.

Hidden manna . . . "more to be desired . . . than gold, yea than much fine gold: sweeter also than honey and the honeycomb." (Psalm 19:10)

HIDDEN TREASURE

• Speaking of "hidden things," Jesus further explained our inheritance this way:

". . . the kingdom of heaven is like unto trea-
sure hid in a field; the which when a man hath
found, he hideth, and for joy thereof goeth and
selleth all that he hath and buyeth that field."
(Matthew 13:44)

It is vitally important that we realize this particular reference to *the kingdom of heaven* is not just referring to a place that the soul of a believer goes to at the moment of death. It is referring as well to a spiritual realm of intimacy with God that we can walk in and live in . . . right here, right now!

In this kingdom realm of God's presence, there is . . .
An eternal fountain of peace,
A never-ending river of grace,
An everlasting supply of mercy,
A boundless, fathomless ocean of love,
And an infinite number of ideas and spiritual concepts . . . creative, inspired thoughts coming from the very mind of God Himself, communicated with words that the Holy Ghost teaches, comparing spiritual things with spiritual.

Words are powerful, even in the natural, but anointed words, even more so, are mighty through God.

Words are the building blocks of the universe, both natural and celestial.

Divinely inspired words contain creative life.

They group together in families, and become life transforming ideas.

Jesus contains the sum total of all the God-authored thoughts, words and spiritual concepts available to us.

• **This Word-treasure was first hidden from us;** then God graciously opened our eyes and we beheld and understood the mystery of **who Jesus is.**

We heard the report of others who found Him, and faith was stirred in us that we could do the same.

We *dug deep* and found this life-giving *treasure* that has been *hidden* in the world for centuries (and, truthfully, He has always been *hidden* — first of all in a little remote town called Bethlehem; then, on a little remote hill called Calvary; and now, in a book often despised and neglected called the Bible).

When we discovered the *great riches* of salvation by grace, out of gratitude and — *"for the joy thereof"* — each one of us had to *"go and sell all we had."*

We had to prove ourselves willing to give up our lives, our hopes, our dreams and our will, in order to "buy," not only the treasure, but also the field that contains the treasure (for through our commitment to God we will one day inherit the earth).

4

• **Now this treasure is hidden in us** . . . (and Paul did say — "we have this *treasure* in earthen vessels, that the excellency of the power may be of God, and not of us"). (II Corinthians 4:7)

This hidden treasure was initially the revelation of *who Jesus is.*

Now, this treasure, having been transferred to our hearts, is the ever unfolding revelation of *who we are "in Christ."*

We must first *discover* (ascertain, determine and unearth) this great wealth of wisdom and knowledge that is veiled in mystery, hidden deep down in the secret chambers of the regenerated spirit; then we must *bring forth.*

Jesus said — *"A good man out of the good treasure of the heart bringeth forth good things."* (Matthew 12:35)

The smallest, inspired insight concerning the riches of our inheritance is truly a "good thing" (yes, a glorious thing).

Every little intricate detail in this eternal revelation is, in a sense, a precious stone . . . a priceless gift from the God who delights in sharing divinity with humanity.

This inward treasure chest will benefit us little though, if it remains an untapped resource — undiscovered and unused.

Again, we must first *discover* this treasure (in many cases, by first beholding and discovering the absolute perfection of these *title-positions* as reflected in the firstborn Son). We then hide this treasure in our hearts, rejoice with joy, pay the price, and then progressively *bring forth,* in our own consciousness and in the consciousness of others, the awareness of "who we are in Christ," what we have inherited, and what therefore we can potentially become.

This "casket of jewels" contains the secret of the ages (the mystery which has been hidden from ages and generations, but now is made manifest to the saints . . . Christ in us, the hope of glory).

Every contributing concept and every individual, heaven-sent idea which surfaces in our hearts is a valuable jewel of divine knowledge . . . producing a spiritual heap of glittering diamonds, rubies, opals, and emeralds, that, once beheld, will surely leave us awestruck.

We can be satisfied with a partial possession of our inheritance and become quite useless to the kingdom and quite stagnant spiritually, or we can persistently and increasingly *discover and bring forth.*

Electricity has always existed, but it had to be *discovered.*

Gravity, friction, inertia, and the other natural laws of the universe have always existed; but they had to be *discovered.*

Someone now must accept the challenge of *discovering* that which is, as of yet, undiscovered spiritually and climb the divine mountain that has never been scaled.

5

Someone must dare to explore the supernatural unknown . . . and then pull back the curtain that others might see.

BEYOND THE VEIL

• In the Old Testament, God gave Moses a plan for something called the tabernacle.

This tabernacle consisted of a fenced-in tent, containing seven main articles of furniture — the altar of sacrifice, the laver, the table of shewbread, the golden candlestick, the altar of incense, the ark of the covenant and the mercy seat.

This tabernacle was the place where Jehovah would visibly and manifestly reveal Himself to Moses and Aaron, *beyond the veil.*

It is a noteworthy fact that, viewed from the outside, the tabernacle looked ugly, undesirable, and actually somewhat repulsive. All that could be seen was a rough-looking tent, a brazen altar covered with blood, and a large laver where the priests washed as they performed their duties . . . and surely the water was quite dirty and bloody.

The tent itself was covered with weather-beaten badger skins, blackened and brittle from the hot, burning rays of the desert sun, and caked with dirt and dust from the winds that whipped across the arid wilderness wasteland.

There was no outward beauty.
There was no apparent beauty.
There was no evidence of beauty — for the beauty was concealed, hidden within, secreted *beyond the veil.*
The view from the outside and the view from the inside were drastically different.

•• Inside the beauty was spectacular.

The walls were covered with the finest linen . . . purple, scarlet, blue and white, embroidered by cunning workmen with images of heavenly cherubim.

The furniture was all overlaid with gold. In the ark were the tablets of stone, written on miraculously with the very finger of God, a golden bowl full of heavenly manna miraculously preserved, and Aaron's rod that miraculously budded.

But most miraculous and wonderful of all was the Shekinah glory that would appear over the mercy seat.

And how thrilling it must have been to experience the celestial illumination in the holy place, a place that was certainly "charged" with the manifest presence of God.

The golden candlestick, with seven bowls full of oil, provided the only light within this sacred place of worship.

There were no windows allowing any earthly light to come into the

6

tabernacle, and the brilliant light that was kept burning daily was of heavenly origin.

At the outset, fire fell from heaven to consume the animal sacrifices that were placed on the altar. (Leviticus 9:24)

It seems certain that the priests then kept that sacred fire burning as they were commanded (Leviticus 6:13) and used it to light the candlestick daily.

Therefore, those who were chosen of God and blessed of the Most High to walk in that holy sanctuary, were literally walking in a resplendent, celestial light that the world has never known!!

BUT WHAT DOES ALL OF THIS HAVE TO DO WITH THE SIGNIFICANCE AND IMPORTANCE OF THE TITLES OF THE CHILDREN OF GOD?

The answer is very simple.

• This tabernacle in the wilderness represents *Jesus,* for He was, and is, the everlasting *tabernacle* of the living God. In like manner, it also represents *the glory of our inheritance position "in Christ"* . . . for, through salvation, we have also become the dwelling place of deity, the temple of Jehovah.

Isaiah prophesied that, when we would behold Jesus, there would be "no beauty that we should desire Him."

Those who have never experienced the supernatural reality of Jesus Christ are looking at the tabernacle from the outside. Merely beholding the strict and selfless life-style of the Son of God, and the strong message that He preached — quite often, at first, seems very unappealing and undesirable.

Viewed from without, the Christian walk may seem too demanding, too austere.

To take up a cross, deny self and follow the Lamb, in devotion to the righteous and holy principles that He upheld, appears too difficult to accept and even repulsive to some.

To live a crucified life, dying to sin and dying to the flesh, cuts directly against the grain of what the world considers important.

But for those who accept the invitation . . .

For those who dare to go *beyond the veil of flesh-consciousness,* into His presence . . .

For those whose eyes are opened . . .

His beauty is indescribable.

His joy is unspeakable.

His peace passes understanding.

And the revelation of His everlasting love surpasses knowledge itself.

When we enter this tabernacle, this place of divine illumination, then the false light that this world produces can no longer confuse, deceive or mislead us. Instead, the heavenly light of the Word illuminates our path.

God communes with us from the mercy seat.

We are enlightened . . . supernaturally.

We see things from a totally different perspective.

We see the beauty of the Lord.

We behold the exceeding greatness and the radiant glory of this eternal Holy One of Israel, whose name is Immanuel (God with us) and then . . . we actually find ourselves "hid with Christ in God."

If we make the wise choice to remain and yield to the transforming influence of the Son of God, we discover a place of wondrous beauty, complete security, absolute stability and future destiny.

God's immutable promises then and there become our blessed hope — "an anchor of the soul, both sure and stedfast, and which entereth into that *within the veil;* whither the forerunner is for us entered, even Jesus . . ." (Hebrews 6:19-20)

We are no longer hopelessly bound to these natural forms — trapped inside of a poverty-stricken fallen nature.

We behold our God-given heritage, as revealed in our *titles,* and this legacy, this **hidden treasure,** becomes our infinite, spiritual possession.

We perceive the portions of the Word that reveal "who we are in Christ" and **hidden manna** becomes our ever-sustaining, spiritual food.

We are born into the light of God's presence and this **holy of holies,** the secret of His tabernacle, becomes our continual, spiritual dwelling place.

WE DISCOVER THE GLORY OF THE FIRSTBORN SON, JESUS, BUT SIMULTANEOUSLY . . . WE DISCOVER THAT HE HAS PURPOSED TO SHARE THAT SAME GLORY WITH US — ETERNALLY.

THIS IS OUR GLORIOUS INHERITANCE . . . NOW AND FOREVERMORE!

And this is exactly what we intend to "discover and bring forth" through the ensuing chapters of this book *as we thoroughly study sixty-eight of our God-given titles.*

Let us therefore begin our spiritual journey *beyond the veil* . . . lovingly borne by the sweet, precious, Holy Spirit who "searcheth all things, yea, the deep things of God." (1 Corinthians 2:10)

Surely we will not leave this book the same persons that we were when we stepped up on the threshold of chapter one.

THE TITLES

May "the God of our Lord Jesus
Christ, the Father of glory . . . give unto
you the spirit of wisdom and revelation in
the knowledge of Him:
The eyes of your understanding being
enlightened; that ye may know what is the
hope of His calling, and what *THE RICHES
OF THE GLORY OF HIS INHERITANCE
IN THE SAINTS.*
And what is the exceeding greatness of
His power to us-ward who believe, accord-
ing to the working of His mighty power."
(Ephesians 1:17-19)

THE APPLE OF HIS EYE

"He found him in a desert land, and in the waste howling wilderness; He led him about, He instructed him, He kept him as **THE APPLE OF HIS EYE.**" (Deuteronomy 32:10)

THE APPLE OF HIS EYE

"He found him in a desert land, and in the waste howling wilderness; He led him about, He instructed him, He kept him as THE APPLE OF HIS EYE."   (Deuteronomy 32:10)

On a primary level, this scripture refers to Israel — the offspring of Abraham, Isaac and Jacob — and the negative, wasted conditions in which God originally found them.

It also reveals how very dear this chosen nation is to the heart of Jehovah.

As we search out the meaning of this pleasant *title,* in all of its intricate detail, several beautiful and profound revelations come to the surface.

On the highest level of interpretation, the revealed light of this passage expands on the horizon, until it fully embraces God's chosen of the New Covenant as well as the Old.

This *title* definitely applies to every son of God.

THE GATEWAY TO GOD'S HEART

• The **apple of the eye** is the pupil — *the round aperture in the iris of the eye.*

The iris is the colored part of the eye that dilates or constricts to let in varying amounts of light.

But the apple is the centermost part.

It is actually a hole in the iris filled with the same water-like fluid that bathes the eye — a substance called *aqueous humor.*

Light passes through this fluid-filled hole and is then refracted through the lens, producing the image on the retina at the back of the eye.

Therefore, it is simple to see that the apple is veritably the gateway of the soul.

It is definitely one of the most precious and the most protected parts of the body.

The area just around the apple of the eye is quite sensitive, easily irritated and subject to acute pain with the slightest injury.

If damaged severely, it is irreplaceable.

We conclude, therefore, that according to biblical symbolism, being "the apple of God's eye" involves being the very center of His attention and the very gateway to His heart.

Those who are kept as the *apple of His eye,* He watches over intensely to guard and protect, for they are His most precious possession . . . *an irreplaceable treasure.*

This is certainly a fitting description of God's feelings toward Israel because for some strange reason the heart of Jehovah was captured by this seemingly insignificant nation.

And history proves that in all their troubles, He kept them!

In all their calamities and woes, He kept them!

In all their backslidings, He kept them!

And in all their blessings and chastisements, He kept them!

He preserved them, granting what seemed to be an endless stream of grace and an inexhaustible river of mercy.

He overshadowed them in compassion when they were submissive to His will. He severely corrected them when they were not.

But, let no one doubt it . . . He kept them; yet, that which is even more amazing, **He kept them as the apple of His eye!**

He maintained an attitude of devotion toward them, renewing His covenant and commitment over and over again.

He did not preserve the Jews through the Egyptian captivity, the Babylonian captivity and all their other woes just because He felt legally bound or obligated to fulfill His covenant promises.

Quite simply, they remained dear to Him, for He declared — *"I have loved thee with an everlasting love."* (Jeremiah 31:3)

It is a fact of Scripture that God did not choose natural Israel and set His love upon them because they were the greatest of all nations (for they were the least of all nations . . . "the fewest of all people"). (Deuteronomy 7:7)

Neither did the Lord choose them because He foresaw that they would be a totally submissive, holy and obedient people, for it is obvious that many were quite the opposite — perpetually rebellious.

In explaining His motives, God simply said — "I will have mercy on whom I will have mercy and I will have compassion on whom I will have compassion." (Romans 9:15)

But too often the Jews took for granted this outpoured favor and this intimate fellowship they shared with the Father of creation.

Following their miraculous deliverance from Egypt, God was forced to judge the sinful among them with fiery serpents and terrible plagues.

Divine fire fell out of heaven, and the ground opened its mouth from beneath to devour some of the worst.

Thousands fell. They provoked God ten times and drove Him to a breach of promise.

This God of unquestionable justice shut up Canaan land to them and caused them to wander in the Wilderness of Sin for forty years.

They reeled under the awful impact of God's rebuke.

But, wonder of wonders, He still went before them as a cloudy pillar by day and a fiery pillar by night.

He still fed them with manna out of heaven and miraculously provided their natural needs, even to the point of preserving their garments the entire four decades, for He is a great God of preservation.

Jehovah still fought their battles against enemy armies and made them invincible, when they were right in their relationship with Him.

In fact, toward the very end of their journey, a Gentile king named Balak called on a prophet named Balaam to curse Israel saying — "peradventure I shall be able to overcome them." (Numbers 22)

• But God in fury and jealousy spoke to the prophet — *"Thou shalt not curse the people, for they are blessed."*

How utterly amazing!

Even under the chastising rod of the Almighty God, exiled for forty years from the Land of Promise, they were still called a blessed people by God — more blessed than any other nation in the world. Why?

Because Jehovah was in their midst.

The Lord God was with them, and "the shout of a king [was] among them" when Israel had no other king but the mighty God.

• In fact, Balaam prophesied to King Balak that God had not even beheld iniquity in Jacob, nor seen perverseness in Israel.

As perverse and wicked as they had been, apparently, after they repented, God justified them, refusing to see their sins and blotting them out forever from His sight.

The eternal plan of the great I AM continued to overshadow them in every circumstance — (a plan that would span centuries and millenniums . . . a plan that would ultimately open the door to everlasting life and the coming of the kingdom of God to earth).

Yes — He kept them — as *the apple of His eye.*

He kept pouring out fresh mercy and reaching for Israel in ever-increasing ways, even eventually becoming incarnate in human flesh, and taking upon Himself the form of a man.

But again they rebelled and received Him not, crying — *"crucify Him"* — *"His blood be on us and on our children."* (Matthew 27:25)

It is almost incomprehensible why the Lord did not completely reject the Israelites after receiving such cruel treatment at their hands, but He did not.

It is true that God answered their plea and, in 70 A.D., a Roman leader named Titus burned Jerusalem to the ground, scattering the Jews all over the world, for they had to reap what they had sown.

It is true that their dispersion lasted almost 1,900 years. But during this time it is also true that God miraculously preserved their identity as a nation, and kept them through numerous times of persecution.

He never stopped watching over His chosen nation.

Then something even more phenomenal took place.

15

They said it could not be done. They said it was impossible.
God did it anyway.

He overruled men's opinions, exercised His sovereign will, and in 1948 the Jews were restored to their homeland.

Since then God has gloriously and supernaturally protected the Jews from every Arab onslaught and will yet shelter them under the shadow of His wings on that prophetic day when all nations will be gathered against Jerusalem to battle. (Zechariah 12-14)

• But most wonderful of all — when Israel's difficulties reach a peak — God has promised to *"pour upon . . . the inhabitants of Jerusalem, the spirit of grace and of supplication"* and God said *"they shall look upon Me whom they have pierced."* (Zechariah 12:10)

Without a doubt, there will be a mass spiritual renewal among the Jews and the Messiah will be revealed to multiplied thousands of them.

A fountain of mercy will be opened up to Israel again as the Son of God, in the last days, restores multitudes back to His bosom from out of the very nation that once rejected and crucified Him.

This is love beyond human comprehension . . . love that surpasses knowledge.

• TO THE VERY END HE WILL KEEP THEM . . . **AS THE APPLE OF HIS EYE!**

David wrote in Psalm 121:

> *"Behold, He that keepeth Israel shall neither slumber nor sleep.*
> *The Lord is thy keeper: the Lord is thy shade upon thy right hand.*
> *The sun shall not smite thee by day, nor the moon by night.*
> *The Lord shall preserve thee from all evil. . . .*
> *The Lord shall preserve thy going out and thy coming in from this time forth, and even for evermore."*

This psalm contains some of God's greatest promises of preservation to His chosen people, Israel.

But now the pertinent question . . . **How does all of this relate to the born again children of the most high God?**

A NEW COVENANT STATUS

The answer to the foregoing question is quite simple.

As it is with Israel, so is it with God's New Covenant offspring.

We have the same God. His personality has not changed. He was a keeper to Israel; He will be a keeper to us.

And besides — by virtue of being born again we became a part of Israel spiritually and thus we became heirs of the very same promises and blessings given to them.

The Old Testament Jews were supernaturally delivered from a natural desert wasteland called the Wilderness of Sin.

The New Testament sons and daughters of God have been supernaturally delivered from a waste, howling wilderness that is far worse . . . the terrible state of separation from God that sin produces.

They were God's natural people — chosen after the flesh.

We are God's spiritual family — chosen after the Spirit.

We can be even more confident and more bold therefore in declaring that we have captured Jehovah's attention, for we have been exalted to a far more eminent position than they.

God has not only chosen to dwell in our midst, as He did with Israel, He has chosen to live in our hearts!

We have been selected as His eternal dwelling place.

We are His delight, His exceeding joy, His prized possession . . . and we are, even in a greater sense now, **the apple of His eye!**

Surely He will keep us from the destructive effects of living in this evil world and we will be **"guarded as the pupil of His eye."** (Deuteronomy 32:10, NIV).

In fact Jesus has already interceded for us saying — "Father . . . I pray not that thou shouldest take them out of the world, but that thou shouldest *keep* them from the evil." (John 17:15)

We are safe from harm as long as we delight ourselves in the Lord.

RETURNING THIS DEPTH OF LOVE

Love begets love, and commitment begets commitment.

If God has committed Himself to us and chosen us as His delight, it is only right that we return like devotion to Him.

This cannot be a one-sided love affair.

He has already given the exhortation —

> *"Keep My commandments and live; and My law as the apple of thine eye.*
> *Bind them upon thy fingers, write them upon the table of thine heart."*

(Proverbs 7:2-3)

17

In other words, fulfilling His Word must become the main *focus* of our attention . . . *the apple of our eye.*

A life of submission and obedience to Him must become our exceeding joy and our supreme delight . . . *the very gateway to our hearts.*

The fellowship that we have with this everlasting Lord of glory must be our prized possession . . . something that we consider *irreplaceable* and watch over intensely to preserve.

OUR VALUE IN HIS SIGHT

Gratefully responding with this kind of commitment is a natural reaction when we really comprehend how extremely valuable we are to Him.

We are quite possibly the only thing in the universe more precious than the precious blood of Jesus — for His blood bought us and brought us back to God, and without controversy, the thing purchased is always more valuable to the buyer than the price paid to secure the item.

He has adorned us with His own glory, the splendor of His presence and the beauty of His holiness, that we might be exceedingly beautiful in His sight . . . *uniquely special.*

And so great is His oneness with us and His infinite love toward us, that when persecution arises because of our adherence to His will, He said — "He that despiseth you despiseth Me; and he that despiseth Me despiseth Him that sent Me." (Luke 10:16)

He is one with us in our burdens and our griefs . . . our rejections and our persecutions.

He carries our sorrows as if they are His own.

When Jesus rebuked Saul on the Damascus Road, who was on his way to persecute the Christians there, the Saviour said — "Saul, Saul . . . why persecutest thou Me?"

He did not say — "Why are you persecuting My people?"

Rather, Jesus, grieved in spirit, cried out — "Why persecutest thou **Me?**" (Acts 9:4)

His compassion was so complete toward those being tortured and persecuted that their pain was actually His pain.

This is easy to believe, for Psalm 105:15 declares that He has even reproved kings for the sake of His chosen, saying "Touch not Mine anointed [those on whom He has poured out the oil of His Holy Spirit] and do My prophets no harm."

• In Zechariah 2:8 He enhances this truth by saying — **"He that toucheth you toucheth the apple of His eye."**

Again — the area around the apple is the most sensitive part of the eye . . . more easily irritated and more subject to intense pain and discomfort with the slightest injury.

So in essence God was saying — "If someone touches My people it is as if that person is injuriously sticking his or her finger in the most sensitive part of My eye."

We can reasonably deduce therefore that there is no greater way of irritating God, arousing His wrath or stirring His jealousy than to persecute or injure one of His beloved sons and daughters.

Surely He will rush to their rescue and speedily avenge His elect.

• In the same chapter of the prophecies of Zechariah, God went on to assure us that He would be — **"A wall of fire round about . . . and the glory in the midst."**

We therefore have nothing to fear.

We have considered the sparrows and the lilies.

We know that we are far more valuable than they.

God's glory is in our midst, even in our hearts.

His love and His eternal ordination for us is like an impenetrable fiery wall around us.

We can rest secure in this knowledge.

A REFLECTION OF HIS IMAGE

• Finally it is important for us to understand that this particular phrase — THE APPLE OF THE EYE — is found only five times in the Bible.

Once it is used literally, three times in reference to God's people, and once, as already mentioned, it is used to symbolically represent the depth of love that we should have for God's law.

• It is also quite significant to note that the main Hebrew word translated **APPLE OF THE EYE** is — *ISHON* (used three times, Deuteronomy 32:10; Psalm 17:8 and Proverbs 7:2).

This Hebrew word literally means — *the little man.*

Apparently *ishon* was used by the Jews to mean *the apple of the eye* because of the small reflection that a person can see of himself in the area of the pupil when gazing into a mirror.

This speaks of the fact that when God gazes into our hearts, He sees a reflection of His own image coming forth.

And was that not His deepest desire from the very beginning . . . to raise up a family of offspring who would eternally reflect His power, His character, His divinity and His attributes?

We are quick to say that if this was God's most predominate passion in the dawn of creation, and it certainly was, then it will undoubtedly be His greatest fulfillment eternally.

We know that this is the plan of God and the purpose of God . . . and when we gaze into the Word, and make it *the apple of our eye,* we see this image of "what we can be" reflected in its pages.

Therefore, we are convinced.

Our God will keep us and watch over us with tender mercy and gentle care until we come forth totally in His likeness . . . **THE APPLE OF HIS EYE,** not only during this earthly sojourn, but also throughout the ceaseless ages.

How does a child of God respond and react to all these blessed truths?

There is no better way than to quote a prayer of David.

> *"Shew Thy marvelous lovingkindness, O Thou that savest by Thy right hand them which put their trust in Thee . . . **keep me as the apple of the eye, hide me under the shadow of Thy wings.**"*
>
> (Psalm 17:7-8)

We have learned.
This is God's promise, His everlasting promise to us.

Therefore, we have determined.
This is our prayer, our never-ending prayer to Him.

BELIEVERS

*"And **BELIEVERS** were the more added to the Lord, multitudes both of men and women."* (Acts 5:14)

BELIEVERS

*"And BELIEVERS were the more added to
the Lord, multitudes both of men and women."*
(Acts 5:14)

The early disciples of Jesus were referred to as *believers* long before they were ever called Christians.

They were easily distinguished from the mainstream of humanity by a believing-spirit that was surely one of their most predominant, noticeable and remarkable qualities.

They believed so fully in the power of the cross that they were perfectly willing to die in defense of their faith.

They believed so completely in the reality of the resurrection that it seemed nothing could ultimately defeat them — not even the grave.

In a dark and depressing world of unbelief, these followers of Christ appeared happy and victorious, even in the worst of circumstances.

In this dungeon of despair, where the captives of time are imprisoned for life in chains of fear and doubt, these vessels of truth loudly proclaimed to the world that the Son had set them free.

They appeared stable and strong even when they were encompassed with situations that make ordinary men crumble in weakness and defeat.

Thus, they were entitled believers.

But it is very certain that — as they were then, so we are now.
We are members of the same family. We have the same Father.
We are heirs of the same conquering spirit.
We have been filled with the same supernatural capacity to *believe*.

*　　　*　　　*　　　*　　　*　　　*

• The original biblical words (Hebrew and Greek) that were translated into the English word **believe,** could also be translated to mean the following:
To be fully persuaded of.
To be steadfast in commitment to.
To fully adhere to, trust in, or rely upon.
To cling to.

From this alone we see clearly that believing involves much more than mere intellectual assent.

A true belief is not something that the mind possesses; it is something that possesses the mind. It is birthed in the heart of a man and spends its life taking over more territory in his spirit.

Real believing involves a deep inner transformation and progressive growth.

23

Jesus gave the inhabitants of this world a wonderful promise when He compassionately pledged — *"He that believeth on Me hath everlasting life."* (John 6:47)

It is certain though that the act of believing referred to by the Son of God involves much more than just mentally assenting to the fact of Jesus' historical existence. It hinges on much more than just mere intellectual acceptance of the story of His crucifixion.

• To really be labeled as *believers,* we must be *fully persuaded* in our hearts that Jesus is the Saviour of the world. We must be *steadfast in our commitment* to the ideals that He upheld. We must *fully adhere* to the truth of the Word, *trust in* His promises, and *rely upon* the power of His grace.

And most of all, we must tenaciously *cling to* the old rugged cross regardless of what comes our way.

No man can reach this depth of faith through mere human willpower; it is the product of a spiritual rebirth.

In fact, it is interesting to note that the word *believe* (including *believed,* and *believeth*) appears 45 times in the Old Testament, but it appears about 250 times in the New Testament. This, in itself, indicates that possessing the spirit to believe is definitely a New Covenant inheritance-blessing.

When we are born again we receive a new nature . . . a Christ-like nature.

It then becomes natural for us to believe in the Messiah and His life-giving promises. It becomes natural for us to desire steadfastness in our commitment to the commands contained in His Word.

When we are transformed by the "washing of regeneration" we begin living in the realm of spiritual realities where believing is a spontaneous and automatic action and reaction.

As we grow in the Lord, we are given the spirit of wisdom and revelation in the knowledge of God that we might know — "the exceeding greatness of His power to us-ward who believe."

This unveiling of God's power floods our lives with excitement and fulfillment. Every day becomes a thrilling experience, for as we journey through time, the God of hope fills our hearts — *"with all joy and peace in believing."* (Romans 15:13)

It is no wonder that we are astounding to the world.

Often, we even astound ourselves.

WE WHO BELIEVE DO CONQUER ADVERSITY
WE RISE ABOVE THE POWER OF SIN

• Psalm 27:13 declares — *"I had fainted, unless I had believed to see the goodness of the Lord in the land of the living."*

We certainly agree with this passage.

Surely we must admit that we would be overwhelmed spiritually and be swallowed up by adverse circumstances often if we never dared to boldly believe God. But we have been enlightened!

We know that the goodness of God initially led us to repentance and that this same goodness is ordained to follow us all the days of our lives. (Romans 2:4, Psalm 23:6)

We know that if we have the Son of God we have life — and "He that believeth on Him is not condemned." (John 3:18)

Just by knowing these things, the goodness of God is poured out on our lives . . . from His cornucopia-like store of plenteous, heavenly blessings. Great mercy, power, restoration-grace, and imparted righteousness resurrect us daily — because we believe! Romans 10:11 declares — "Whosoever believeth on Him shall not be ashamed."

Yes — we have risen above the power of sin. We have risen above the power of circumstances.

We are free from condemnation for we are "in Christ" and in Him is life.

We have conquered the power of guilt.

Faith, firmly set in the goodness of God displayed at Calvary, has made us more than conquerors — *therefore we will not faint!*

WE WHO BELIEVE DO REPEAT HIS WORKS

Just before ascending into heaven, Jesus declared that — "These signs shall follow them that *believe;* In My name shall they cast out devils; they shall speak with new tongues . . . they shall lay hands on the sick, and they shall recover." (Mark 16:17-18)

These are only a few of the many supernatural signs that are supposed to follow **true believers.**

Jesus is the total Word of God; He is the embodiment of all God's exceeding great and precious promises.

To believe in Him automatically involves tapping into the supernatural and receiving of what He is.

Jesus said if we believe in the light, we become the children of light.

In like manner, if we believe in miracles, then we become children of miracles.

If we believe in the authority in Jesus' name, we become children of authority.

If we believe in Jesus, we become identified with what He is . . . and His nature, His character, His attitudes and His abilities overflow into our lives.

• No wonder Jesus promised — "Verily, verily, I say unto you, He that BELIEVETH on Me, the works that I do shall he do also; and greater works than these shall he do; because I go to My Father." (John 14:12)

In the early church it happened.

The blind saw. The deaf heard.

The dead were raised. Miracles abounded.

Now God is doing it again. The requirement is still the same. *"He that cometh to God must believe. . . . "*

WE WHO BELIEVE DO ENTER INTO HIS REST

What is this mysterious high goal of a believer referred to as *the rest of God?*

The Bible warns us to fear lest we fall short of it, and to labor that we might enter into it.

But without a doubt, if we are to fully enter into, attain, and possess this *rest of God,* we must first have a clear understanding of what it really is. This revelation is found primarily in the epistle to the Hebrews, chapters three and four.

• For the Jews of the Old Covenant entering *the rest of God* meant two things. First of all — it meant entering the Promised Land (a natural place of protection, security and abundant provision) that God had promised to give them for an inheritance, right here in this world. But secondly, it was a reference to Abraham's bosom — the spiritual abode of the righteous after death.

In the days of the Old Testament this temporary paradise was located in the lower parts of the earth.

The Jews who rebelled against Moses were excluded from both of these places of rest, both natural and supernatural. They died in the wilderness of Sin naturally and we assume that many of them perished forever spiritually.

• Because they repeatedly rebelled against the Lord and against His Word, God swore in His wrath saying . . . *"They shall not enter into My rest."*

• The Bible clearly reveals that . . . *"They could not enter in because of unbelief."*

• The Bible further explained that although the Gospel was preached to them — *"the word preached did not profit them, not being mixed with faith in them that heard it."*

These followers of Moses sinned atrociously against Jehovah in numerous and various ways. But it is quite apparent that the main sin which prevented them from receiving their glorious inheritance was not so much their stubbornness, their rebellion, their adultery or their idolatry, for these transgressions, though disgusting and abominable, were still forgivable, had they repented and believed.

Their primary transgression was rather the terribly offensive yet subtly corrupting sin of unbelief.

26

This sin of unbelief was definitely the root of all other sins committed.

What an awful calamity!

How tragic it is that they could not believe.

How amazing it is that they could witness some of the most phenomenal, supernatural displays of divine power that the world has ever seen . . . and still draw back into perdition and destruction through unbelief.

How true it is that we are doubly chargeable before heaven if we walk in their footsteps.

They did not possess the faith-nature as we do, for they were yet of the flesh, bound in carnality.

We are so blessed in comparison.

We have received the spirit to believe.

The Word of God has been planted in our hearts, opening up a wellspring of daring hope and loving trust.

We have been born again. We are of divinity; we are of faith. We have been loosed into spirituality.

The Word has entered into us, that we might enter into the Word.

We are convinced that — *"All things are possible to him that believeth."* (Mark 9:23)

We view impossible situations and obstacles in our way but we boldly declare — we can do it, in Jesus name!

*   *   *   *   *   *

• The concept of *the rest of God* means something quite different to New Testament believers.

First of all, it relates to a spiritual land of inheritance — a certain place of bold confidence in God that we can obtain right now in this life.

Secondly — *the rest of God* refers to our eternal home in heaven.

We will only deal with the first level of interpretation.

It is necessary to understand that all that happened to the Jews in their conquest of natural Canaan's land is symbolic of a spiritual quest in which we are engaged.

We are searching for spiritual stability and the unsurpassed peace that comes with it.

We are pursuing the calm assurance that comes by living the faith-life.

As the eagle labors to mount up into the high atmospheric currents where it can soar effortlessly on the wings of the wind, so we, with firm resolve, are constantly laboring to enter into *the rest of God.*

We labor by fighting the good fight of faith.

We labor by waging war against the doubts and fears that plague our minds.

We labor by persistently claiming, confessing and pursuing the promises of God.

•• We fully attain the rest of God when we possess just as much confidence in God as God has in Himself (a goal that we will obviously never reach FULLY until the resurrection).

The Bible declared that — *"God did rest the seventh day from all His works."* (Hebrews 4:4)

It is important to understand that God did not just rest from those works which were then visibly, perceptibly and tangibly manifested in the beginning. He rested the seventh day from *all* His works, those works already revealed, and also those works yet to be generated or brought forth into actual existence.

It is absolutely certain that *all* the works of God were— *"finished from the foundation of the world."*

Even as a child actually exists in the womb of its mother until its appointed time of birth, so also the ordained works of God actually exist in the womb of eternity, in the mind of God, until their appointed time of manifestation. And it is certain . . . if something takes place in the mind of God, it is as good as done! It will definitely come to pass!

Of course, not everything that happens in the realm of time can be referred to as an ordained work of God.

• Only God Himself knows fully where to draw the line between the works of God and the works of man.

Even in the religious realm, it can be truthfully stated that many Christian activities and endeavors are simply works done *for* God.

But when something is spawned in the mind of God from the beginning, its fulfillment is absolutely certain, and it is correctly entitled — *a work of God.*

As we look back through time we can easily pick out some of the happenings that would most probably fit under this category.

The calling of Abraham was *a work of God.*

Sarah bearing Isaac in her old age was definitely *a work of God.*

The parting of the Red Sea, the opening of Jordan, the conquest of Canaan and the collapse of the walls of Jericho were all products of the everlasting plan of God . . . *works of God.*

The deliverance of Meshach, Shadrach, and Abednego from the furnace of fire was an ordained *work of God.*

The Pentecostal outpouring of the Holy Spirit on the one hundred and twenty in the upper room was, without question, ordained of God, a sovereign act of El-Shaddai . . . the All-Sufficient One.

The final binding of Satan, the coming of the Lord, the resurrection of the dead and the entrance of the kingdom of God into this world are all predestined spiritual happenings . . . *works of God.*

Nothing could stop these former works of God from coming to pass:

nothing can hinder His future works from being fulfilled.

When Adam and Eve transgressed in the beginning, it appeared that the plan of God had a disastrous head-on collision with sin and rebellion.

It looked as though God's original purpose was being thwarted by the devil's evil devices.

But the God of all foreknowledge was not caught by surprise nor weakened by the intrusion of sin into the Garden of Eden.

Being omniscient (all-knowing) He had prepared far in advance and formulated an unconquerable and irreversible plan.

Atonement would be provided and God's original purpose ("*Let us make man in our image*") would be brought to an even greater fulfillment through the resurrection.

This was all predetermined.

It is perfectly and scripturally sound to believe the following bold and profound declarations of our faith.

• The Lamb of God was slain from the foundation of the world! (Revelation 13:8)

• We were chosen in Christ before the foundation of the world! (Ephesians 1:4)

• The kingdom that we shall inherit has been prepared for us from the foundation of the world! (Matthew 25:34)

• Our names have been written in the Lamb's book of life from the foundation of the world! (Revelation 17:8)

• And again — the works of God were finished from the foundation of the world! (Hebrews 4:3)

•• **All these things are a part of God's irreversible and unconquerable plan.**

Therefore, it is quite reasonable to conclude that God is not the least bit nervous. He was not worried when Adam initially fell. He is certainly not worried now.

God is not even slightly anxious.

God does not view the future with fearful apprehension.

From the beginning God has *rested* in the calm assurance and the absolute confidence that His original plan would be completely fulfilled . . . not one jot and not one tittle will pass until all be fulfilled.

Not one grain will fall to the ground. (Amos 9:9)

Not one tare will be gathered into the garner.

Jesus is the beginning and the end of all things, natural and spiritual. He is Alpha and Omega — the great I Am.

• He existed long before the start of natural creation and He will exist long after the renovation, recreation and restitution of all things.

His very existence encircles, encloses and embraces the plan of God — therefore, it is already completed within Him, deep within His heart.

Over the centuries and millenniums, from time to time, He has sent forth His Word through the veil, into the world, to accomplish the good pleasure of His will.

He is not like the fisherman, baiting a hook, who hopes to get a strike.

He is not like the man, drilling for oil, who hopes to hit a gusher.

He is not like the businessman, investing in some enterprise, or venturing into some business deal, hoping to clear a profit.

God already knows.

God has absolute confidence in the stability, security and effectiveness of His Word-plan, for His Word is forever settled in the heavens.

This quick and powerful sword of the Word penetrates infinitely into the past and infinitely into the future to determine, dictate and create circumstances and events as He wills.

God's investment is secure.

His Word will not return unto Him void.

It will accomplish that which He pleases.

It will prosper in the purpose for which it was sent. (Isaiah 55:10-11)

Therefore, we can remain steadfast in confidence for we have blessed assurance.

We can have just as much confidence in God and in His plan as He has in Himself.

- **THIS IS THE REST OF GOD!**
- THIS IS THE HIGH CALLING OF THE BELIEVER!

This is more than faith in God.

- THIS IS THE FAITH OF GOD!!

The very same rest that our Father possesses has now arisen in our hearts . . . for we are His offspring.

If we have been born again, we can be unshakeably certain of these things, for we are more than believers in the plan of God.

We are actually a part of His eternal plan!

No wonder the Bible strongly asserts — "He that believeth on Him shall not be confounded."

Our eyes have been opened.

It is becoming increasingly more difficult to accept and be bound by the weakness of the Adam-nature.

We have discovered a wellspring of strength.

We have learned to see things from God's perspective, therefore we will not be confounded *(frustrated, baffled, confused or destroyed)* by the events of life.

We see that the work has already been done and the victory has already been won.

With His stripes, we were healed.

By His blood, we were delivered.

We behold the promise of God and the fulfillment as one complete circle.

When this takes place, we cease from our own works as God did from His; our doubts dissolve and faith reigns supreme in our hearts and lives.

Unreserved trust in the finished work of Calvary lodges firmly in our spirit. We enter into the rest of God.

• More than ever, we can confidently affirm that healing belongs to us, forgiveness belongs to us, restoration belongs to us, imparted righteousness belongs to us, for almost two thousand years ago Jesus clearly proclaimed — *"It is finished."*

The plan of God was sealed by the blood of the Lamb at that moment and now there is absolutely no way that it can fail.

God will preserve His elect people who trust in Him. God will see His original purpose brought to ultimate fulfillment.

So certain is the entrance of the kingdom of God into this world that when John the Revelator saw, in a vision, the holy city coming down from God out of heaven, he heard the voice of the Lord saying — *"It is done."* (Revelation 21:6)

• The Lord did not say that it *will be* done, He said — *"It is done!"*

As far as God is concerned, this future event has already taken place . . . so God can rest in joyous anticipation, trusting in His own infallible, immutable Word.

Now we have received a challenge from the Most High God.

We have been exhorted to enter His rest (not just a spiritual rest that comes from God but actually *the rest of God,* the same rest that He experiences).

It is certain that we can do it for we have discovered the key to obtaining this peace that passes all understanding.

Jesus said (John 7:38) — "He that *believeth* on me . . . from out of his belly shall flow rivers of living waters." (And remember, something that is alive is something that is growing, enlarging and reproducing itself.)

The issues of DIVINE LIFE just keep flowing and growing in the heart of that person who dares to KEEP BELIEVING.

This is the answer. This is the key.

We have learned a vital secret from God . . . *"without faith it is impossible to please Him."*

And if this be true, then the opposite is true also.

With faith we are very pleasing to Him.

Having learned this, we are more than ready to accept the challenge and the resulting *title,* for this is exactly what God has called us to pursue and fulfill.

WE ARE BELIEVERS!!!

THE BELOVED

HIS DARLING

THE DEARLY BELOVED OF HIS SOUL

"I will call them My people, which were not My people; and her BELOVED, which was not beloved."
(Romans 9:25)

"Deliver My soul from the sword; MY DARLING from the power of the dog."
(Psalm 22:20)

"I have given THE DEARLY BELOVED OF MY SOUL into the hand of her enemies."
(Jeremiah 12:7)

THE BELOVED
HIS DARLING
THE DEARLY BELOVED OF HIS SOUL

*"I will call them My people, which were not
My people; and her BELOVED, which was not
beloved."*   (Romans 9:25)

*"Deliver My soul from the sword; MY
DARLING from the power of the dog."*
         (Psalm 22:20)

• The word — *beloved* — means **dearly loved.**
In the New Testament, two Greek words are translated into the word
beloved . . . agapao and *agapetos.*

It is very clear that both of these words spring from another Greek
word — *agape* — which is translated into the English word — *love.*

It is also important to note that the English language is quite deficient when it comes to expressing this idea of love.

We use the same word to describe how we feel toward God, our
family, a favorite car, or a good meal.

The Greeks had three main words for our one . . . *eros, phileo and
agape.*

Eros is sensual love, a selfish, self-seeking love that grasps for that
which satisfies and gratifies the flesh.

Phileo is brotherly love and normally requires a measure of acceptance in return.

But *agape* is a brand of love that was never fully revealed in this
world until Jesus came.

Agape-love is a totally selfless love, divine in origin, that is not controlled or determined by the reaction of those to whom it is sent.

It is freely given.

This is the kind of love that compelled Jesus to heal His own enemy
in the Garden of Gethsemane.

This is the kind of love that constrained Him to taste death for every
man, even the most rebellious sinner, on Calvary.

This is the kind of grace-filled love that has lifted us from the dunghill and raised us up to sit together with Christ in heavenly places.

This is the kind of merciful compassion that has literally poured
into our lives to make us — **"accepted in the beloved** *(the agapao)."*

ISRAEL AS THE BELOVED

Originally Jehovah referred to the entire nation of Israel as *His beloved*.
The Psalmist David "stood in the gap" for the offspring of Abraham praying — "Be Thou exalted, O God, above the heavens: and Thy glory above the earth; that *Thy beloved* may be delivered: save with Thy right hand, and answer me." (Psalm 108:5-6, See also Psalm 60:4-5)

Yet another Psalm reveals Jehovah's feelings toward His people on an individual level saying — "He giveth *His beloved* sleep" — and another translation — "He gives to *His beloved* even in his sleep." (Psalm 127:2, AV, NAS)

This passage speaks of God's abundant provision and watchful care over all those who have been brought to His bosom in a covenant relationship.

But evidently, many in Israel took such intimacy with their Creator for granted. Insulting Him with their rampant idolatry and sin, Jehovah was compelled to declare — "What hath *My beloved* to do in Mine house, seeing she hath wrought lewdness with many?" So great was their transgression against Him that the Lord even demanded of Jeremiah — "pray not thou for this people, neither lift up a cry or prayer for them."

And He expressed His great heaviness over such a choice when He admitted — "I have given **THE DEARLY BELOVED OF MY SOUL** into the hand of her enemies." (Jeremiah 11:14-15, 12:7)

What a horrible end result for that nation at one time called the apple of God's eye!

But really, this was only to be expected.

"For the law made nothing perfect, but the bringing in of a better hope did." (Hebrews 7:19)

Under the Old Will, God's desire for His own was definitely unrealized. But for this cause — and to change this condition — Jesus came.

JESUS AS THE BELOVED

The term — *beloved* — was next used in reference to Jesus.

The espoused bride in the Song of Solomon refers to the groom often as her *beloved* (for example — *"My beloved is white and ruddy, the chiefest among ten thousand"*).

The Song of Solomon is a highly poetical and prophetical book that speaks of the love relationship between Jesus and the church (His bride).

We read also of the heaven-sent confirmation that took place on the day of Jesus' baptism.

> *"And Jesus, when He was baptized, went up*
> *straightway out of the water: and, lo, the heav-*

ens were opened unto Him, and He saw the Spirit
of God descending like a dove, and lighting upon
Him.

And lo a voice from heaven saying, this is My
beloved Son, in whom I am well pleased."
(Matthew 3:16-17)

The Father presented the Jewish nation with irrefutable evidence, both visible and audible, confirming Jesus' identity as the beloved Son and confirming that the good pleasure of God rested upon Him.

This is an undeniable fact, but it is also just as undeniable that Jesus' purpose in coming was to establish us in the same relationship with the Father that He had.

THE CHURCH AS THE BELOVED

In His great intercessory plea for the church (John 17) Jesus cried — *"Father, I will that they also whom thou hast given Me, be with Me where I am."*

This petition, that was soon to become the soul-piercing passion of Gethsemane, was uttered at the base of the Mount of Olives, just across the brook Kidron.

Surely Jesus was not praying that all believers would be gathered with Him in that physical place.

He was rather referring to a spiritual place.

This *spiritual place* related first of all to paradise (the third heaven) where the souls of departed saints live gloriously and joyously in the very manifest presence of the Almighty God.

But this *spiritual place* is also a certain spiritual position of intimacy with the Father and power over Satan, that we can live in right now!

Jesus occupied this position alone initially.

But now He has invited every born again child of God to dwell with Him . . . in the secret place of the Most High, under the continual shadow of the Almighty God.

He left this spiritual position of authority in this world, ascended to heaven, and told us to occupy until He comes. Yes, we have been commanded by God to assume the reins — to take over where Jesus left off — and to do it all for His glory.

We are so blessed! We have been linked to the source of all life and all love. We are actually a part of Him.

In the mind of the Father we share complete identity with the first-born Son. We are in Christ, and He is in us!

•• **Therefore because we are in Him . . . we are in "the beloved."**
We now share Jesus' identity and inherited position.

37

The good pleasure of God now rests upon us. (Ephesians 1:9)
We are accepted!
We are no longer rejected.
We are no longer outcasts — exiled from the presence of God.
The impossible barriers have been removed!

The veil before the holy of holies was rent from the top to the bottom when Jesus died. Prior to that blessed day, only the high priest could enter the inner sanctuary.

Moreover, the Gentiles were not even allowed in the temple area, except in the court of the Gentiles.

In fact, there were notices placed on this wall of separation pronouncing death on all Gentiles who dared to enter. (VED)*[1]

But this *middle wall of partition* was broken down, in a symbolic sense, when the blood of the Lamb was shed.

Now, everything has been drastically altered.

Now, all men are accepted and welcomed into the presence of the Almighty, if they approach Him in sincerity, humility and faith, believing fully in the redemptive price that Jesus paid.

• Hosea prophesied how we would be included, saying — *"I will call them My people which were not My people; **and her beloved,** which was not beloved."* (Romans 9:25)

When we are begotten of the Word, we are presented "holy and without blame before Him in love" . . . receivable in His sight. (Ephesians 1:4)

His blood makes us pure, even as He is pure.

His grace makes us righteous, as righteous and as holy as He.

Therefore we that are saved are just as accepted in the presence of the Father as Jesus, our Elder Brother.

So complete is this miracle of identification that Jesus' *title (the Beloved)* has now also been transferred to us.

God could well speak over the entire body of Christ now, saying — "This is My *beloved,* in whom I am well pleased."

We have been cleansed. We have been justified . . . just as if we never sinned.

We are joint-heirs with Christ.

•• **We are just as beloved of the Father as He.**

This is a faith-fact that is easily proven.

Listen again to a portion of the prayer that preceded Gethsemane.

> *"Father . . . the glory which Thou gavest Me
> I have given them; that they may be one, even as
> We are one.
> I in them, and Thou in Me, that they may be
> made perfect in one; and that the world may know*

38

that Thou hast sent Me, and hast loved them, as
Thou hast loved Me."   (John 17:22-23)

According to this passage, Jesus prayed that the world would fully recognize how very precious and dear we are to God . . . as precious, beloved and dear to the Father as the firstborn Son.

It is an amazing fact, though, that many of the sons of God have not even yet received this life-transforming revelation, much less the world.

But more and more we are being illuminated concerning this wondrous gift called grace *(unmerited love)* and our hearts are increasingly being filled with praise.

Once this beautiful truth is unveiled, we are never the same again.

We become strong in faith.

We become rigid in determination.

We become unshakeable in confidence, for we recognize our inherited position.

Jesus is our Forerunner; He led the way.

Jesus walked in deep personal communion and absolute oneness with the Father when He was on the earth.

• In the depth of prayer, He would address the Almighty using the phrase — *"Abba, Father."* (Mark 14:36)

This is an affectionate Aramaic word *(a term of endearment)* similar to our English word — *papa.*

But it is definite that Jesus has not reserved this right of intimacy with the Father unto Himself alone.

For the Scripture now declares that God has sent forth the Spirit of His Son into our hearts crying — *"Abba Father."* (Galatians 4:6)

As regenerated sons of God, we have inherited the divine right to approach the Father in the same fashion.

We ask in the name of Jesus.

We pray in the name of Jesus.

In other words, we come before the throne in His righteousness, praying as He would pray, and expecting to be received as He would be received, for we come in His name.

WE STAND UNAFRAID AND UNASHAMED IN THE PRESENCE OF THE FATHER BECAUSE JESUS STANDS WITH US AND IN US.

HIS LOVE HAS COVERED THE MULTITUDE OF SINS!

BEING MADE PERFECT IN LOVE

I John 4:16 declares that — "We have known and believed the love that God hath to us."

We have received the mind-realization of His wondrous love *(we have known).*

But even more so, we have received the heart-revelation *(we have believed).*

We now realize that if He has considered us worthy to receive **His love** *(His agape)* then we are worthy to be included in **His Beloved** *(His Agapao).*

Crippling fear and dread despair have left our lives for we are being "made perfect in love."

In other words, we are entering into a full, complete and mature revelation of the depth of God's love.

This perfect love erases our guilt and casts out all of our fears.

One translation (NEB) declares that this perfect love actually — "banishes fear" — literally forcing it out of our hearts.

Another translation (PME) says that — "Fully-developed love expels every particle of fear." (I John 4:18)

How powerful this love-revelation really is!

What a mighty effect it has on our thinking and our attitudes.

It quickly crushes the satanic onslaught of condemnation that buffets our minds.

It swiftly conquers the torment that tears at our souls.

This perfect love is a nail-scarred hand, stretched forth against the storms in our lives, and a gentle yet commanding voice that says — *"Peace be still."*

The revelation of this perfect love, this perfecting love, establishes us in perfection and in our sonship inheritance . . . now and forevermore.

•• In fact, John the Revelator emphatically stated — **"Herein is our love made perfect, that we may have boldness in the day of judgment: because as He is, so are we in this world."** (I John 4:17)

Our hearts are flooded with an inexpressible joy and an indescribable peace. Though it seems almost beyond belief, we know it is true.

Because He is holy, we are holy.

Because He has power over the devil, we have power over the devil.

Because He has intimacy with the Father, we have intimacy with the Father.

Because He is accepted, we are accepted.

"As He is, so are we in this world."

We are not afraid anymore.

We are not afraid of the power of sin.

We are not afraid of the power of sickness.

We are not afraid of success or failure.

We are not afraid of the weakness of our flesh, or the strength of the devil.

We are not afraid of circumstances.

We believe in the strength of humility and faith more than we believe in the strength of the adversary.

We have tapped into the greatest source of power that exists.

This *perfect love* is the supreme power and the bond of perfectness that keeps lifting us higher. Through this perfecting love we are free from condemnation . . . and *"Beloved,* if our heart condemn us not, then have we confidence toward God. . . ." (I John 3:21)

Knowing this, and believing this, will give us *"boldness in the day of judgment."* (I John 4:17)

It must be said that this enlightening and somewhat astounding Scripture refers to two different yet related concepts. Both are extremely important and both are worthy of our attention.

BOLDNESS IN THE DAY OF CHASTISEMENT

First of all — 1 John 4:17 speaks of those times in which we are brought under judgment and chastened, because our walk with God is not what it should be. (Hebrews 12:1-14)

Every child of God, at one time or another, has experienced the displeasure of the Almighty and His corrective measures . . . "for what son is he whom the Father chasteneth not? But if ye be without chastisement, whereof all are partakers, then are ye bastards and not sons."

Chastisement awakens us spiritually and makes us much more sensitive to what pleases and displeases God.

Chastisement yields the peaceable fruit of righteousness, for it spurs us into action.

Chastisement is sent to sons of God to keep them and preserve them unto life eternal.

The Bible definitely states that when God is forced to discipline us this way He does it *"for our profit, that we might be partakers of His holiness."*

Of course, it should not be necessary for God to always have to pressure us this way into surrendering our will to His.

If we are sincerely grateful for the gift of eternal life, we should automatically respond by disciplining ourselves and ridding ourselves of those things that make us unfit spiritually.

I Corinthians 11:31 assuredly declares that — "If we would judge ourselves, we should not be judged."

41

In other words, if we would take the responsibility of keeping our hearts sanctified before the Lord, God would not have to bring us under judgment.

We all agree this is the best route to take.

But regardless we know that — "when we are judged, we are chastened of the Lord, that we should not be condemned with the world."

Knowing these things will surely give us **boldness in the day of judgment** (the day of chastisement) — boldness to believe that all things really do work together for our good, our benefit.

We can boldly "Lift up the hands which hang down, and the feeble knees."

We can boldly — "make straight paths for our feet" knowing that God is for us, so who and what can be against us.

We can gladly believe that God does not want us to be condemned with the world so He sends forth — *"judgment unto victory."* (Matthew 12:20)

When we are bruised, He will heal us; when the fire is burning low in our hearts, He will rekindle it.

We can praise Him in every circumstance for we are sure that when we yield to God's discipline, the end result will always be *victory! Victory! Victory!*

O, how strong we become when this faith-fact and this love-revelation is firmly rooted in our hearts.

Depression and discouragement are then easily conquered foes.

BOLDNESS BEFORE THE THRONE OF GOD

Secondly — the Day of Judgment refers to that time when all men will stand before God and be judged according to the deeds done in the body.

The sinner, on that day, will tremble with guilt and cringe in horror.

The rebellious will recoil in heart-rending fear at the dreadful sound of God's voice as He pronounces their eternal doom.

But the blood-washed throng will lift their voices in joyful adoration, boldly and gratefully declaring their salvation inheritance.

We will stand boldly before the throne of the Almighty God, not in the filthy rags of our own attempt at goodness, but in the white robes of God's imparted holiness.

We will be clothed eternally in that righteousness which is — *"of God, by faith."* (Philippians 3:9)

We will possess the very boldness in the Day of Judgment that He promised would be ours.

We will be **HIS DARLING** forever, delivered eternally from — **"the power of the dog"** — *(the accusing, condemning, corrupting, devouring power of Satan).* *²

This must come to pass for it was Jesus' prayer from the cross, given prophetically by David in Psalm 22.

> *"My God, My God, why hast Thou forsaken Me? . . .*
>
> *For dogs have compassed Me: the assembly of the wicked have enclosed Me: they pierced My hands and My feet . . .*
>
> *But be not Thou far from Me, O Lord: O My strength, haste Thee to help Me.*
>
> *Deliver My soul from the sword; MY DARLING from the power of the dog."*
>
> (Psalm 22:1,16,19,20)

The first part of this prayer-psalm ("My God, My God, why hast Thou forsaken Me?") was definitely recorded in the gospels as one of the seven final statements Jesus made while hanging on the cross.

We do not know whether or not the rest of the words contained in this Psalm were ever finally uttered by Jesus on Calvary's hill, but we do know that every line of this prophetic prayer will ultimately be fulfilled.

We will be *His Darling* throughout the ceaseless ages, for He has definitely referred to us this way in His prophetic Word. (See also Song of Solomon 5:2, NAS)

The false church — the Jezebel church — will ultimately be devoured by "dogs" out of hell, just as it literally happened to wicked Queen Jezebel of old when the judgment of God fell on her. (II Kings 9, Revelation 2:20; 17, 18)

But we — the true church, the bride of Christ — will come forth *totally delivered.*

This is the revelation of the promise of God . . . for *the dearly beloved of His soul* in the end will not be given into the hand of her enemies. Quite the contrary, she will crush them underfoot.

Therefore, we are sure that Jesus will continue in His fervent and watchful care over us, ever living to make intercession for our souls.

Until the dawning of the new age, He will rebuke the devourer for our sake. (Malachi 3:11)

He will set us free from every bondage and finally liberate us to praise Him forever.

We will worship God boldly in the glory of His Shekinah presence.

We will shine boldly like the sun in the kingdom of our Father.

We will be bold, eternal examples of the great power of God's love — "that in the ages to come He might shew the exceeding riches of His grace in His kindness toward us through Christ Jesus." (Ephesians 2:7)

We will dwell eternally in New Jerusalem — *"the beloved city."* (Revelation 20:9)

We will be thoroughly convinced of our importance to God.

We will be the central focus of His attention and love . . . His bride . . . HIS DARLING . . . HIS BELOVED . . . HIS AGAPAO . . . and THE DEARLY BELOVED OF HIS SOUL . . . forever and ever.

---

¹Vine's Expository Dictionary, under *Partition,* page 163, New Testament words.

*²The word — *dogs* — in the Scripture is used to describe Gentiles (Matt. 15:26) homosexuals (Deut. 23:18) profane persons (Matt. 7:6) cruel enemies (Jer. 15:3) and all who will be ultimately shut out of heaven (Rev. 22:15). This term, therefore, is indicative of all who are vile, unclean, rebellious and apart from God. A Christian going back to his former sins is portrayed as a dog returning to its vomit. But who was it that gave this dog-like nature to fallen man? None other than Lucifer himself who, as a dog, feeds on filth and seeks to devour new prey every day. Therefore this phrase — *the power of the dog* — is most likely a reference to the power Satan has that enables him to devour men and women in that sin-nature which in the end renders them disgustingly dog-like. From this Jesus has graciously delivered us, for we are *His Darling . . .* filled with His righteousness and heirs of His divine nature.

THE CHILDREN OF ABRAHAM

THE CHILDREN OF PROMISE

HEIRS OF PROMISE

HEIRS ACCORDING TO THE PROMISE

A GREAT NATION

ABRAHAM'S SEED

ABRAHAM'S CHILDREN

TRUE DESCENDANTS OF ABRAHAM

TRUE HEIRS OF HIS PROMISE

"Know ye therefore that they which are of faith, the same are THE CHILDREN OF ABRAHAM."
(Galatians 3:7)

"Now we, brethren, as Isaac was, are THE CHILDREN OF PROMISE."
(Galatians 4:28)

"Wherein God, willing more abundantly to shew unto THE HEIRS OF PROMISE the immutability of His counsel, confirmed it by an oath:"
(Hebrews 6:17)

". . . and I will make of thee A GREAT NATION."   (Genesis 12:2)

"And if ye be Christ's, then are ye ABRAHAM'S SEED, and HEIRS ACCORDING TO THE PROMISE."
(Galatians 3:29)

THE CHILDREN OF ABRAHAM
THE CHILDREN OF PROMISE
A GREAT NATION

"Know ye therefore that they which are of faith, the same are THE CHILDREN OF ABRAHAM."   (Galatians 3:7)

"Now we, brethren, as Isaac was, are THE CHILDREN OF PROMISE." (Galatians 4:28)

When Abraham was seventy-five years old, he was yet without a son by his barren wife Sarah.

The Almighty God visited him saying — *"Get thee out of thy country, and from thy kindred . . . unto a land that I will shew thee: and I will make of thee a great nation."* (Genesis 12:1-2)

Abraham believed and immediately "departed, as the Lord had spoken unto him." As a result God promised Abraham that his seed would be — *"as the dust of the earth."* (Genesis 13:16)

Approximately fifty years later, about twenty-five years after the promised son had been born, God visited Abraham again demanding that he offer his son as a burnt sacrifice on Mount Moriah. (UBD)

Abraham knew that God had promised through Isaac there would come forth *a great nation.* And he knew that the promises of God are immutable and unchangeable: they must come to pass. So, in reality, when Abraham attempted to obediently sacrifice Isaac, he did so believing that God was able to raise his son from the dead.

This measure of resurrection-faith pleased God so greatly that He reconfirmed His covenant with Abraham promising that his seed would be — *"as the stars of the sky in multitude, and as the sand which is by the seashore innumerable."* (Hebrews 11:12)

This triple analogy speaks of much more than just the great number of offspring that Abraham would have.

• This was a prophecy of two kinds of offspring . . . a natural people *(represented by both sand and dust)* and a spiritual people *(represented by the stars).*

Both would claim to be *children of Abraham;* both would be a multitude without number; and the faithful of both one day would make up that *great nation* that God spoke of in the beginning.

• It is quite clear that Abraham (whose very name means *father of a multitude)* is not just the father of the natural Jewish nation; Romans 4:11 announces that he is *"the father of all them that believe,"* and that includes all who are born again, both Jews and Gentiles.

Abraham is called the father of the believing and the blessed, first of all, because he and his natural descendants were chosen to be the *Messianic line* (the family line that would bring forth the Messiah).

Now we, as believers, are considered to be the spiritual offspring of this same Messiah (Jesus) — so, in a spiritual sense, it is logical to say that we are *the children of Abraham.*

• Secondly, Abraham can be called the father of the believing and the blessed because his example of believing, and his experience with God, *begets* like faith in us, through the seed of the Word being planted in our hearts.

There is a spiritual transfer.

Paul experienced something similar to this with his converts. To the Corinthians he wrote — *"I have begotten you through the gospel."* (I Corinthians 4:15)

The seed of the Word travelled through Paul on its journey into their hearts.

There was a spiritual transfer of revelation knowledge from his life to theirs . . . so, in a certain sense, they became his spiritual children.

The same thing has happened between Abraham and all those who believe. The *living Word* came through him on its journey into our hearts and lives.

We have inherited his revelation of El-Shaddai, the All Sufficient One.

We have therefore become his spiritual descendants.

THE BLESSING OF ABRAHAM

•• The Bible declares that if we be Christ's then we are — **"ABRAHAM'S SEED, and HEIRS ACCORDING TO THE PROMISE."** (Galatians 3:29)

Another translation of the same passage said — "And if you belong to Christ, you are **true descendants of Abraham,** you are **true heirs of his promise."** (PME)

If we are the seed of Abraham, and we are, then it is quite correct to assume that we are also his heirs.

The Bible declares that Jesus was actually made a curse for us — *"that the blessing of Abraham might come on the Gentiles through Jesus Christ."* (Galatians 3:14)

Now think of that. Jesus thought it was so vitally important for *Gentiles* to inherit the blessing of Abraham that He was willing to become a curse in order for *such a transfer* to take place.

Now this covenant of blessing is such an integral part of the spiritual makeup of *both Jews and Gentiles, who are born again,* that we have actually been entitled — **THE CHILDREN OF PROMISE** and **HEIRS OF PROMISE.** (Galatians 4:28, Hebrews 6:17)

Many of God's promises to Abraham are being expressed and fulfilled in us daily. If we are children of Abraham, then we are children of blessing.

We are begotten of the very promises that God gave to him.

We have every pledge embedded in our spirits.

And we have a dual reason for total confidence in their fulfillment. First, we know that God cannot lie. And second, we know that in an amazing way God actually swore by Himself, confirming these Abrahamic promises by an oath . . . "that we might have a strong consolation." (Read Hebrews 6:13-20)

•• We are of faith . . . and we know that — *"they which be of faith are blessed with faithful Abraham."* (Galatians 3:9)

Let us therefore explore the blessings and promises given to this great patriarch, that we might discover and appropriate that which rightfully belongs to us. (Genesis 12-22)

AGGRANDIZEMENT

To **aggrandize** means *to magnify, enlarge or greatly exalt.*

This is what God promised to do to Abraham.

•• He said — **"I will bless thee, and make thy name great; and thou shalt be a blessing."** (Genesis 12:2)

Foundationally, this promise was fulfilled in Abraham's great material prosperity for "Abram was very rich in cattle, in silver, and in gold."

But God certainly had much more than that in mind. God blessed him even more with spiritual prosperity; he was rich in peace, joy, righteousness and faith. He was rich in the Spirit . . . so rich that he could share with multiplied thousands of others what God had originally given to him.

God also promised to make his name great.

At one time Abraham was a relatively unknown desert dweller, a nomad, wandering through the wilderness of the Middle East.

Now three of the world's major religions (Judaism, Mohammedism and Christianity) revere him and speak his name with great respect.

We know that Abraham never sought this kind of fame; he simply served God out of sincerity and true devotion.

But Jehovah rewarded him and now his life, his obedient spirit, and his love for God, have become a source of inspiration to multitudes.

God blessed him that he might be a blessing.

All of this earthly recognition, honor, and glory that God gave Abraham is close to nothing, though, compared to the eternal glory of being included in the heavenly hierarchy.

In the kingdom to come surely Abraham's name will be great in the sight of the very angels of God and all who share the delights of eternal life . . . forever and ever.

This is all parallel to the inheritance we have received also.

God has blessed us and given us the power to bless others, which is truly the greatest blessing of all.

We can win the lost, deliver the oppressed, and comfort the downtrodden.

The Bible said that this God we serve "comforteth us in all our tribulation, that we may be able to comfort them which are in any trouble, by the comfort wherewith we ourselves are comforted of God." (II Corinthians 1:4)

We can expect to prosper, materially and spiritually, and then joyously give of our material and spiritual abundance to others.

We have been transformed by the power of God, and now God has given us the power to transform others — by the Word and the Spirit.

We are blessed of God, that we might be a blessing!

But our God has done even more for us.

Our names have been greatly exalted, for our very names have been written in heaven, in that celestial roster called the Lamb's book of life.

There is no greater honor that could be given to any man than this, therefore we can truthfully say — we are *"blessed with faithful Abraham."*

DIVINE RECOMPENCE

God gave the following glorious promise to Abraham during the first visitation.

•• Jehovah pledged — **"I will bless them that bless thee, and curse him that curseth thee."** (Genesis 12:3)

How magnificently this has been fulfilled over the centuries for natural Israel alone.

Every nation that has consistently blessed Israel and stood with Abraham's seed has always ended up being mightily blessed of God as a result. And every nation that has ever attempted to curse Israel has ended up falling under the terrible curse of God and the vengeance of the Almighty.

Behold Egypt in the days of Pharaoh (humbled in judgment).

Behold Amalek (destined to be destroyed forever).

Behold the Canaanites (conquered by the Jews and subdued supernaturally).

Behold Germany under Hitler's rule (finally crushed by the Allied Powers).

Behold the Arab nations (humiliated and defeated, over and over again, by this little nation whose population they vastly outnumber).

And behold the prophetic day, near at hand, when a great northern army (called Magog in Ezekiel 38) will make the grave error of attempting to destroy Israel.

Because this army will think an *"evil thought"* and seek to come against God's chosen and beloved natural nation, she will see five-sixths of her army destroyed in one day — supernaturally destroyed by hail, fire and brimstone pouring out of heaven.

Yes, history has proven, and will yet prove, that it is literally impossible to ultimately defeat this nation that God loves so intensely.

It is important to note though, that this is not necessarily because of the goodness or the worthiness of all Jews.

This is just the blessing of Abraham overflowing from one generation to the next.

Now, if the *transfer of blessing* works this powerfully when it involves just the natural offspring of the patriarch Abraham, then *how much more* powerfully should it go into effect when the contributing circumstances involve the spiritual offspring of the Almighty God.

No person can bless a child of God without being blessed in return.

Neither can any person curse or mistreat a child of God without a curse of recompense returning to them as a result, unless they sincerely repent before the Lord.

Of course we do not wish harm on anyone and we even pray for our own enemies, but still we know that this law is in effect.

Therefore we need not fight our own battles, for the battle is the Lord's. (I Samuel 17:47)

We serve the same Almighty God who boasted — "Vengeance is Mine; I will repay, saith the Lord." (Romans 12:19)

The God that slew one hundred eighty-five thousand Assyrians in one night by the angel of the Lord will surely defend us also.

The prophet Isaiah prophesied to that heathen nation that defied Israel saying — "Whom hast thou reproached and blasphemed? and against whom hast thou exalted thy voice . . . even against the Holy One of Israel." (Isaiah 37:23)

By fighting against Israel, the Assyrians were actually fighting against God, therefore it was impossible for them to win.

•• Again, if this works for the natural sons of Abraham, then how much more should it work for His spiritual posterity!

When the Jewish elders of the Sanhedrin court were intent on killing the disciples, Gamaliel, a great teacher in Israel, gave them a stern and urgent warning, saying — "Refrain from these men, and let them alone: for if this counsel or work be of men, it will come to nought: but if it be of God, ye cannot overthrow it; lest haply ye be found even to *fight against God."* (Acts 5:38-39)

This was the blessing of Abraham resting on the early disciples. To fight against them was to fight against the God that lived in their hearts and who can possibly fight against God and win!

This is the same blessing that rests upon us even now!!!

The Bible has also made it quite clear that this recompense can be eternal (for those who bless or curse a true child of God) . . . for on the Day of Judgment, Jesus will make the pronouncement — "Inasmuch as ye have done it unto one of the least of these My brethren, ye have done it unto Me." (Matthew 25:40)

This is the miraculous and wondrous way that Jesus Christ identifies with His believers.

This is the blessing of Abraham in manifestation . . . eternally.

In light of these things, we are convinced that Satan fights against us in vain. People that set themselves against us can never ultimately harm us.

All things will ultimately work out to our benefit for we are — *"blessed with faithful Abraham."* (Galatians 3:9)

DIVINE PROTECTION AND REWARD

After winning a phenomenal victory against four kings with only three hundred men, Abraham received another visitation of God.
•• The Lord came to him in a vision saying — **"I am thy shield and thy exceeding great reward."** (Genesis 15:1)

This is the blessing of Abraham manifesting in two new ways.

First of all, it speaks of divine protection.

This blessing rested upon David, and Goliath fell defenseless before him.

This blessing rested upon Jonathan and when he went out against the Philistines there was — "no restraint to the Lord to save by many or by few." (I Samuel 14:6)

This blessing rested upon Daniel and the lions in the pit became docile and harmless creatures.

This blessing rested upon Meshach, Shadrach and Abednego and the raging fire had no authority over them.

This is our inheritance as well . . . for we are children of Abraham.

Our God is a *shield of protection* against the powers of Satan, for He ever lives to make intercession for us. He gives us power over all the power of the enemy.

Our God is a *shield of protection* against sickness and disease, for He is Jehovah-Rapha. He promised not to even bring upon us the diseases of Egypt if we obey His statutes. (Exodus 15:26)

Our God is a *shield of protection* against emotional and mental oppression. He has promised that if we will always pray and let our requests be known unto God, the peace of God that passes all understanding will keep our hearts and minds through Christ Jesus. (Philippians 4:6-7)

Yes, we can have security in any and every situation. Regardless of what happens naturally (whether we get healed or not, whether we are delivered or not) we know that still, in all things, we are shielded and preserved unto eternal life.

The Lord has given His angels charge over us to keep us in all our ways.

No weapon formed against us shall prosper.

• Secondly, this *shield-promise* given to Abraham also included the pledge that the Lord would be his *exceeding great reward.*

He had shunned any reward from the king of Sodom for his great victory and for the return of Sodom's goods. (Genesis 14)

He was amazingly unselfish, therefore the Lord became his portion and walking in intimacy with God became his *exceeding great reward.*

It works the same with us.

Jesus rebuked the Pharisees who did their alms before men to be seen of them, as well as those who prayed long prayers and fasted in such a way that they would be noticed. (Matthew 6:1-21)

Jesus shockingly declared — "They have their reward."

Their reward was the cheap, ear-tickling, heart-bloating flattery with which they were corrupted.

They were puffed up with spiritual pride.

The leaven of hypocrisy took its toll.

They sold out for tinsel.

They sold out for nothing.

They totally lost the return reward they could have received had they worshipped God sincerely.

What a tragedy this is!

They were so close, yet so far, from the kingdom of God.

But we have seen the valuable for what it is.

• We know that it means far more to have the favor of God and the fellowship of His presence than all the empty adulation that men can give.

Knowing this, we can echo the heart cry of Jeremiah who declared — "The Lord is my portion, saith my soul; therefore will I hope in Him." (Lamentations 3:24)

Surely just having this *reward* alone (the spiritual opportunity of walking with God in this life) makes us — *"blessed with faithful Abraham."*

53

But there is yet more that needs to be said.

Abraham sought to keep his values and attitudes right because he was also seeking for a heavenly reward. He was looking — "for a city which hath foundations, whose builder and maker is God." (Hebrews 11:10)

He was not satisfied with merely what the earth had to offer, nor was he seeking only for those things of God available to believers during this earthly sojourn.

He was looking for an eternal inheritance and so are we.

We expect and desire to one day — "sit down with Abraham, Isaac, and Jacob, in the kingdom of heaven." (Matthew 8:11)

We know that God is not unmindful of our work and labor of love.

We know that our works are not in vain.

If they are performed in the name of the Lord, they have eternal merit and value.

Jesus said — "Behold, I come quickly; and my *reward* is with Me, to give every man according to as his work shall be." (Revelation 22:12)

Paul said, concerning that great day, that — "every man's work shall be made manifest; for the day shall declare it, because it shall be revealed by fire; and the fire shall try every man's work of what sort it is." (I Corinthians 3:13)

• If our works remain, we receive a *reward,* and God called it **an exceeding great reward.**

Surely there are no words available that can sufficiently describe the glorious destiny awaiting us in the kingdom to come where — "the glorious Lord will be unto us a place of broad rivers and streams." (Isaiah 33:21)

Unutterable splendor and unspeakable glory, O, surely it will come.

• But one of the most amazing things is the fact that we can determine the degree of heavenly reward awaiting us by what we do in this life.

We can actually lay up treasure in heaven. (Matthew 6:20)

O, what a blessing it is not to be locked inside of the law of the flesh any longer, where — *"all is vanity, and vexation of spirit."*

Our greatest earthly achievements were empty and vain before, disintegrating in front of us like crumbling cobwebs with one sweep of the hand.

But now we have finally discovered that which is valuable, meaningful, worthwhile and fulfilling . . . infinitely. We have learned how to sow seeds of devotion and service to God — seeds that we can reap an exceeding great reward from eternally. What a blessed opportunity!

This is wonderful . . . yet, this is even more than wonderful!

This is the blessing of Abraham resting upon us now!!!

EXCELLENT FRUITFULNESS AND BLESSED SECURITY
AN EVERLASTING POSSESSION

• God said to Abraham — "I will make thee **exceedingly fruitful** . . . and I will **establish My Covenant** between Me and thee and thy seed after thee . . . for **an everlasting covenant.**" (Genesis 17:6-7)

Now, the accepted definition of the word **covenant** is — *a formal, solemn, and binding agreement between two or more parties, especially for the performance of some action.*

So a covenant is already something that is considered binding and sure, but God went one step further and said that He would establish this agreement . . . everlastingly.

If God Himself avows something to be everlasting, then it has no beginning and no end.

It is so much a part of God that it is forever settled in the heavens like the Word itself.

Remember, a covenant almost always involves expectation of performance.

The Bible declared that Abraham was fully persuaded that what God had promised — "He was able also to perform." (Romans 4:21)

We are fully persuaded also.

We know that God will watch over His Word to perform it. We know that He will even hasten His word to perform it. (Jeremiah 1:12)

Paul said — "Being confident of this very thing, that He which hath begun a good work in you will perform it until the day of Jesus Christ." (Philippians 1:6)

God did not intend to do a temporary work when He came into our hearts; His intentions were eternal. We entered into *an everlasting covenant* with the Creator Himself, *an established covenant;* and we received *an everlasting possession* as a result.

We know that God pledged to Abraham — *"I will give unto thee, and to thy seed after thee, the land wherein thou art a stranger, all the land of Canaan, for **an everlasting possession.**"* (Genesis 17:8)

The fulfillment of this promise is both natural and spiritual.

Natural Canaan land belongs to the Jews now, but it will also surely be the everlasting possession of those saints who will be in the thousand year Millennial Kingdom of God to come.

It is a true saying that Canaan land will then be the spiritual and political center of the earth.

Jerusalem will be the capital city and the center of worship for all the inhabitants of the earth.

The throne of the King of kings will be there.

Certainly God will dwell with His people and His people will dwell with Him.

This, in itself, is most blessed.

But our everlasting possession involves much more than just a natural land of mountains and valleys and plains.

Our everlasting possession is presently a spiritual land, a land of life-giving, eternal promises that we have inherited as children of Abraham, as well as a vast, celestial, promised kingdom, yet to come.

We can boldly claim these promises knowing that God will surely bring them to pass.

• It is quite interesting to note that one of the promises God gave to Abraham and to us was the promise of being *exceedingly fruitful.*

Now it is vitally important to realize that the word **exceed** means — *to go beyond a limit, to surpass, transcend, excel and outdo.*

Foundationally, Abraham's promise of great fruitfulness was fulfilled in the multitude of his natural descendants (a natural nation that is still growing in number).

Secondly, it was fulfilled, and is being fulfilled, in the great multitude of his spiritual offspring (a spiritual nation that is still enlarging and multiplying itself).

But the third and greatest fulfillment of this promise to Abraham of abundant fruitfulness is found blossoming forth in and through the Son of God Himself.

Just look at the great fruitfulness that has already resulted from the life, death and resurrection of the Messiah, who is called **the Seed of Abraham.** (Galatians 3:16)

Behold how the law of sin and death was abolished, and *the perfect law of liberty* was exalted in its place, to reign over humanity.

Behold the breaking forth of grace into the realm of time . . . and all because of Calvary.

Survey the millions of miracles, deliverances, and healings that have already transpired in the lovely and powerful name of Jesus.

But look even further . . . into the future . . . and behold the fulfillment of our blessed hope, the resurrection of the dead and the translation of the living believers.

Behold the kingdom of God being established in this earth for a thousand years and the binding of Satan in the bottomless pit.

View this wilderness world becoming an Eden paradise again.

Then, as the fruitfulness keeps increasing, behold the eventual, ultimate renovation of all creation — the bringing forth of the new heaven and the new earth.

Then, throughout eternity, only God knows the continuing growth

56

in fruitfulness that will take place — far above and beyond anything we could ask or even think.

• In consideration of all these things, it is no wonder that God said to Abraham — "in thee shall all families of the earth be blessed" — "and in thy seed shall all the nations of the earth be blessed." (Genesis 12:3, 22:18)

• And it is no wonder that God used the Word *exceedingly* when He described Abraham's *ultimate fruitfulness* — for it surpasses and transcends anything that Abraham could have ever imagined possible. It is fruitfulness, eternally increasing, that goes beyond any limit — for there is no stopping point with God.
• It is fruitfulness that goes beyond the natural into the supernatural, ultimately abounding in that which is glorified and eternal.
We can perceive by this that the fruit of the suffering of Calvary will never cease to multiply itself in God's great universe.
As long as God exists, He will increase, therefore the results of what God has done in our lives will also eternally increase in excellence. And the fruitfulness that we give birth to, through suffering with Christ, will continue to multiply itself forever. This is precisely why — "the sufferings of this present time are not worthy to be compared with the glory which shall be revealed in us." (Romans 8:18)

For the suffering itself will eventually come to an end, but the reaping of the reward will never end!
Even as the potential to multiply in a seed is endless, so the increase-potential in a regenerated heart is endless (for the seed of eternal life has been planted within).
Therefore, we will never reach a stopping point: we will pass from glory to glory . . . throughout the ceaseless ages.
• This is the blessing of Abraham manifesting in us . . . *the blessing of being exceedingly fruitful . . . eternally fruitful . . . unceasingly and increasingly fruitful.*

No wonder Jesus said — "Abraham rejoiced to see My day: and he saw it, and was glad." (John 8:56)
Abraham apparently looked up from his paradise vantage point to the surface of the earth and saw God's solemn pledge to him coming to pass, when the Son of God walked in Judea . . . delivering the oppressed and setting the captive free (bearing spiritual fruit).
O, how Abraham's spirit must have soared into the heights of worship as he rejoiced with joy unspeakable over what he saw at the dawning of the New Covenant.

But now — how the fruit is greatly increasing!
The name of Jesus is filling the earth and the results are manifesting in phenomenal ways.

How much more then should high praises be erupting in the celestial realms now . . . for God is proving over and over again that He is still watching over the promises He gave to Abraham to keep them.

And God is still verifying, over and over again, that without a doubt, we are included, and that we are therefore — *"blessed with faithful Abraham."*

ULTIMATE VICTORY
ROYAL RESULTS

•• God promised Abraham — **"thy seed shall possess the gate of his enemies."** (Genesis 22:17)

The phrase — *thy seed* — refers primarily to Jesus.

His enemies are the satanic forces that have controlled, possessed and defiled the hearts and minds of men since the fall of Adam.

Until Jesus came, Satan ruled over the inhabitants of the earth with an iron fist.

This world was like an impregnable fortress of death . . . the gateway to the raging hell that burns in its heart.

Being born in this realm automatically meant, for almost all of humanity, the wretched state of being spiritually blind and mentally and emotionally dead . . . with no hope for anything better. But then the Captain of our Salvation invaded this enemy territory and began to wage war against sin, deception and the powers of evil.

Through death He destroyed him that had the power of death, that is the devil, and began the process of delivering those — "who through fear of death were all their lifetime subject to bondage." (Hebrews 2:14-15)

The prince of darkness had set up his kingdom here and had no intention of relinquishing control, but through the crucifixion and the resurrection, Jesus — "spoiled principalities and powers and . . . made a shew of them openly, triumphing over them in it." (Colossians 2:15)
To spoil is to plunder — to strip a defeated foe of his possessions.
This is exactly what Jesus did to the devil.

In a spiritual sense, He knocked down the gate of hell. He recaptured the keys of hell and of death. (Revelation 1:18) He re-established His dominion and lordship in this world. He stripped the devil of his authority. He reclaimed the human race and began restoring those who chose to yield to His influence.

He rebuilt the broken-down bridge spanning the gap between time and eternity, between heaven and earth.

He won the battle of the ages.

Ultimate victory was secured and sealed by His agony in Gethsemane and His passion at Calvary.

Now we are His occupational force . . . going forth into all the world, spiritually taking control of the territory that already rightfully belongs to the kingdom of God.

We know that the powers of hell will mount up against us, attacking us in certain areas of our lives (through certain emotional, mental, physical or spiritual gates) but in the name of Jesus, **we possess the gates of our enemies** (the channels through which evil spirits attack us), and we bring these personal battles under control . . . by the Word, by the Spirit, and by the blood.

Though Satan rages, he is engaged only in a futile, last-ditch effort to reclaim the control that he lost forever almost two thousand years ago.

He cannot stop the inevitable.

Jesus will complete the work that He has started, in the earth and in us.

The gates of hell cannot prevail against the Rock of ages, nor the church that has been built on the rock. (Matthew 16:18)

- We will ultimately prevail. We will possess the gates of our enemies even in a worldwide sense — for the very cities and nations that seem to be presently under Satan's control will ultimately come under our dominion forever. (Matthew 25:14-30, Luke 19:12-19)
- We are *the meek* who are destined to inherit the earth. (Matthew 5:5)
- We will definitely come into this inheritance . . . for it is the very inheritance-destiny that God promised to Abraham's seed. This blessed expectation is very much a part of the blessing of Abraham for he was called to be the heir of the world and such a status has, of course, been passed on to us as well. (Romans 4:13-14, refer also to RSV)

- In the beginning, Jehovah gave the patriarch a royal promise that — *"kings shall come out of thee."*

Now, it is true that this was fulfilled on a lesser level, in the natural kings that ruled over the Jews during the Old Covenant age.

But the perfect fulfillment of this promise is spiritual and eternal.

Jesus is the King of kings, and it is certain that all of His seed inherit His royal nature.

We are the kings over which He rules and through which He will set up His kingdom.

It is a prophetic fact that Satan has lost all hope: his evil empire is disintegrating right before his eyes.

It is also a prophetic fact that we will reign with Jesus forever . . . in the earth and throughout his vast universe in the New Creation to come.

This is the blessing of Abraham manifesting in *royal results* and *ultimate victory!*

THE WORKS OF ABRAHAM
AND THE MOST MIRACULOUS BLESSING OF ALL

We have already established that — "they which are of faith, the same are the children of Abraham." (Galatians 3:7)

•• But we also know that according to James 2:20 — **"faith without works is dead."**

Therefore, it is logical to conclude that if we really have the Abraham-kind of faith, then we will also manifest works similar to his.

This New Testament writer went on to say:

> *"Was not Abraham our father justified by works, when he had offered Isaac his son upon the altar?*
> *Seest thou how faith wrought with his works, and by works was faith made perfect?*
> *And the Scripture was fulfilled which saith, Abraham believed God, and it was imputed unto him for righteousness: and he was called the Friend of God.*
> *Ye see then how that by works a man is justified, and not by faith only."* (James 2:21-24)

Real faith always results in works.

This is the difference between dead faith and living faith; this is the indicator.

We are only — *"blessed with faithful Abraham"* — if we are of faith; and we are only of faith if we have the manifestation of certain works.

"For as the body without the spirit is dead, so faith without works is dead also."

Jesus confirmed this in a heated discussion that He had with certain Jews that were somewhat offended at His preaching. (John 8:31-39)

He explained to them — "If ye continue in My word, then are ye My disciples indeed; and ye shall know the truth, and the truth shall make you free."

They answered Him — "We be Abraham's seed, and were never in bondage to any man: how sayest Thou, Ye shall be made free."

60

• Jesus then uttered a profound statement that should still be echoing in the hearts of believers today, spurring us into action. He said — *"If ye were Abraham's children ye would do the works of Abraham."* (John 8:39)

Many of those who heard Jesus that day just could not measure up to this demand.

They were not walking in faith; they were merely under the law, students of Jewish theology. It is apparent that they did not have a personal relationship with the God that Abraham served. They were bound by spiritual pride, enslaved by sin, and blinded by a certain false sense of religious self-sufficiency. Thus, it was impossible for them to even see their own need.

They could not manifest the works of Abraham, because they did not have the faith of Abraham, nor the fullness of the revelation of the Almighty God that he possessed.

We that are born again are a different breed altogether.

We are walking in faith, for we are of faith.

We know Jehovah-Jireh, *the God who will provide.*

He has poured His essence into us . . . the very divine nature that influenced Abraham and shaped his actions and attitudes.

Abraham was greatly affected by his revelation of the Almighty God, but we are begotten of that revelation.

Therefore, how much more should we manifest works similar to those manifested by the patriarch of the Jewish race himself!

It behooves us therefore to search out what these works of Abraham were, to which Jesus referred, and then zealously and fervently strive to see similar works reproduced and perfected in our own lives.

*   *   *   *   *   *

• The works of Abraham could be described as the *acts or actions* that resulted from certain *admirable attitudes* that Abraham cultivated and developed within himself. Romans 4:17-25 gives us a list of some of these attitudes.

When Sarah was yet barren, and the promised son had not yet come, the Bible said that — "against hope [Abraham] believed in hope, that he might become the father of many nations."

Another translation said that — "when hope seemed hopeless" Abraham kept believing. (NEB)

Hope is desire married to expectation.

It is apparent that Abraham worked at maintaining this admirable attitude.

Abraham also worked at being persistent in his believing. The Bible said that "He staggered not at the promises of God through unbelief; but was strong in faith."

His strong, persistent faith pushed him over the top.

Abraham worked at maintaining a heart fixed on the positive promises of God. "He considered not his own body now dead . . . neither the deadness of Sarah's womb."

In other words, Abraham refused to even contemplate on the outward and inward hindrances to the plan and purpose of God in his life. He knew that God could and would do it, so he rested in confidence. Instead of considering the greatness of the opposition, he considered the greatness of his God.

Finally, Abraham worked at being unselfish, he worked at giving glory to God, and he worked at loving God unreservedly and obeying Him implicitly.

But even though Abraham worked at developing and maintaining all these personality traits — if they existed only in his spirit, as of yet unmanifested, they would still be, in a certain sense, insufficient of themselves to justify him before God.

These qualities of character, though praiseworthy, could never really be labeled *works of Abraham* until they were tangibly manifested in some *act or action.*

Of course, real hope will always ultimately manifest in works. Real unselfishness, real faith, real love, and real obedience will all eventually manifest in works.

• *Works are positive and tangible proof of the existence of certain intangible and unseen character qualities.*

Abraham proved for instance his unselfishness by giving Lot the best land.

Abraham proved his devotion and his desire to give God the glory when he paid tithes to Melchizedek from the spoil procured in the battle with Chedorlaomer and his three confederate kings.

• But supremely Abraham proved his faith, his obedience and his love for God by immediately responding and submitting to God's first demand that he leave his homeland and later on to the demand that he sacrifice one of the very things he loved the most in this world — his beloved son, Isaac.

In fact, when the knife was raised in Abraham's hand, poised above Isaac's chest, surely Abraham proved himself to God, more than ever before.

By works he was justified, and not by faith alone.

His works clearly indicated, demonstrated, and evidenced his faith.

He proved his commitment, for he put the will of God first above his own feelings, and he proved the depth of his faith, for he knew God would have to raise Isaac from the dead to fulfill his original promise.

•• As a direct result, Abraham received what is possibly the greatest of all the promises of blessing that God gave to him — *the blessing of imputed righteousness.*

This happened in the beginning too.

• When God promised that Abraham's dead body, and Sarah's dead womb, would actually bring forth life, Abraham believed, and the Bible said that God — *"counted it to him for righteousness."* (Genesis 15:6)

• Whenever Abraham manifested resurrection-faith (believing that God could actually bring life out of death) this blessing would come.

This same imparted righteousness is presently available to us also, for we too believe that our God can bring life out of death. (Romans 4:23-25)

We believe He can actually turn our sorrows into joy.

We believe that He can take the greatest trials and tribulations of our lives and bring forth good out of them all. (Romans 8:28)

We believe that He is ever able to resurrect us from the death-grip of sin by His precious blood. We believe that He will preserve us from the wicked one who seeks continually to devour us with mental, emotional and spiritual death.

We believe that ultimately His power will resurrect us from the grave, or translate and glorify us if we are alive at His coming.

We prove that we believe these things, by obediently sacrificing, when God demands it, some of the things in life we may love or desire the most. But we deny ourselves in order to please God.

Yes, we prove that we really believe the gospel when we strive to sincerely obey His Word-commands, both written and living.

By maintaining this ABRAHAM-KIND OF WORK (obedience and self-denial), we prove that we truly have the ABRAHAM-KIND OF FAITH, and we thereby inherit and receive the ABRAHAM-KIND OF BLESSING.

We are counted righteous in the sight of God. (Romans 4:23-25)

We are justified first by faith in the crucifixion and resurrection of Jesus, but then we prove our faith by maintaining a willing spirit, submissively attempting to come out of the world and be a separate people.

By doing this, we place ourselves in a *position of receptivity* where we can receive, by faith and not by works, exactly what God has for us.

It is a true saying that only those who make this kind of sincere attempt at righteousness can rightfully claim and receive the imparted righteousness of God.

Only those who seek and strive are counted blameless before the throne of the Almighty God . . . but blameless and holy they are, in the name of Jesus!!

We are bold to say that this is certainly the most miraculous of all the blessings of Abraham that we have inherited!!

How glorious it is that men and women, once bound by the filthiness of sin can claim perfection in Christ now, and the ultimate destiny of being perfected in the holiness of God forever!!

This is our heritage and this is our faith.

We seek to imitate the positive character-qualities that Abraham possessed, and we prove our acquisition of them by works.

It is then that we fully walk into the abundant blessings of the Abrahamic covenant.

THE CONCLUSION OF THE WHOLE MATTER

It is important now that we review and summarize all of the vitally important points covered in this essay.

We are *of faith,* therefore we are *the children of Abraham.*

If we are *the children of Abraham,* then we will do the *works of Abraham,* thereby inheriting the *blessing of Abraham.*

The *blessing of Abraham* will manifest itself, in our lives, in the following ways, if we sincerely strive to walk in submission and obedience:

God will bless us materially and spiritually, and make us a blessing to others (which is the greatest blessing of all).

God will prosper us eternally and make our names great.

God will recompense both those who bless us and those who curse us.

God will provide His abiding presence as a shield of protection.

God will grant us an exceeding great reward, in this present world and the world to come, for the works we do in His name.

God will make us exceedingly fruitful (eternally, increasingly fruitful) granting us an everlasting covenant and an everlasting possession!

God will cause us to possess the gates of our enemies. We will also receive the earth as our inheritance.

God will exalt us as kings, and raise us up to reign with Him. But, most miraculous of all, God will grant us a standing of righteousness in His presence . . . now and forevermore.

It is certain that all these things can be labeled *present possessions,* as well as a future inheritance potential.

Therefore, we happily arrive at the following definite conclusion.

Refusing to waver, we affirm once and for all . . . WE ARE **THE CHILDREN OF PROMISE!**

YES — WE ARE **THE CHILDREN OF ABRAHAM!**
WE ARE THAT **GREAT AND ETERNAL NATION,** SPRING-
ING FORTH FROM THE SEED OF ABRAHAM (JESUS) — ULTI-
MATELY DESTINED TO INHERIT ALL THINGS.

We **have been** as the dust of the earth.
We **shall be** as the stars of heaven.

*　　　　*　　　　*　　　　*　　　　*　　　　*

> *"Wherein God, willing more abundantly to
> shew unto the **HEIRS OF PROMISE** the immu-
> tability of His counsel, confirmed it by an oath:*
> *That by two immutable things, in which it was
> impossible for God to lie, we might have a strong
> consolation, who have fled for refuge to lay hold
> upon the hope set before us:*
> *Which hope we have as an anchor of the soul,
> both sure and stedfast, and which entereth into
> that **WITHIN THE VEIL"***
>
> (Hebrews 6:17-19).

THE CHILDREN OF GOD

THE CHILDREN
OF THE RESURRECTION

"But they which shall be accounted worthy to obtain that world, and the resurrection from the dead, neither marry, nor are given in marriage.

Neither can they die anymore: for they are equal unto the angels; and are **THE CHILDREN OF GOD,** *being* **THE CHILDREN OF THE RESURRECTION."** (Luke 20:35-36)

THE CHILDREN OF GOD
THE CHILDREN OF THE RESURRECTION

"But they which shall be accounted worthy to obtain that world, and the resurrection from the dead, neither marry, nor are given in marriage.
Neither can they die anymore: for they are equal unto the angels: and are THE CHILDREN OF GOD, being THE CHILDREN OF THE RESURRECTION."   (Luke 20:35-36)

All animal species, and every certain race of humanity, pass on their nature and their attributes to their offspring.

Wolves do not bring forth sheep, neither do sheep bring forth wolves.

Vicious wolves will beget like vicious offspring.

Docile, gentle sheep will beget lambs just as docile and gentle.

There is a *transfer of nature* as well as an inheritance of like physical appearance.

And what is true naturally is also true spiritually.

We are the children of God; we have been born again.

Divine nature has been transferred to us and generated in us.

Jesus is the everlasting Word — He is the Living Word and the embodiment of the written Word.

• This eternal Word *(logos)* now lives in our hearts. We actually have been begotten of this infinite Word of life, therefore we have received a Word-nature (the same nature that our Father possesses).

We are vessels of authority, for authority abides in the Word, and the Word abides in us.

The words of Jesus were and are stronger than death.

The words of Jesus are spirit and they are life . . . resurrection life! (John 6:63)

Because we are Word-children, this same resurrection life has become an integral part of our spiritual makeup.

This is exactly why we can confidently laugh at famine, death and destruction! (Job 5:22)

God is for us; who and what can possibly be against us?

We are winners; the Word in us cannot be conquered — neither can we be conquered as long as we yield to its influence.

JESUS — RESURRECTION AND LIFE

• The Bible declared that death could not hold Jesus in its terrifying grip — *"because it was not possible that He should be holden of it."* (Acts 2:24)

•• Three main things brought Jesus out of the grave — the Word, the Spirit, and faith.

First of all, the *written Word* had already foretold in prophecy that Jesus' soul would not be left in hell, neither would His flesh see corruption. (Acts 2:22-35)

Surely, because of this, and in light of this, Jesus dared to go one step further and speak the living Word in the face of death itself.

He boldly announced to a crowd of unbelieving Jews — "Destroy this temple, and in three days I will raise it up." (John 2:19)

Of course, when He used the word *temple,* He was referring to His own physical body that was soon to be mutilated almost beyond recognition.

But His words, packed full of creative faith and resurrection life, went before Him, entering into the grave with Him. Three days later this *word of faith confession* brought Him out victorious and triumphant!

Secondly, the Bible declared also that He was *"quickened by the Spirit."* (I Peter 3:18)

And thirdly, the Spirit and the Word rescued Him and lifted Him from the very jaws of destruction, simply because He believed!

Resurrection life is always triumphant over corruption! Resurrection life is always victorious over depression, oppression and darkness.

This divine life is always stronger than death . . . but what is even more wonderful, this quality of divinity is at work in us now!

This is exactly why a child of God just cannot be kept down!

We have been begotten of the Word and born of the Spirit . . . both the Word and the Spirit have penetrated us to the very core of our being.

It is an undeniable and eternal fact that both of these mediums of divine expression contain, manifest and impart to us the resurrection life of God.

Therefore, we have nothing to fear if we are sincere in our commitment to the Father.

Powers and principalities are subject to us . . . in the name of Jesus!

We are stronger than anything hell can manufacture. There is an overflow of victory from the grave of resurrection flooding our hearts and overflowing our lives right now.

IT IS JUST AS IMPOSSIBLE FOR US TO BE SWALLOWED UP BY DEFEAT AND PERMANENTLY HELD IN THE GRIPS OF DEATH AS IT WAS FOR JESUS, THE FIRSTBORN SON OF GOD (IF WE KEEP OUR ATTITUDES RIGHT BEFORE GOD).

If we are among the living believers who are instantly translated at the coming of the Lord, or if we have to temporarily go the way of the grave, still either way we can shout the victory!

We have been enlightened! We joyously declare that we have the same spirit that raised Christ from the dead.

We are persuaded therefore that He will raise us up also, if we place our trust unreservedly in His indwelling presence.

• The Captain of our salvation has already declared — *"I am the resurrection, and the life: he that believeth in Me, though he were dead, yet shall he live."* (John 11:25)

Even apart from the physical aspect, we know that death will often seek to ensnare us in one of its vicious traps (mental death, emotional death or even spiritual death).

But this ruthless, tyrannical master of the human race cannot hold a sincere, blood-washed child of God under its sway — if that child of God will dare to believe, boldly speak, and energetically appropriate the promises of God (promises of mercy, grace, forgiveness, righteousness and restoration).

These promises are weapons that are mighty through God.

Jesus made it so clear — *"he that believeth in Me, though he were dead, yet shall he live."*

If a believer for a season seems to almost *die* emotionally, mentally or even spiritually . . .

If a believer is temporarily overwhelmed . . .

• If a believer is temporarily pulled down to the bottom, into some kind of spiritual grave, the believer still has a challenge to *be at the bottom believing!!*

We can have the blessed assurance that God will bring us out, for we know that He has already spoken — "I will open your graves, and cause you to come up out of your graves . . . and ye shall know that I am the Lord, when I have opened your graves, O My people." (Ezekiel 37:12-13)

Through this Scripture we understand, on one definite and valid level of interpretation, that all the graves Satan digs for us are actually golden opportunities for our God to prove how mighty He really is in our behalf.

In the day that He brings deliverance to us, we will be all the more convinced that He really is God and that He really is the resurrection and the life — Lord of all power and might!

We have concluded therefore that no matter what happens, faith is the key!

Faith in the Word pulls us back up again. Faith in the Spirit propels us to victory.

Faith in the Word, and faith in the Spirit will always put us over the top and raise us up in power and authority, if we keep our hearts right.

Faith never recognizes defeat. Faith brings restoration.

Faith never considers circumstance. Faith keeps us spiritually alive.

Faith is resurrection life in action.

Faith releases the quickening power of the Word and the Spirit into our lives . . . into the past, into the present and into the future.

Faith can definitely change the unchangeable.

Faith is our normal way of reacting now, for the personality of deity has pervaded our spirits.

We do not know how to stay down for we have not inherited a quitting spirit!

Peter said that we have been begotten again unto a **lively hope** (a living, eternal hope — an undying, imperishable, indestructible, constant, ever-continuing hope) by the resurrection of Jesus Christ from the dead. (I Peter 1:3)

Because death was swallowed up in victory then, we cannot be swallowed up by death now.

Death has lost its sting.

No matter how rough things get we know that our hope can be constant. We know that without Jesus life is a hopeless end, but with Jesus life is endless hope!

We abide in His life-giving presence. He has rebuked the devourer for our sakes.

We know that immediate restoration is always available to us in the Spirit, if we remain sincere in our love for God.

No wonder, the Scripture declares — *"Rejoice not against me, O mine enemy: when I fall, I shall arise; when I sit in darkness, the Lord shall be a light unto me."* (Micah 7:8)

IDENTIFYING WITH CHRIST

•• **We are identified with Christ.**

Because He lives, we can live also! (John 14:19)

Of course, it hasn't always been this way. In fact, we perished in Adam before we were ever born, for the sperm seed that would eventually bring us forth was hidden in his loins when he fell from his state of oneness with God.

In a very real way therefore, we were separated from God the very moment that he was, because we were in him.

In a parallel way, we that are born again identify with Jesus spiritually. We identify with His great victory!

It is certain that when Adam lost, we lost; but it is also just as certain that when Jesus won, *we won!*

The Word-seed that eventually entered into us, causing the new birth, has always been "hid with Christ in God!"

At the appointed time, this Word-seed was planted in our spirits, causing a sacred conception and resulting in the birth of a new creation.

But this divine part of us has always been a part of Him!

So in a very real way, when He arose out of the grave, we arose triumphantly with Him, and in Him!

When He conquered death, in a sense we conquered with Him and in Him.

When He ascended up on high, far above all principalities and powers, we ascended with Him and in Him.

Right now, He is seated on a throne of authority in the heavenlies.

It is certain that, spiritually speaking, we are presently seated with Him.

• The Bible emphatically states that God has — *"raised us up together, and made us sit together in heavenly places in Christ Jesus."* (Ephesians 2:6)

Therefore we share His position of *rest, victory and authority* . . . right now!

This very revelation gives us a dogged determination to arise and shine, no matter how dark the darkness gets.

We have — "the promise of life that now is." (I Timothy 4:8)

We are clean, unrebukable, and unreprovable in His sight — right now!

We are free from condemnation — right now!

We are holy and blameless — right now!

We are perfect in Christ — right now!

We are "in Him" and "in Him" is life (John 1:4) — creative life, renewing life, restoring life, the life of imparted righteousness.

We believe that this resurrection life will one day overflow from the spiritual into the natural, and its transforming work will then come to completion in us.

For — "when He shall appear, we shall be like Him, for we shall see Him as He is!"

• The Bible went on to say that — "every man that hath this hope in him **purifieth** himself, **even as He is pure!"** (I John 3:2-3)

This is absolutely wonderful!

By maintaining faith in the resurrection power of God, we are kept sanctified and purified . . . resurrected spiritually every moment we spend in His presence.

• Therefore, through the precious blood of Jesus, and the resurrection life of God that is in the blood, we have a new beginning every day and the dawning of a new day every moment.

What an edifying truth! What a spirit-lifting revelation! What a life-changing discovery!

No wonder the Bible emphatically states — "Happy is that people whose God is the Lord." (Psalm 144:15)

QUICKENED ETERNALLY

• The Scripture teaches us that — "as in Adam all die, even so in Christ shall all be made alive." (I Corinthians 15:22)

The Greek word — *zoopoieo* — is translated into this two-word English phrase — *made alive.*

It is interesting to note that *zoopoieo* is also translated in several other passages of Scripture into the English words — *quickening, quickeneth and quickened.*

To be **quickened** means — *to be revived, to be stimulated, to be animated, or to be made alive.*

This is exactly what Jesus has done for us.

•• I Corinthians 15:45 states that — *"The first man Adam was made a living soul; [but] the last Adam [Jesus] was made a quickening spirit."*

It is a faithful saying that no human being can come into intimate spiritual contact with this Jesus without being *quickened* as a result (raised from death unto life).

Ephesians 2:1 states — "And you hath He *quickened* who were dead in trespasses and sins."

He came into our hearts fully intending to express Himself this way (an ambitious and determined life-giver . . . *a quickening spirit).*

He created us alive with the very life of God.

He resurrected us into divinity in the inner man.

He revived us then and continues to revive us daily on our journey to heaven.

This was never meant to be merely a one-time experience; this is a continuing process . . . as steady, persistent and necessary as the beating of the heart.

He continually stimulates us by His Word and by His Spirit.

We are animated now, full of spiritual activity and movement. We have more than a blood covering, for the blood of Jesus flows through us constantly . . . renewing us constantly, for life is in the blood.

We are in the resurrection family — the family of deity. We are very much like our Father and very much like our Elder Brother.

• The Bible said that — "as the Father hath *life in Himself;* so hath He given to the Son to have *life in Himself."* (John 5:26)

The Greek word that was translated *life* in the above passage was not *psuche* which means **natural life;** it was *zoe* — meaning *divine life.*

We have obtained a similar inheritance also, for we are joint-heirs with Christ.

Jesus Himself pledged — "I am come that they might have *life,* and that they might have it more abundantly." (John 10:10)

The word rendered *life* in this passage is again *zoe,* for we have received the priceless gift and the precious treasure of possessing *divine life within ourselves.*

Now in reference to God, this kind of statement speaks of His total self-sufficiency and self-reliance . . . for He is the Self-Existent One. He possesses *life within Himself.* But in reference to us, such a statement means that because we are linked to Him, we find total sufficiency in Him. We need no other source.

We rely on Him utterly and draw our spiritual *life* out of Him who knows no limitation.

THE WELL OF LIVING WATER

• The very moment that the Spirit of God entered into us at salvation, something mysterious and miraculous took place, deep within our hearts.

A wellspring of divinity was created within us, as infinitely deep as God Himself!

A river of resurrection life began flowing out of us, as consistent, unlimited and perpetual as God Himself.

Yes, 'this is a river that never runs dry, therefore we will never lack, as long as we yield to its influence.

This river of life keeps us *quickened,* enlivened with the very *life* of the Almighty God.

Jesus was surely referring to this gift of inherent divine life in His sermon to the woman at the well. (John 4:1-30)

• He said — *"Whosoever drinketh of the water that I shall give him shall never thirst; but the water that I shall give him shall be in him a well of water springing up into everlasting life."* (John 4:14)

This river of living water is not flowing from without . . . in, it is flowing from within . . . out.

We realize that this river of Holy Spirit life (resurrection life) will keep flowing out of our hearts, into our lives, as long as we seek after obedience, and as long as we keep believing.

• Jesus said — *"He that believeth on Me, as the Scripture hath said, out of his belly [his innermost being] shall flow rivers of living water."* (John 7:38)

Surely, if we maintain faith, humility and sincerity, this river will keep lifting us, resurrecting us, into our rightful place of inheritance and harmony with God.

• It must be said that even as two natural elements (hydrogen and oxygen) make up natural water, so two spiritual elements (the Word and the Spirit) make up this spiritual water.

And Jesus did promise that if we drink of this water we will never thirst.

This does not mean that once we are saved we become so satisfied that we never desire anything deeper in God; it rather means that if we have this inward gift of eternal life we will never want for sufficient grace and power to meet our needs. No matter how great our thirst gets spiritually, there will always be enough spiritual water available to quench that thirst, even as there was always enough water in the rock to sustain the Jews in the wilderness.

We could also view this "never-thirsting promise" another way.

At the moment we are converted, we merely lift the cup of salvation to our lips and take the first refreshing sip.

From that moment forward, it is apparent that, contrariwise, we never cease to thirst . . . in fact, more often than not, our thirst, our deep craving for God, tends to increase yet more and more.

But every day we eagerly and gratefully lift *the golden cup* again and again.

Surely this omnipotent and sovereign Lord of our lives has our allotted time, and our allotment of grace, so ordered that the very last day we spend in this earth realm — we will also finally drink this soul-fulfilling cup to the dregs.

Then in a certain sense, we will set this cup aside and depart from this realm . . . *never to thirst again!*

But until that day we must avail ourselves of every opportunity to drink in more of the Word and more of the Spirit (the same spiritual elixir that sustained Jesus when He walked over the sun-parched and sin-parched sands of time).

Nothing that the firstborn Son ever faced in the valley of death's shadow ever conquered Him — because He stayed full of life.

Now He has challenged us to walk in His footsteps and do the same.

• But to enjoy these privileges of being *risen with Christ,* and *quickened* in Him, it is imperative that we set our — "affection on things above, not on things on the earth." (Colossians 3:1-2)

We will only know Him in the power of His resurrection, if we are willing to know Him in the fellowship of His suffering — "being made conformable unto His death." (Philippians 3:10)

Having reached this point, and having achieved this attitude, we no longer progress by our own strength and power.

We are carried forward to our eternal goal by a deep, strong current of the love of God.

We know that — *"all the rivers run into the sea"* — and that this is true in the spiritual as well as in the natural. (Ecclesiastes 1:7)

The vast ocean of eternal life is wooing, drawing and compelling this *river of divinity* that flows out of the unfathomable depth of the regenerated heart.

• The life of God without is an irresistible force constraining the life of God within to complete its journey and finally pass from time into eternity.

This inward river is stronger than anything in its path; it will cut through spiritual granite rock (the most immovable opposition that Satan can muster against us).

This inward river is the divine personality, the same thing that carried Jesus victoriously through death, hell and the grave, so surely it will do the same for us!

We are well able! We are masters of circumstances! We are champions and overcomers!

We cannot lose, for we are of the truth!

• The obstacles have already been removed, for Jesus rolled the stone away almost two thousand years ago, for Himself and for us also.

We are thrilled about our present inheritance of perpetual blood-bought victory that has come as a result, but we are even more ecstatic about our future destiny.

We are speedily approaching the day of total restoration, redemption and recreation.

We are seeking to apprehend something that is actually apprehending us. (Philippians 3:12)

Soon, Jesus will appear, descending from above.

"All that are in the graves shall hear His voice." (John 5:28)

The heavens will rend.

Resurrection power will erupt in us — fully overpowering, subduing, then recreating our Adam-flesh.

We will rise to meet Him in the air. We will be changed in a moment, in the twinkling of an eye.

We will be glorified!

Death will finally receive a death-dealing blow itself, ultimately to be cast into the lake of fire. (Revelations 20:14)

•• THIS AWFUL SENSE OF SEPARATENESS FROM GOD WILL BE GONE FOREVER, FOR THIS INWARD RIVER WILL FINALLY EMPTY INTO THE INFINITE OCEAN AND BE ABSORBED IN THE INDESCRIBABLE BLISS OF ABSOLUTE ONENESS WITH GOD.

Resurrection life will carry us successfully and triumphantly all the way through.

We will win . . . ultimately, completely and eternally.

We have to! Winning is a part of our nature now.

WE ARE THE CHILDREN OF THE RESURRECTION!
WE ARE THE CHILDREN OF THE ALMIGHTY GOD!

A CROWN OF GLORY

A CROWN OF BEAUTY

A ROYAL DIADEM

"Thou shalt also be A CROWN OF GLORY in the hand of the Lord, and A ROYAL DIADEM in the hand of thy God." (Isaiah 62:3)

A CROWN OF GLORY
A CROWN OF BEAUTY
A ROYAL DIADEM

*"Thou shalt also be A CROWN OF GLORY
in the hand of the Lord, and A ROYAL DIA-
DEM in the hand of thy God."* (Isaiah 62:3)

The supreme accomplishment of a person's life is spoken of as his *"crowning glory."*

A person's greatest achievement is what crowns him with honor and joy and gives him a feeling of worth . . . a warm sense of fulfillment.
• If this is true, and it is, then certainly God's *crowning glory* — His greatest achievement — in time and eternity, is the glorious salvation of His elect and chosen people from their sin, and the glorious destiny and inheritance they have received from Him.

Everything in God's creation is miraculous . . . from the unfolding of the smallest flower blossom, to the wondrous and curious formation of life in the womb, to the swirling of the mightiest galaxies in the heavens.

But the most remarkable work, the most miraculous divine act of all, is the awe inspiring transformation that comes to human beings who dare to believe the blessed gospel of Jesus Christ and receive His saving grace.

Sin slaves destined for damnation, in a moment's time become heirs of the very righteousness of God, destined to share His glory forever.

Spiritual beggars, controlled by dead minds and carnal passions, are suddenly born into a royal family of overcomers. These regenerated men and women, once referred to as losers, are suddenly spoken of as being more than conquerors, through the love of God overflowing their hearts and lives.

Bankrupt souls, spiritually poverty-stricken, are suddenly accepted in an elite group, the richest of the rich — destined to inherit all the countless, boundless, limitless treasures that are hid with Christ in God.

The patriarch Joseph, in one day's time, was lifted from the lowest place in Egypt (the king's dungeon) to the highest position in the land (sharing Pharaoh's throne).

This drastic and sudden turn of events was undeniably miraculous, yet what God is doing for every born again believer is even more miraculous.

We were trapped in a prison house of human flesh; bars of bones enclosed our souls in spiritual darkness and ignorance.

We were like unclean beasts, our hearts polluted with the sin-nature. At our best state we were altogether vanity!

But wonder of wonders . . .
He remembered us in our low estate.
His heart burned in compassion toward us.
He reached down with His nail-scarred hand and opened the prison doors. He set us free.
He brought us out of the deep — the violent, churning waters of eternal death in which we were drowning.
He has promised to lift us from this cesspool of sin and deliver us from this place that is certainly, apart from hell itself, the lowest sink-hole of despair in the universe.
He has covenanted to elevate us to the highest position available in creation — sharing the throne of the Almighty God!

• We that were wretched and poor spiritually will ultimately obtain awesome kingdom responsibilities, governing vast realms, quite possibly and eventually both natural and spiritual, at the behest of God.

We will be suddenly changed . . . participants in one of the most drastic turn of events that the universe will ever witness.
And certainly, through it all, the depth of God's love and power will be unveiled . . . in a depth that will never be surpassed.

•• **Therefore, there is absolutely nothing in the creation that can prove God's greatness as well.**
No blazing, radiant sun mysteriously holding planets in their orbits by an unseen power.
No majestic mountain penetrating the sky, embraced with the warm glow of the dawning of a new day.
No eagle soaring spectacularly on the wings of the wind.
No crisp and clear autumn night, aglow with innumerable starry lights.
No throng of angelic ministering spirits, arrayed in the splendor of celestial garments, lifting their voices to make heaven resound with the thunder of their praise.

None of these things can prove God's glory and heap honor on Him as well as those who have been brought out of darkness into His marvelous light . . . washed from their sins in the precious blood of Jesus and made to become heirs of eternal life.

Therefore, we are HIS DIADEM OF BEAUTY . . . for the beauty of His character is clearly revealed by the way he has compassionately dealt with us.

We are HIS CROWNING GLORY . . . His everlasting trophy, His memorial of victory, the proof of His greatness!

We are His greatest source of praise.

We are His prized possession forever . . . His eternal crown!

He has pledged that we belong to Him forever and that we will — "no more be termed forsaken." (Isaiah 62:4)

We are compelled to lift our voices, in praise to Him, for this wondrous gift from on high!

*   *   *   *   *   *

Now all these things that have been spoken are wonderful and true, but it is important that we realize — this is a reciprocal thing; it works both ways.

The bringing-forth of the bride of Christ is certainly the Lord's greatest singular achievement . . . *His crown of glory,* or, as the NAS translates it, *His crown of beauty.*

But responding to the wooing of His Spirit, receiving Him in our hearts, and following Him in submission and obedience is our supreme accomplishment in life.

As the world plunges into the dark abyss of the severe, final judgments of God, we will see, all the more clearly, the great value of our choice to serve the Master.

Isaiah prophesied again saying — "IN THAT DAY SHALL THE LORD OF HOSTS BE FOR A **CROWN OF GLORY,** AND FOR A **DIADEM OF BEAUTY,** UNTO THE RESIDUE OF HIS PEOPLE." (Isaiah 28:5)

Listen to these inspired words for it is certain that on the highest level of fulfillment, they will soon come to pass.*[1]

In the last days, the residue of the church will be *crowned* with the glory of God and beautified with the manifestation of His power and presence . . . in wonderful depth!

But this will happen manifestly only for those who recognize the Most High as a *crown of glory* and a *diadem of beauty* — in other words, those who magnify the Lord as our only source of glory and the only means by which we can be numbered among the royal seed.

Those who pay the price of discipleship, extolling His highness and praising His greatness this way will certainly blossom in God, in glory and beauty.

On the contrary, the false church, referred to as a crown of pride, shall discover her "glorious beauty . . . a fading flower," trodden underfoot by the Antichrist ("a mighty and strong one, which as a tempest of hail and a destroying storm . . . shall cast down to the earth with his hand"). (Isaiah 28:1-4)

But God's latter day remnant will be drawn close to His bosom.

We will be separated unto God and endued with *"the crown of the anointing oil."* (Leviticus 21:12)

He will flow through us in great love and authority.

We will be adorned with His infinite wisdom.

He will surely bestow upon His bride the very best of all that He has to give, and surely we will return the same to Him!

A man and woman, made to be one in the act of marriage, in a sense, *crown* each other with love, by *completing* one another.

Proverbs 12:4 says — *"a virtuous woman is a **crown** to her husband."*

Ephesians 5:23 declares — *"the husband is the head of the wife."*

And as it is in the natural, so shall it be in the spiritual.

The creation, transformation and exaltation of the spotless bride of Christ is the Lord's most perfect and successful act of *completing* Himself . . . *crowning Himself with glory.*

But yielding to His creative, transforming and exalting influence is our ultimate *crown of success* . . . bringing us to *completion* and perfection spiritually and eternally.

We are confident that this is the prophetic plan and purpose of God, and that it is surely being fulfilled in this hour . . . more and more as we draw near to that glorious day of resurrection and final glorification of the church.

THEN ETERNALLY . . . WE WILL BE **HIS ROYAL DIADEM OF BEAUTY,** AND HE WILL BE OURS!

We will be His supreme accomplishment in time and eternity, and He will be ours!

WE WILL BE **HIS CROWN OF GLORY!**

But even more so, He will be ours . . . forever and ever!!!

---

*¹On a lesser level of fulfillment, this passage is a reference to how Ephraim, the northern kingdom, was totally destroyed by the Assyrian invasion, but Judah was miraculously spared. Though much was destroyed at that time, the remnant that remained knew not to glory in the flesh any longer but rather in their God. He became "a **crown of glory and . . . a diadem of beauty**" unto the residue of Israelites left in the land. God **glorified** Himself by destroying 185,000 Assyrians in one night, smiting them by an angel of the Lord.

HIS DOVE

HIS LOVE

HIS UNDEFILED

"I sleep, but my heart waketh: it is the voice of my beloved that knocketh, saying, Open to Me, My sister, MY LOVE, MY DOVE, MY UNDEFILED."
(Song of Solomon 5:2)

His dove
His love
His undefiled

> *"I sleep, but my heart waketh: it is the voice of my beloved that knocketh, saying, Open to Me, My sister, MY LOVE, MY DOVE, MY UNDEFILED."*   (Song of Solomon 5:2)

• The bride of Christ is represented in this passage as a dove.

• To fully appreciate this symbolism, it is important to remember that in other passages of Scripture, both Jesus and the Holy Spirit are also depicted this way.

The Old Testament sacrifice of a dove for a burnt offering or a sin offering foreshadowed Jesus as the supreme sacrifice for our sins. (Leviticus 5:7-11)

Furthermore, the Bible tells us that when Jesus was baptized, He — "went up straightway out of the water: and, lo, the heavens were opened unto Him, and He saw the Spirit of God descending like a dove, and lighting upon Him." (Matthew 3:16)

So we see that scripturally, the bride of Christ, the Son of God and the Holy Spirit are all portrayed, in different instances, as a *dove*.

Surely, there is a reason for this divinely authored symbolism, a definite, meaningful reason that needs to be unveiled.

First, we must recognize that the Holy Spirit contains the personality of God, and that the divine personality actually contains certain *dove-like qualities*.

Next, we must realize that the first begotten Son of God contained, and still contains, all the fullness of the Holy Spirit . . . and certainly that *dove-like divine temperament* found fullness of expression in Him.

Finally, we must understand the mystery that — "of His fullness have all we received."

This dove-like personality has been transferred down through the Godhead into us.

We have inherited the indwelling of the Father's Spirit, the very personality of deity that was first revealed in Jesus and is now being expressed in every son and every daughter of God.

• No wonder the bridegroom (Jesus) complimented the bride (the body of Christ) in the Song of Solomon, saying — *"Behold, thou art fair, My love . . . thou hast dove's eyes within thy locks."* (Song of Solomon 4:1)

In other words, the bride is being praised for she has become so one with the Lord, and so filled with His Spirit, that she now *sees* things as He would see them.

She has *dove's eyes* . . . eyes like His eyes *"washed with milk, and fitly set."* (Song of Solomon 5:12)

She views circumstances from His heavenly perspective and she has learned to react with his divine attitudes, for her eyes have been *washed* with the *milk* of the Word and rigidly *set* with a firm determination to reach her heavenly goal.

She perceives the constant loving flow of revelation truth underlying every circumstance in life.

Her eyes like His are *"as the eyes of doves by the rivers of waters"* reflecting the deep still current of eternal wisdom in every passing ripple of that infinite river called time.

She has *dove's eyes* . . . eyes that are shining with faith, even when disaster appears imminent, eyes that are clear with purity, intense with fervency, and bright with compassion.

She has *dove's eyes* . . . eyes that are like inner spiritual mirrors reflecting the beauty and the glory of the Lord . . . eyes that reveal the dove-side of the character of God that is blossoming within.

Yes, the bride of Christ possesses eyes that mirror innocence, tenderness, tranquility, faithfulness, gentleness, forgiveness and calm assurance.

She has *dove's eyes* . . . eyes that look beyond faults and weaknesses, eyes that are captured by humility, eyes that see the potential for good hidden in the hearts of men.

REFLECTING HIS GENTLENESS AND PEACE

•• **The dove is one of the most gentle and peaceful birds in the animal kingdom.**

• From the days of Noah, when the dove came back to the ark with an olive leaf plucked off, this bird has represented *peace with God, reconciliation and a time of new beginnings.*

A dove is a creature who has no ability to retaliate: it does not possess the nature to fight back.

Surely it was this expression of the Holy Spirit in the Son of God that gave Him the nature Isaiah prophesied about — "He was oppressed and He was afflicted, yet He opened not His mouth."

How astoundingly gentle Jesus was with His own enemies, even healing the severed ear of a man who sought, along with others, to hale Him to the torturous treatment awaiting Him in Pilate's Hall.

How amazingly merciful He was when He interceded for His own murderers saying "Father forgive them; for they know not what they do''.

How generous in kindness Jesus was with the dying thief, who had cursed Him only a few moments before, but then repented and pleaded with the Son of God to be remembered.

How wonderfully compassionate Jesus was to say — ''Thou shalt be with Me in paradise.''

How confidently peaceful this Lord of lords was even in the face of death, committing His spirit into the care of the Father.

How pleasant and challenging it is to behold the beautiful, pure and powerful revelation of the character of the Son of God!
Astoundingly gentle,
Amazingly merciful,
Generously kind,
Wonderfully compassionate,
and confidently peaceful.

Jesus, Calvary's sacrificial dove, provided us with an example . . . a living example of extreme gentleness and undisturbed peace.

Now we are called to be imitators — reflecting the tender, loving and peaceful nature of this Lord of grace *(His dove-nature)*.

We must seek to be always motivated by love . . . even to the point of loving our enemies.

We must learn to feel the infirmities of others . . . even praying for those who despitefully use us.

We must refuse to retaliate, but rather be quick to forgive . . . even blessing those who curse us.

We must reach out to humanity with meekness and tenderness . . . even doing good to those who hate us.

We must also discipline our spirits that we might maintain unshakeable peace, steadfastness of faith, in the worst of circumstances.

We can do these things, for we have received the visitation of the heavenly dove (the Holy Spirit) into our lives.

We know also that the sweet Holy Spirit is not called the Condemner — He is called *the Comforter*.

He tenderly upholds and graciously consoles us in times of tribulation and temptation.

He gently comforts us in our sorrows.

He lovingly alleviates our pain and our grief.

We expect it to be this way, for this is *the dove-nature, the gentle nature of our God*.

It is quite interesting to note that the same Greek word — *parakletos* — that was translated — *comforter* — (in John 14, 15, and 16) was also translated into the English word — *advocate* — (in I John 2:1).

When *parakletos* is translated — *comforter* — it refers to the Holy Spirit, but when it is translated — *advocate* — it is referring exclusively to Jesus and it means a *defense attorney.*

John, under the inspiration of the Spirit of God, wrote — "If any man sin, we have an *advocate* with the Father, Jesus Christ the righteous: and He is the propitiation for our sins. . . . "

It is an amazing thing that in times of weakness we have a Defender of the weak who fights for us. He is not against us, if we are sincere in our commitment to Him. He is not a prosecuting attorney dedicated to exposing our faults and proving our guilt.

He is our Champion — the Captain of our salvation.

"He giveth power to the faint; and to them that have no might He increaseth strength." (Isaiah 40:29)

As an expert defense attorney, He seeks to prove our innocence before the throne of God, by the atonement covering of His precious blood.

This is the dove-nature, the gentle nature of our God.

He delights in granting us peace with God (harmony and reconciliation with the Father).

He delights in restoration, and so will we, when we become like Him in our attitudes.

This is exactly what our calling is.

- We are called to be comforters and advocates.

We are called not to condemn men, but to set them free.

We are called to share the suffering and heal the hurts of those around us.

We are called to defend the weak and deliver the oppressed.

We are called to forgiveness and mercy.

We are called to gentleness and peace . . . *for this is the dove-nature, the gentle nature of our God, emerging in us.*

This is our nature now, for God Himself has spoken it . . . *we are His dove.*

REFLECTING HIS BURDEN

•• **The dove has a unique, cooing, mourning song — a grieving, sorrowful sound that is far different than the song of any other bird.**
This is an important fact to consider, for if the dove of the Holy Spirit really takes up residence in our hearts, in a spiritual sense, we will surely echo the same kind of song inwardly.

When the Holy Spirit fills a believer, it is true that He produces a deep sensation of peace and an ecstatic feeling of heavenly joy — but, all the while under the surface, there is a deep travail for the lost of this world and the tragic condition of the human race.

No person can be in intimate contact with the Lord Jesus *(heaven's sacrificial dove)* without feeling this spiritual grief — *"For in much wisdom is much grief."* (Ecclesiastes 1:18)

Paul said it this way:

> *"I say the truth in Christ, I lie not, my conscience also bearing me witness in the Holy Ghost, That I have great heaviness and continual sorrow in my heart."*
>
> (Romans 9:1-2)

This is the result of selfless love and the burning of conviction in the inner man.

This is the soul-piercing, blood-sweating passion of Gethsemane gripping another vessel of prayer.

This is the fellowship of His suffering.

This is the burden of the Lord.

This is the love-burden that drove Jesus to Calvary and constrained Him to actually become a curse for us, tasting death for every man.

Paul, experiencing an overflow of this very same constraining burden of compassion, went on to say — *"For I could wish that myself were accursed from Christ for my brethren . . . who are Israelites."*

In other words, Paul was saying that he dearly loved his lost Israelite brethren to such degree that, if it were necessary, he would almost be willing to perish in hell himself if it would deliver them from such a dreadful fate.

O, what an unfathomable love this is.

How it seizes the soul of that person who has been enlightened concerning the eternal state!

What an anguish it is to know that multitudes of men and women will be tormented in a burning hell, weeping and wailing and gnashing their teeth!

What a painful thing it is to realize that the damnation of the wicked is irreversible and unchangeable once it takes place!

How important it is that we reach every person with the life-transforming gospel of Jesus Christ before it is too late!

What a holy charge we have received!

What an inexpressible weight of responsibility!!

It is no wonder that the prophet Jeremiah cried — "Oh that my head were waters, and mine eyes a fountain of tears, that I might weep day and night for the slain of the daughter of my people." (Jeremiah 9:1)

Surely it was the Spirit of God that stirred the prophet to the very core of His being . . . and surely those who are sensitive to God now feel the very same kind of heart-gripping pain.

We that have dove's eyes *see* the nearness of prophecy therefore we are compelled to travail in prayer until we *see* as well the birth of the greatest spiritual awakening that the world has ever witnessed.

This desperateness in intercession is unquestionably an absolute prerequisite for revival.

For it is only when Zion travails that children are brought forth and born into the kingdom. (Isaiah 66:8)

We see the need. The lost must be saved. The oppressed must be delivered.

The church must be awakened out of deception, indifference and spiritual lethargy.

Therefore there is only one route to take — we must rend our hearts.

• We must *"weep between the porch and the altar and . . . say, Spare Thy people, O Lord . . . give not Thine heritage to reproach."* (Joel 2:17)

We cannot be at ease in Zion!

We have been made sensitive to the inner anguish of the Holy Spirit, who travails in prayer within us, in — "groanings which cannot be uttered." (Romans 8:26)

We groan inwardly to be sanctified and clean before the Lord . . . fit vessels.

Our hearts are throbbing with the very heart throb of deity.

We are burdened with His burden.

We are containers of His emotions.

We are one with Him.

• Isaiah 59:11 declares that *"We roar all like bears, and mourn sore like doves."*

We sing the Lord's song of lamentation, mourning and woe . . . for this is the song that echoes day and night deep within our inner being.

We were born to be gripped in such a way.

This is normal. This is the spirit of prayer.

We travail again in birth until Christ be formed in us. We travail again in birth until the kingdom of God be born in this world.

This is the song of the dove within us.

This is our nature now for . . . *we are His dove.*

REFLECTING HIS FAITHFULNESS

• **This dove is an amazingly faithful bird.**

Experts believe that the dove remains faithful to its mate unto death.

This is commitment.

This is the faithfulness of the Son of God toward us.

We are His bride; we are His mate forever.

He has solemnly pledged — "I will never leave thee nor forsake thee."

He has given the promise of security — "Lo, I am with you alway, even unto the end of the world." (Matthew 28:20)

We know that we will face various temptations and tribulations, but we also know that the Lord will deliver us out of them all. (Psalm 34:19)

Regardless of what we go through, He has already assured us saying — "My grace is sufficient for thee."

Grace is God's faithfulness in action.

Faithfulness is so much a part of the character of the Son of God that it has become His name.

• John the Revelator beheld Him in a vision and said — *"I saw heaven opened, and behold a white horse; and He that sat upon him was called Faithful and True."* (Revelation 19:11)

The word — *true* —means *dependable, constant, trustworthy and loyal.*

These adjectives are all beautifully descriptive of Jesus . . . for when we fail, or when we succeed, He is still constant in His devotion toward us.

When we are weak, or when we are strong, He is still loyal in His commitment to us.

Even as He faithfully sent fresh manna daily to the Jews for forty years in the wilderness, when they were worthy and when they were not, so He has faithfully and daily supplied our needs.

This is the dove-nature, the faithful nature of our God.

Now it must be said that if we are in the bride of Christ this faithful nature will be reflected in us.

We will take up our cross willingly to follow Jesus.

We will gladly submit ourselves to the will of God, deny self and be crucified with Christ.

The same thing that held Jesus to the cross will hold us there also, and it was certainly not the nails.

Love compelled Him. Love constrained Him.

His faithful commitment to the will of the Father was represented by the vertical beam of the cross (the beam reaching from earth to heaven).

His faithful commitment to humanity and to the body of Christ was represented by the horizontal beam (the beam reaching to either side).

In a symbolic sense, the first and greatest commandment held Him on the vertical beam — ("Thou shalt love the Lord thy God with all thy heart, and with all thy soul, and with all thy mind").

The second greatest commandment held Him on the horizontal beam — ("Thou shalt love thy neighbor as thyself").

• Jesus said — "On these two commandments hang all the law and the prophets." (Matthew 22:37-40)

Jesus was without a doubt the embodiment of all the Law and all the prophecies of the prophets for He was the Word made flesh.

• He literally hung on an old rugged cross on Calvary's hill, but in all reality He was really hanging on two love-commandments.

Those two commandments, those two beams, held Him suspended between heaven and earth until He paid the full purchase price to bring redemption to man.

He was *"faithful* to Him that appointed Him" — and He was *faithful* unto us. (Hebrews 3:2)

Now we are called to exhibit the same spirit, for — "They that are with Him are called, and chosen, and *faithful."* (Revelation 17:14)

We must be *faithful* in our commitment to God and *faithful* in our commitment to others . . . *faithful* even unto death.

We know that our future eternal inheritance veritably defies description, and we also know that it is definitely hinging on our development of this very quality.

We know that we are heirs of God and joint-heirs with Christ.

Only God knows fully what this will include, but we do know according to Matthew 25:14-30 that the *faithful* servant who is *faithful* over a few things will be made ruler over many things, and enter into the joy of the Lord.

This is the reward of commitment.

This is the key to our destiny.

And this is the dove-nature, the faithful nature of our God . . . unveiled in us . . . eternally.

REFLECTING HIS HOLINESS

•• **The dove is one of the cleanest birds in the animal kingdom.**

• Its feathers are daily cleansed by a unique process: a continual flow of oil comes out of its pores and covers its entire body.

This is representative of the daily spiritual renewal that takes place in the life of a believer.

"For which cause we faint not; but though our outward man perish, yet the inward man is *renewed* day by day." (II Corinthians 4:16)

• This word — *renewed* — means — *to be made new all over again.*

The inward man is the new creation man, the son of God part of us — the hidden man of the heart.

There is a continual, life-giving oil-flow of the Spirit of God in and through this inward man, just as there is a continual flow of life-giving blood in the outer man.

Natural blood ceaselessly revitalizes and renews the natural body with oxygen from the lungs, and necessary nutrients from the digestive system.

Through this miraculous process our bodies stay strong and healthy.

But the oil of God's presence is persistently, incessantly revitalizing and renewing our spirits, with sanctifying power to blot out our sins, and justifying power to make us righteous and holy in His sight.

Through this miraculous process we are kept strong and healthy spiritually.

We are kept in harmony with God.

We are immersed and continually bathed in a spirit of victory!

The indwelling of His Spirit imparts divine life; it imparts righteousness . . . continually.

The Spirit of God is creative life.

We release the Spirit to do His wondrous creative work in us by maintaining humility, sincerity and faith before the throne of God.

This — *"threefold cord is not quickly broken"* — by Satan or by circumstance. (Ecclesiastes 4:12)

Every moment that we spend in the presence of God, with this interwoven set of spiritual attitudes, we are being made new all over again.

We are being resurrected spiritually every day — yes, every moment.

We are *"being born again,* not of corruptible seed, but of incorruptible, by the word of God, [and by the Spirit of God] which liveth and abideth forever."* (I Peter 1:23)

This word — *being* — implies not just an initial experience, but a continuing process.

As the oil of God's presence flows through us we are constantly being *born again* into new peace, new joy, new righteousness and new life.

• This is exactly why we can be called **His Undefiled.**

Though the world around us continually battles against us, in an attempt to defile and to pollute us spiritually, still the oil of God, intermingled with the precious blood of Jesus, is so much stronger.

• In times of great distress and sore temptation we have learned to pray as David did in Psalm 57:

> *"Be merciful unto me, O God, be merciful*
> *unto me: for my soul trusteth in Thee: yea, in the*
> ***shadow of Thy wings** will I make my refuge until*
> *these calamities be overpast."*

Yes, under the shadow of Jesus' wings we, His earth-bound brood, contentedly and constantly discover our purity renewed and innocence restored, for the oil-flow from Him passes into us and we become as holy as He.

This miraculous transfer could have never been made possible had the firstborn Son been defiled (corrupted by the world).

When Jesus stood before Pilate — *"harmless as a dove"* — the Roman governor's testimony was altogether correct.

He dared to defy the tumultuous crowd who sought to crucify Jesus by declaring — *"I find in Him no fault at all."* (John 18:38)

It is somewhat amazing that even an unbelieving Gentile in that day had enough spiritual discernment to perceive that this gentle heaven-sent dove was truly without spot and without blemish.

Jesus Himself sealed the testimony when He told His disciples right before His death — "Hereafter I will not talk much with you: for the prince of this world cometh, and hath nothing in Me." (John 14:30)

• In other words, Jesus was affirming the fact that even though He was "in all points tempted like as we are" still He came forth from it all "without sin" — *undefiled!*

Now, because we are identified with Christ, we are blessed beyond measure to share in this . . . His status of utter righteousness.

We now obtain, by faith, His acceptability in the presence of the Father.

We now partake of all the good obtained through His vicarious sufferings on Calvary.

And we now partake of all the overcoming power procured through His victorious resurrection three days later, for our faith has literally broken through the barriers of time and space.

We are inseparably linked to this Holy One of Israel, who has arisen over our lives — *"with healing in His wings."*

We have found "the secret place of the most High" where we "abide under the shadow of the Almighty." (Psalm 91:1)

And in this place . . . where sin abounds, grace does much more abound. And where weakness abounds, the strength of God's promises does much more abound.

• One of the most glorious promises is the fact that when sin is blotted out by the precious blood of heaven's sacrificial dove, it is not merely forgiven . . . as far as God is concerned, it is annihilated . . . it does not exist anymore.

We are justified . . . just as if we had never sinned.

This is why we can claim to be — *"holy and without blame before Him in love"* — *undefiled.* (Ephesians 1:4)

• And this is why we can look forward, with such great expectancy, to that wondrous day when He will come again and call to us from heaven, saying:

> *"Arise, My love, My fair one, and come away. **O My dove,** thou art in the clefts of the rock, in the secret places of the stairs [the steep pathway], let Me see thy countenance, let Me hear thy voice; for sweet is thy voice, and thy countenance is comely."*
>
> (Song of Solomon 2:13-14, AV, NAS)

Jesus is the Rock of Ages cleft for us and Jesus is the steep and narrow pathway (sometimes difficult, but always rewarding) that leads from earth to heaven.

We are hidden in Him . . . the everlasting Rock and the infinite Stairway.

He is the Word . . . impregnable and rock-hard, unchangeable and rock-sure.

And, as an inviting, challenging, and *never-ending stairwell,* He beckons us to climb higher in Him every day and for all eternity.

He has lifted us from the very bottom and is joyously in the process of taking us to the very top . . . and we are so grateful.

We long to see his countenance and hear His voice when He descends to change us into His flawless image.

But what is more wonderful than words can express . . . He desires to see our countenances and to hear our voices as well and even more so . . . for our voices, like the sound of many waters, will be sweet music to His ears, and our countenances, so ecstatic with eternal life, will be exceedingly comely in His sight.

Yes, His supreme joy will be to grant us the wings of a dove that we might *"fly away and be at rest."* (Psalm 55:6)

• In Psalm 68:13 He gave the gracious promise:

> *"Though ye have lien among the pots, yet shall ye be as **the wings of a dove** covered with silver, and her feathers with yellow gold."*

This passage has been translated many ways and in some, the words — thorns, dung and brickkilns — were used instead of pots. (DARB)

Regardless of the translation, the essence of what God was seeking to communicate remains the same . . . that He has lifted us from a state of utter degradation and misery to an inheritance that will yet cause us to spectacularly emerge even as **a beautiful, infinite and glorified dove,** our feathers as it were overlaid with the shining silver of His redemptive love and our wings tipped with the lustrous gold of His divine nature.

97

Yes, this is our wondrous heritage and our eternal calling for we are . . . **HIS LOVE, HIS DOVE** AND **HIS UNDEFILED.**

"Thanks be unto God for His unspeakable gift!"*¹

---

*¹**An important afterthought:** In the fourteenth chapter of Leviticus, we find certain Mosaic ordinances that dealt with the cleansing of lepers. These laws are quite significant to us, for the dreaded disease called leprosy is itself a symbol of the far more dreadful condition of being "dead in trespasses and sins." If a leper was found to be clean, the priest was to first take two birds, presumably doves — "alive and clean, and cedar wood, and scarlet, and hyssop." Then one of the birds was to be "killed in an earthen vessel over running water." This speaks of Jesus sacrificing Himself on Calvary (God incarnate in an "earthen vessel") and pouring out His blood over the "running waters" of eternal life (the deep, still current of God's eternal purpose). Next, the priest was commanded to tie the living bird, along with hyssop, to a piece of cedar wood, using the scarlet thread. He would then dip the living bird, first in the blood and then in the water, sprinkling the leper with both. Finally, the priest would release the living bird (which typified the resurrected Christ) and send the leper away "justified." The cedar wood speaks of that which is eternal, the scarlet thread speaks of both redemption and the love that bound Jesus to His cross, while the hyssop denotes the generous transfer of the wondrous effects of Jesus' death and resurrection to those who believe. This is all a beautiful Old Testament type of the glorious work that God has wrought in us through the sprinkling of the blood of Jesus, heaven's sacrificial dove. After this ritual, two turtledoves or two pigeons were also sacrificed, one for a sin offering and the other for a burnt offering. This speaks of Jesus becoming sin for us and being consumed with the fire of divine judgment that we might be delivered from the "leprosy" of the sin-nature.￣

• THE ELECT •

GOD'S ELECT

HIS OWN ELECT

THE VERY ELECT

THE ELECT OF GOD, HOLY AND BELOVED

THE ELECTION

"And He shall send His angels with a great sound of a trumpet, and they shall gather together His ELECT from the four winds, from one end of heaven to the other." (Matthew 24:31)

*"Paul, a servant of God, and an apostle of Jesus Christ, according to the faith of **GOD'S ELECT,** and the acknowledging of the truth which is after godliness."* (Titus 1:1)

*"And shall not God avenge **HIS OWN ELECT,** which cry day and night unto Him, though He bear long with them."* (Luke 18:7)

*"For there shall arise false Christs, and false prophets, and shall show great signs and wonders; insomuch that, if it were possible, they shall deceive **THE VERY ELECT.**"* (Matthew 24:24)

*"Put on therefore, as **THE ELECT OF GOD, HOLY AND BELOVED,** bowels of mercies, kindness, humbleness of mind, meekness, longsuffering."* (Colossians 3:12)

*". . . Israel hath not obtained that which he seeketh for; but **THE ELECTION** hath obtained it, and the rest were blinded."* (Romans 11:7)

THE ELECT

*"And He shall send His angels with a great
sound of a trumpet, and they shall gather together
His ELECT from the four winds, from one end
of heaven to the other."*   (Matthew 24:31)

• The word — **elect** — means . . . *that which is picked, chosen, selected and exclusively preferred.*

This expression is found only twenty times in the Bible (King James Version).

Two variations of the word, **election** and **elected,** are found six times and one time, respectively.

It must be mentioned that in the New Testament the Greek word that is rendered **elect** *(eklektos)* is also translated into the word — **chosen** — a total of seven times (for instance, when Jesus said, "many be called, but few are **chosen.**" Matthew 20:16)

The Hebrew word in the Old Testament that is translated **elect** *(bachir)* — is also translated as meaning — **chosen** — a total of eight times.

So we see clearly that the words **elect** and **chosen** are synonymous and interchangeable.

We will center our attention though only on the times that the words *bachir* and *eklektos* have been translated to mean — **elect.**

• **This word is used twice in reference to Jesus, including the first time that it appears in the Scripture.**

Isaiah prophesied of the Messiah saying — "Behold My servant, whom I uphold; *Mine elect,* in whom My soul delighteth; I have put My spirit upon Him: He shall bring forth judgment to the Gentiles." (Isaiah 42:1)

Peter later called Him the — "chief corner stone, *elect,* precious. . . . " (I Peter 2:6)

• **This term is used once in reference to the angels that remained faithful when Satan fell.**

Paul exhorted Timothy saying — "I charge thee before God, and the Lord Jesus Christ, and the *elect angels,* that thou observe these things . . ." (I Timothy 5:21)

• **This term is used once in reference to Israel.**

In Isaiah 45:4 Jehovah talked about controlling the Persian empire and revealing Himself to Cyrus, the ruler of that nation, for the sake of *"Israel Mine elect."*

•• **But this expression is used sixteen times in reference to all of those individuals, who are born of the Spirit and included in the family of God.**

Paul said — "I endure all things for *the elect's* sake, that they may also obtain the salvation which is in Christ Jesus with eternal glory." (II Timothy 2:10)

From this scripture we infer that Paul knew there were certain people elected and chosen from the foundation of the world to respond to his preaching, though the vast majority would doubtless reject his message.

All who heard Paul preach would have the opportunity to willfully respond by accepting the gospel, but there were certain individuals, foreknown of God, who definitely would believe and receive.

This is not fatalism.

This just simply means that God knows the end from the beginning, and that His counsel will stand. (Isaiah 46:9-10)

Therefore, Paul was encouraged to endure any necessary persecutions or afflictions, for he knew that the original plan and purpose of God could not and would not fail.

•• **This whole idea of being elected of God can be compared to an architect submitting blueprint plans for a large building to the president of a construction firm.**

The builder sees in advance what the building will ultimately look like and if this **foreknowledge** pleases him, he will then sign the plans, thus setting the project in motion toward its **predestined** goal.

There has to be a plan.

It would be absurd for the builder to go out in a field and just start digging footers, pouring concrete slabs, and laying blocks at random . . . anywhere that anybody pleased.

It is absolutely necessary to first create, and then proceed by, a predetermined pattern and design.

Of course, this still leaves room for changes and subtle alterations.

But irregardless, the final product is, as much as is humanly possible, an exact visible reproduction of what was initially a somewhat invisible dream, schemed out in great detail in some architect's mind.

Now if finite man can do such a thing to insure success in the natural, and he definitely does, is it not possible for an infinite God to follow suit, yet of course on a much higher plane?

The answer unquestionably must be a loud, resounding *yes!*

This does not necessarily mean that God ordains one group to be saved and another group to be lost, and there is nothing that any human being can do to alter this predetermination.

It rather means that God, from the start of creation, knew every detail of what would result from the creation, the fall, and the subsequent redemption of mankind.

The infinite and omniscient Holy Spirit/Architect, not being confined within the walls of time, foresaw **the end from the beginning** and then, in a certain sense, submitted this "insight into the future" to the Master Creator and Builder as a foundational "blueprint plan."

This would be the ultimate outcome of it all.

This would be the progression of events leading up to the grand finale of the New Creation.

Surely, God saw all the woeful misery, the pain, the suffocating spiritual darkness and ignorance, but He also beheld the sure resulting victories and a certain number of redeemed people, emerging as heirs of God and joint-heirs with Christ, coming forth in the image of the Creator Himself.

And the good evidently outweighed the bad, for those who passed through the valley of the shadow of death successfully would end up far better off in many ways for having experienced such an earthbound time of exile.

So God, in a sense, placed His signature, seal and stamp of approval on "the project outline" and, by doing so, He set the wheels of creation in motion.

•   By electing to proceed, God firmly and irrevocably chose from the foundation those who would eventually choose and elect, of their own free will, to later respond to His call.

Admittedly, the only weakness in the preceding analogy is the fact that cinder blocks, steel beams, bricks, planks of wood and glass panes do not possess a free will.

Man does.

And without a doubt, this thing called *freedom of choice* is a gift of God.

This God-given ability gives meaning to life, and without it, our sojourn in the realm of time is clearly a cold, cruel and unfair experience.

Even on the positive side, if our highest achievements in God can only be traced back to divine authorship, with no input necessary on our part, then our passage through this world has been a waste.

Nothing has been accomplished.

Yet, without a foundational plan of election, creation would be nothing but utter chaos.

So, there is only one logical conclusion to make.

•   There must be *a mysterious blend* of the sovereignty of God and the free will of man, and only God knows where the line of demarcation falls.

If there was no such thing as divine election, why would the Bible boldly declare, concerning the revival in Antioch, that — "as many as were **ordained** to eternal life believed." (Acts 13:48)

And why would God encourage Paul to ignore opposition and continue preaching in Corinth, for God said in advance — "I have much people in this city." (Acts 18:10)

And, of course, God spoke these words long before most of the Corinthian Christians were ever converted.

Yet, even before their decision, God claimed them and elected them as His own.

He knew from the very foundation that they would come in, and He knew that He would receive them by and through His grace.

PRESERVATION, PROTECTION AND SURE VICTORY

Let me reemphasize a very important point.

• The same word — **elect** — is used in reference to Jesus, Israel, the holy angels, and the church . . . (and again being elected of God always insures an inheritance of divine stability — for certain events of life are God-shaped and divinely authored).

Therefore, because we all bear the same *title,* we assume that our election is just as certain and just as effective as the election of the angels, of Israel, or even to a certain degree, the Lord Jesus Christ Himself.

We are bold to say that our election is not in the least bit inferior.

• The bond and seal of ordination, given to any of the chosen sons and daughters of God, is just as dependable and just as potentially powerful in propelling us forward in victory as it was in carrying Jesus triumphantly through death, hell and the grave!

As long as we yield to the ordination through humility and faith, and as long as we are sincere in our desire to follow Jesus, our preservation is just as sure as the miraculous preservation of Israel over the centuries.

And we are just as much an irreplaceable part of heaven as the holy angels themselves.

In fact, it is significant to note again that the word — *elect* — was used much more often in reference to those who have been ordained of God from the beginning to be a part of the church (actually sixteen times) so we, even more than the angels or the nation of Israel, should abide in absolute confidence.

If Jehovah could successfully preserve the national identity of Israel (a people who, to a great degree, initially rejected the Messiah) during almost 2,000 years of dispersion, and if He could then reestablish that nation securely in 1948 (a miracle of restoration the likes of which has never taken place for any other nation in the world) — then we surely must believe that He is able to preserve those Jews and Gentiles who love the Messiah and serve him in sincerity and truth. Surely He can reestablish and restore us when it is necessary. Surely He will build a hedge of protection around us.

We are confident of this for we know that it is El-Shaddai, the Almighty God, who has selected us.

We are winners. We are His preferred choice.

We are more than winners!

We are the elect of God!

By an act of divine will He has granted us grace *(unearned favor that imparts divine ability)*.

"And if by grace, then is it no more of works: otherwise grace is no more grace." (Romans 11:6)

We must recognize that God is sovereign — He is omnipotent and omniscient in His dealings with men — all powerful and all knowing.

•• The Bible plainly states that God has — "saved us, and called us with an holy calling, not according to our works, but according to His own **purpose** and **grace,** which was given us in Christ Jesus **before the world began.**" (II Timothy 1:9)

In other words, before any of the natural creation existed, God gave each one of His elect sons and daughters a general as well as a specific purpose, and what is even more wonderful, God gave us grace in advance to fulfill that purpose!*[1]

Our God anticipated every trial and every opposition that we would ever face and, from the very beginning, He gave us an ample amount of grace to come forth from all these circumstances and to victoriously fulfill His blueprint plan for our lives.

Therefore, we will never face anything in life out of which we cannot emerge as conquerors if we tap into that which is rightfully ours.

God ordained for us, in advance, certain works that we should perform in His name. Then He sealed us into success by giving us the grace, the divine enablement, to fulfill each ordained task from the foundation of all things!

What greater proof of ultimate victory could we ask for? God is for us, who and what can be against us?

Jesus was elected and ordained from the beginning to face Calvary and to arise three days later from the grave for He was "the Lamb slain from the foundation of the world!"

• We cannot ignore the fact that He could have rebelled against this election, just as we can rebel against ours, but instead He chose to go to Gethsemane and then later "by the grace of God" to taste death for every man. (Hebrews 2:9)

Even He had to receive grace to endure what seemed impossible to endure, and He had to make a choice.

Yet, surely this grace was given to Him long before there was "planted a garden eastward in Eden."

He was God's Elect.

He was given a purpose and grace before the world began.

We are God's elect as well.

No matter how difficult it seems to be, we can fulfill God's design for our lives.

We believe that Jesus meant what He said when He told Paul and subsequently revealed to us — *"My grace is sufficient for thee."*

THE SOVEREIGNTY OF GOD

• Before the twin brothers, Jacob and Esau, were born to Isaac and Rebekah, it was prophesied by the Lord in advance that — "The elder shall serve the younger." (Genesis 25:23)

Later, after their birth, God explained — "Jacob have I loved, but Esau have I hated." (Romans 9:13, Malachi 1:2-3)

In explaining the reason for this strange predetermination, the Bible declared — "the children being not yet born, neither have done any good or evil, that the purpose of God according to **election** might stand, not of works, but of Him that calleth." (Romans 9:11)

> *"What shall we say then? Is there unrighteousness with God? God forbid.*
>
> *For He saith to Moses, I will have mercy on whom I will have mercy, and I will have compassion on whom I will have compassion.*
>
> *So then it is not of him that willeth, nor of him that runneth, but of God that sheweth mercy."* (Romans 9:14-16)

• God definitely does have an ordained people that He has created for the purpose of receiving His mercy, in order to reveal that side of His nature . . . eternally!!!

And God definitely does have an ordained plan involving certain key ordained figures who were quite evidently chosen by God in a more manifest and profound way, before they ever came forth from the womb.

Paul could write very convincing arguments upholding this point of view because he was living proof himself — for he was on his way to actually kill Christians in Damascus when suddenly a light from heaven shone around him and Jesus revealed Himself — to a murderer who hated His name.

Paul's conversion had to be an absolute election of grace.
The facts plainly prove it.

It was definitely not Paul's choice to find Jesus.
Rather, it was God's predetermined choice to find Paul and to bring him into the revelation of, and the fulfillment of, the divine plan for

106

his life.

Therefore, in the light of this irrefutable truth, we arrive at a certain conclusion . . . that there are some persons God elects in advance to eventually *accept and receive* at their request, while others God elects in advance to ultimately *manifest Himself to* whether they request it or not, for He knows their hearts.

•• Both of these are true and valid descriptions of the way that God moves and deals with human beings, and both are easily proven by the Scripture.

So it must be said that a balanced and correct view of divine election will always, of a necessity, include both of these definitions of the same term, for both concepts are complementary to the point of being inseparable.

They are married to each other; they are two petals of the same flower, two notes of the same chord and two separate distinct particles (proton and neutron) that make up one singular atom.

To be correct in our theology, we definitely must look at the "whole picture."

We know that God is "not willing that any should perish, but that all should come to repentance." (II Peter 3:9)

We know that He said — "Look unto Me, and be ye saved, all the ends of the earth. . . . " (Isaiah 45:22)

And we know that the Bible did not say — "God so loved *the elect* that He gave His Son." It rather declares loud and clear that — "God so loved *the world,* that He gave His only begotten Son, that *whosoever* believeth in Him should not perish, but have everlasting life." (John 3:16)

• But we also know that often God **seeks out** certain individuals, as He did Paul, with a bold display of power and what seems to be an almost irresistible revelation of Himself.

This is God's prerogative . . . He can make such a decision and predetermine such a purpose if He so chooses.

Though it doesn't always appear to work this way, still many of us could reach the same conclusion concerning the initial visitation, and the ensuing revelations, that we have received from God.

In many cases, it was evidently not so much our choice to find Him; it was rather His choice, His election, to find us . . . and yet still intertwined in the whole affair is that personal and weighty responsibility on our part to willingly surrender.

This is all more easily understood when we see that the nation of Israel had waited prayerfully, hundreds of years, for the coming of the Messiah.

It was their choice to see this Christ, this Anointed One, lead the Jewish nation back to her former glory, for He was called the *"Repairer of the breach, the Restorer of paths to dwell in".* (Isaiah 58:12)

They diligently searched the Scripture for clues concerning His coming. They fully expected to receive Him.

They fully intended to surrender to His authority.

They fully intended to follow Him and worship Him.

But when He finally did come, it is apparent that a great many were instead offended at Him.

They were appalled at His gentleness toward erring sinners.

They were horrified at His bold defiance of certain Jewish laws and customs.

They were confused by His parables and the depth of His preaching, unable to see the truth He unveiled.

They were upset because He did not raise up an army to deliver them from the Romans; He rather preached that we should love our enemies.

Above all, they were alarmed at the way He publicly censured their conduct and upbraided them for their unbelief.

The two-edged sword that proceeded out of His mouth cut too deeply when He painfully exposed their hypocrisies and ripped to pieces the covering of every religious facade that they hid behind.

This was not the Messiah that many of the Israelites had expected and certainly not the one they wanted . . . so the most peculiar, ironic and heartrending turn of events took place.

Instead of gratefully falling at His feet in adoration, they screamed out against Him, declaring Him to be an imposter — and put Him to death, the torturous death of the cross.

They did not obtain what they sought for "But **THE ELECTION** hath obtained it, and the rest were blinded (According as it is written, God hath given them the spirit of slumber, eyes that they should not see, and ears that they should not hear) . . ." (Romans 11:7-8)

Though the Jews were a part of God's **elect** natural nation, still many of them missed the key to their salvation — for they "being ignorant of God's righteousness, and going about to establish their own righteousness" did not "submit themselves unto the righteousness of God" (the plan, purpose and present revelation of the New Covenant). (Romans 10:3)

But God had a spiritual elect number of Jews and Gentiles, foreknown from the beginning, whose eyes had to see, and whose ears had to hear . . . their visitation from heaven was simply inevitable.

And as it was then, so it is now!

God emphatically and mysteriously declared it with these words — "I am sought of them that asked not for Me; I am found of them that sought Me not." (Isaiah 65:1)

JUSTIFICATION AND DEFENSE

•• No wonder Paul protested — "Who shall lay any thing to the charge of God's **elect?** It is God that **justifieth.** Who is he that condemneth?

It is Christ that died, yea rather, that is risen again . . . who also maketh intercession for us.'' (Romans 8:33-34)

To be **justified** is to be counted righteous in the presence of God, to be accepted as clean and unrebukable (just as if we had never sinned) free from condemnation!

This divine act of justification is a predetermined gift of God that comes at the precise moment that regeneration and salvation comes to a repentant sinner.

It is maintained in the daily walk of every sincere believer through the indwelling of the Spirit, the washing of the blood, and through Jesus' ministry of intercession.

This is a wonderful truth and a grand heritage for those He calls *His preferred choice!*

We have a right to be emotional in praising our God!

Jehovah-Jireh has done great things for us.
We are forgiven! Our sins have been blotted out!
We are clean and holy in His sight.
The past has no authority over us.

The accuser of the brethren may try to condemn us and accuse us, but his efforts are in vain.
He cannot viciously undo what God has graciously done.

We trust in the Saviour of the world who came for the purpose of forgiving us, delivering us, restoring us, transforming us and building hope in us.

Certainly we admit that we are not totally free from pressure now. In fact, the pressure may be greater in some ways now than it was before we were saved. Of course, the spiritual warfare really begins in full force only after salvation . . . for it is then that we become a threat to the devil.

We are buffeted on every side.
We are beset by powers and principalities . . . spiritual wickedness in high places.
We are cast down at times.
We are weak and weary . . . overwhelmed by a continual barrage of tribulations and temptations.
• But we hear a blessed voice echoing from another century saying . . . ''Shall not God avenge **His own elect,** which cry day and night unto Him, though He bear long with them? I tell you that He will avenge them speedily.'' (Luke 18:7-8)
Jesus will fight our battles for us.
Jesus will not fail nor forsake His ordained, for all things have been created for their sakes. The universe, and all events in the realm of time, revolve around God's eternal purpose in His elect people.

So, without a doubt, strength is on our side.

THE ELECTION OF GRACE

In the days of Elijah the prophet, when almost all of the Jews were being carried away into idolatry and apostasy, God spoke and assuredly declared — "I have *reserved* to Myself seven thousand men, who have not bowed their knee to the image of Baal." (Romans 11:4)

These men were exclusively selected, reserved, preserved, and preferred by Jehovah-God Himself.

They did not compromise, for God, in advance, gave them the unction to have an attitude and spirit different from the rest.

•• In reference to this fact, Paul boldly stated *"Even so then at this present time also there is a remnant according to the election of grace."* (Romans 11:5)

God always has a remnant in every era that He preserves — an elect people who are foreknown and called out by God to be different from the mainstream of humanity, and at this present time, different from even the mainstream of what is commonly called Christianity.

Especially now in the last days this is true — for deception is going to increase, and the human race is going to polarize, going to one extreme or the other. Men will be either totally overwhelmed by darkness, or fully illuminated by the light of God.

In fact, Jesus only used this word — **elect** — seven times in His teachings in the gospels. Six of those times it refers distinctly to those *chosen* believers who will be alive on this earth in the last days (Matthew 24, Mark 13) . . . *God's final remnant.*

• Jesus forewarned us that in this hour — "there shall arise false Christs and false prophets, and shall shew great signs and wonders; insomuch that, if it were possible, they shall deceive **THE VERY ELECT."** (Matthew 24:24)

But we must say that *the very elect* of the last days will not be deceived; it will be utterly impossible for them to be seduced by doctrines of devils. As long as they remain sincere and faithful before the Lord they will have the Spirit, the Comforter, to lead them and guide them into all truth and He will not fail them.

The human race is going to reel under the devastating impact of judgment blows from the throne of God — famines, plagues, natural disturbances and finally a nuclear war will ravage this planet.

• Jesus warned — "Except those days should be shortened, there should no flesh be saved; but for **THE ELECT'S** sake those days shall be shortened." (Matthew 24:22)

• But then, right at the critical moment, when it seems that all hope is gone, Jesus will — "send His angels with a great sound of a trumpet, and they shall gather together **HIS ELECT** from the four winds, from one end of heaven to the other." (Matthew 24:31)

Regardless of what comes, there is one thing for certain . . . Jesus will always grant a generous and bountiful supply of grace to meet the needs of His chosen.

The Bible said that — "God is able to make all grace abound toward you; that ye, always having all sufficiency in all things, may abound to every good work." (II Corinthians 9:8)

Remember, grace is *divine ability* that gives us strength to stand, but it is also *unmerited love* that will pick us up and restore us, if we happen to falter.

To abound is to have more than enough.
To have a sufficiency is to have just enough.

In this scripture Paul is boasting that the God we serve will supply to His chosen people more than enough grace to make sure that we have just enough.

This is absolutely glorious . . . a faith-fact that certainly sends our spirits soaring through heavenly places.

But still we must remember that God only gives grace to the humble and the sincere.

Being elected of God is not a free ticket to heaven, regardless of the life-style of the believer.

Neither does the election of God make a proud, egotistical, arrogant, self-centered or self-assured attitude excusable.

• Colossians 3:12-13 says — "Put on therefore, as **THE ELECT OF GOD, HOLY AND BELOVED,** bowels of mercies, kindness, humbleness of mind, meekness, longsuffering; forbearing one another, and forgiving one another. . . ."

• We are — "elect according to the foreknowledge of God the Father through sanctification of the Spirit, **unto obedience**. . . ." (I Peter 1:2)

In other words, the completion and fulfillment of our election hinges on our willingness to obey God, maintaining a melted, submitted spirit before the Lord — a broken and contrite heart. (See Titus 1:1)

We can thrust ourselves out of the ordination of God by allowing our hearts to become — "hardened through the deceitfulness of sin." (Hebrews 3:13)

But even then, God will go to extreme measures to preserve His own.

If necessary, God will even send major chastisements to bring an elect person back to conviction of sin and a sincere commitment to God, at times even delivering a person unto Satan for the destruction of the flesh, that the spirit might be saved in the day of our Lord Jesus Christ. (I Corinthians 5:1-5)

We believe these scriptural truths wholeheartedly, but we also believe that no person should seek to live haphazardly and then try to claim and take advantage of these sacred promises. We cannot use or abuse God's goodness.

We recognize that even if backslidden believers return and repent, they still forfeit a certain portion of their potential reward and some of their works are burned up.

The Bible declared that they are saved, **yet so as by fire** (the fiery trial that it takes to stir them and spur them into consecrating their lives again). (I Corinthians 3)

But this need not be the case!

Let us rather be ever willing and ever yielded — that we might completely fulfill our God-given purpose in this world, and that we might reach our hundredfold potential as sons of God.

Let us ever remember Jesus' pledge to His elect offspring — "My sheep hear My voice, and I know them . . . and I give unto them eternal life; and they shall never perish, neither shall any man pluck them out of My hands." (John 10:28)

But even with startling words as strong as these (falling like diamonds from the lips of Truth Incarnate) — let us also daily rehearse in our minds Peter's stern exhortation concerning our personal responsibility — "GIVE DILIGENCE TO MAKE YOUR CALLING AND ELECTION SURE." (II Peter 1:10)

And how is this done? Very simple. Maintain a spirit of faith, keep your heart melted in humility before the Lord, and always be zealous to actively pursue the ministry or work for which you have been ordained.

---

*¹The *general purpose* is fulfilling God's original desire that man be brought forth in His image. The *specific purpose* involves the details of the specific plan of God for each one of our lives.

THE FULLNESS OF HIM THAT FILLETH ALL IN ALL

"And hath put all things under His feet, and gave Him [Jesus] to be the head over all things to the church,
Which is His body, THE FULL-NESS OF HIM THAT FILLETH ALL IN ALL."　　(Ephesians 1:22-23)

THE FULLNESS OF HIM THAT FILLETH ALL IN ALL

> *"And hath put all things under His feet, and gave Him to be the head over all things to the church,*
> *Which is His body, THE FULLNESS OF HIM THAT FILLETH ALL IN ALL."*
> (Ephesians 1:22-23)

• The word *fullness* means *the highest state of being or completion . . . the maximum.*

• The word *fullness* means *something taken to the utmost extreme or the absolute limit . . . the peak product.*

• This word is certainly descriptive of the firstborn Son of God — "For in Him dwelleth all the *fullness* of the Godhead bodily." (Colossians 2:9)

Jesus was, without controversy, God manifested in the flesh, the form of God who thought it not robbery to be equal with God.

He is, and He always has been and always will be, the express image of the invisible God . . . the exact, precise, explicit, and full image of the Almighty . . . the total expression of the personality of deity.

He is therefore the container of all divinity, all serenity and all tranquillity.

All the love of God finds its medium of revelation in Him and through Him.

He contains all joy, all happiness and all creativity.

• He is the Word . . . the sum total of all the words and ways in which God has expressed Himself or will yet express Himself.

He is *the fullness*.

All power in heaven and in earth resides in Him. All creation came out from Him and is sustained by Him.

He was, and is, the embodiment of all the countless, boundless treasures of wisdom and knowledge that exist.

He is the perfection of all that is good and pure and beautiful.

He is the infinite understanding and unlimited wisdom . . . all wisdom.

He is infinite enlightenment and unlimited knowledge . . . all knowledge.

He is the ultimate and absolute, for — "it pleased the Father that in Him should all *fullness* dwell." (Colossians 1:19)

• These are definitely awe inspiring statements of fact, but there is another true and faithful saying that triggers an even greater sense of awe in our hearts: the wondrous revelation and realization that *"of His fullness have all we received."* (John 1:16)

This all powerful and supreme Lord of the universe now lives in our hearts.

We have been begotten of the Word (the fullness of the Word).
We have been born of the Spirit (the fullness of the Spirit).
By the Word, and by the Spirit, God is in the process of fully expressing Himself in us . . . unto perfection, even as our heavenly Father is perfect.
This is the good pleasure of His will.
It pleases the Father that now all *fullness* should dwell in us.

• We have the inborn potential of emerging fully in the likeness of the firstborn Son, at the resurrection, and being just as utterly one with the Father as He (for this was His prayer).

God has given the five-fold ministry to the body of Christ (apostles, prophets, evangelists, pastors and teachers) for the sole reason of promoting this eternal purpose in us.

• ". . . Till we all come in the unity of the faith, and of the knowledge of the Son of God, unto a perfect man, unto the measure of the stature of *the fullness of Christ.*" (Ephesians 4:13)

Our peak potential therefore runs somewhat parallel to Jesus' peak potential, for it is His peak potential in us, gradually being unveiled.

We will be manifested as fully mature sons of God when we arise in His likeness.
This is a glorious calling and an unspeakable gift.
Our hearts are seized with wonder that He would even include us.
We are brought to our knees in gratitude and devotion . . . for He has opened our eyes.
We behold the mystery that has been hidden from ages and generations — Christ in us, the hope of glory.
•• And this is our hope of glory — that, by receiving His *fullness,* we can finally, ultimately, reach our *fullness* (the maximum manifestation of our inheritance rights in Him, in this world and the world to come).

Without Him we were very much incomplete, but, by granting us *His fullness,* He became *our fullness* (our completion).
We can now gratefully announce that we are *"complete in Him, which is the head of all principality and power."* (Colossians 2:10)
We have no lack. We have no want . . . for we have Him.
The Lord is our portion and abundant life is His provision.
We are joint-heirs with Christ . . . the *fullness* of the Godhead that initially dwelt in Him alone, now dwells in every true son of God.
I Corinthians 4:8 assuredly declares that — "Now ye are *full,* now ye are rich. . . . "
This is a present possession (a right-now fact concerning our inheritance) as well as a future potential.

116

There is definitely more that can be discovered and brought forth in each one of us spiritually.

And there is definitely an infinitely-increasing revelation of the nature of God that we will spend eternity exploring.

But, in a very real sense, there is absolutely nothing that can be added to us now to make us any more complete in the sight of God, if we are truly committed to Him.

We can truthfully say that if we have Jesus we have it all!

No greater spiritual treasure can be found, unearthed, acquired or possessed.

We have been made rich with the riches of His grace and glory — the unsearchable riches of Christ!

There is nothing that can enrich our lives more than knowing the Lord and yielding to Him.

We have reached the ultimate!

• We intend to spend our lives and all of eternity absorbed totally in the ever-unfolding revelation of the love that surpasses knowledge, that we might be *"filled with all the fullness of God."* (Ephesians 3:19)

Knowing, understanding, experiencing and sharing this great love of God is the master key that unlocks all the individual doors leading to different aspects of **OUR GLORIOUS INHERITANCE.**

If we are not *"rooted and grounded"* in this revelation of divine love then we cannot be *"filled with all the fullness of God."*

We know, without a doubt, that God has created and purposed such magnificent things for us that adjectives such as bountiful, glorious and abundant really fall far short of sufficiently describing the splendor of our future heritage.

Eyes have not seen, nor ears heard, neither has it entered into the hearts of men, the things which God has prepared for them that love Him. (I Corinthians 2:9)

Paul, in his writings, even testified that "the sufferings of this present time are not worthy to be compared with the glory which shall be revealed in us." (Romans 8:18)

• The *things* that we will inherit eternally in themselves defy description, but even far greater is the state of being *(the nature and character)* that He has promised to manifest within the sons and daughters of God.

We have obtained His *fullness* — therefore we are heirs of the greatest gift and the highest calling of God available in heaven and earth.

This in itself is sufficient reason to praise His matchless name forever, but there is yet a more complete unfolding of the blossom and a deeper, more profound unveiling of truth.

•• Ephesians 1:23 declared the church to be — *"the fullness of Him who fills the whole creation!"* (JB)

This is simply breathtaking!

• Not only has He become our *fullness* (our completion), we have become His.

Even as Adam and Eve complemented one another and completed one another, so it is with this eternal Saviour and His eternal bride.

The bride of Christ is nothing less than — *"an help meet for God"* — His eternal companion, His completion.

We are the ultimate satisfaction of the deepest longing of His heart (the burning desire to give of Himself fully in a rapturous relationship of holy love).

It is very simple to see that we are definitely incomplete without Him but amazingly the opposite is also true.

• He is definitely, by His own choosing, incomplete without us, for we are married to Him.

We are His *fullness.*

We are channels of His creative life . . . eternally we will be full expressions, peak products, of His creative genius.

Jesus came to reconcile us (to restore us to the intimate relationship with God that Adam once possessed).

Jesus came to bring us back into harmony with the Father — now and forevermore.

He pleads with us to be reconciled, and not only for our sakes, but for His sake also, for He is seeking to be completed through this eternal spiritual union with His bride.

This is the central reason for the incarnation, the final outcome of the crucifixion and the great power of the resurrection.

• When Jesus came out of the grave He — *"ascended up far above all heavens, that He might fill all things."* (Ephesians 4:10)

This passage speaks of the final redemption of creation, for all redeemable things will ultimately be filled with His presence again, yet only in the church will He bring forth His fullness . . . *for we are His fullness.*

It is true that the creation itself will be — "delivered from the bondage of corruption into the glorious liberty of the children of God." (Romans 8:21, AV, RSV)

The land will be called Beulah (which means *married)* for the earth and nature itself will be married to God's Spirit and immersed in His everlasting love.

All things will be filled with the life of God and brought into perfection of beauty in Him.

But He has reserved something far better for the sons and daughters of God.

God will not reveal His character in mountains and hills. God will not pour the full unveiling of His divine nature into the lakes, rivers and oceans.

Flowers will not blossom with the personality of deity.

Trees will not grow in revelation knowledge and spiritual enlightenment.

Animals will not be vessels of His authority or channels of His voice.

Again, all these things will be utterly filled with the life of God, but His personality and character will be completely manifested only in the children of the Most High . . . *"in the dispensation of the fullness of times."* (Ephesians 1:10)

We stand even now on the threshold of this prophecy being fulfilled.

We are living in an hour of fullness.

We have arrived at the climax.

The harlot, apostate church system, described in Revelations 17, will soon drink from a golden cup *full* of abominations and filthiness of her fornication.

We are also told that the transgressors will "come to the full." (Daniel 8:23)

In other words, rampant sin and stiffnecked rejection of the truth will bring this world to a peak of guiltiness in the sight of God. This will especially be so when the abomination of desolation takes place — (the Antichrist being worshipped as God).

This act of supreme rebellion will bring the desolation of a nuclear holocaust on this world — for "the inhabitants of the earth [will be] burned, and few men left." (Isaiah 24:6)

But we, the sons of God, can look past all this fullness of judgment to the mark of the prize of the high calling of God that we will finally apprehend when Jesus comes.

This *"grand finale"* in the realm of time will bring the kingdom of God *fully* into this world and lift us victoriously into the eternal, glorified state where Christ will be *fully* formed in us.

We will be "the completion of Him who Himself completes all things everywhere." (Ephesians 1:23, TEV).

We will finally *fully* arrive at — "the measure of the stature of the *fullness* of Christ."

• And we will come into the *full* understanding of what it means to be entitled — **THE FULLNESS OF HIM THAT FILLETH ALL IN ALL.**

And what shall we say to all these things?

Our hearts are filled with adoration and praise. We lift our hands shouting — *"Glory to God in the highest! His infinite purpose will prevail in the end."*

• HEIRS •

HEIRS OF GOD

HEIRS OF GOD THROUGH CHRIST

HEIRS ACCORDING TO THE HOPE OF ETERNAL LIFE

• JOINT-HEIRS WITH CHRIST •

HIS MANY BRETHREN

• THE LORD'S PORTION •

HIS OWN INHERITANCE

THE LOT OF HIS INHERITANCE

HEIRS OF THE KINGDOM

"The Spirit itself beareth witness with our spirit, that we are the children of God: And if children, then HEIRS, HEIRS OF GOD, and JOINT-HEIRS WITH CHRIST . . ."
(Romans 8:16-17)

"Wherefore thou art no more a servant, but a son; and if a son, then an HEIR OF GOD THROUGH CHRIST."
(Galatians 4:7)

"That being justified by His grace, we should be made HEIRS ACCORDING TO THE HOPE OF ETERNAL LIFE."
(Titus 3:7)

"For whom He did foreknow, He also did predestinate to be conformed to the image of His Son, that He might be the firstborn among MANY BRETHREN."
(Romans 8:29)

"Blessed is the nation whose God is the Lord: and the people whom He hath chosen for HIS OWN INHERITANCE."
(Psalm 33:12)

HEIRS OF GOD
JOINT-HEIRS WITH CHRIST
THE LORD'S PORTION
THE LOT OF HIS INHERITANCE

"The Spirit itself beareth witness with our spirit, that we are the children of God: and if children, then HEIRS; HEIRS OF GOD, and JOINT-HEIRS WITH CHRIST . . ."
(Romans 8:16-17)

"For THE LORD'S PORTION is His people; Jacob is THE LOT OF HIS INHERITANCE."　　　　(Deuteronomy 32:9)

•　Legally, an **heir** is . . . *one who receives, or is entitled to receive, any properties, possessions, endowments, or qualities from a parent or predecessor: the heir is the rightful future recipient or possessor.*

The question is this . . . If we are heirs of God, then what possessions, properties, or qualities have we inherited from Him?

•　The answer is overwhelmingly simple and simply overwhelming: it seems quite certain that we have inherited *all that God is* and *all that God has*. We have inherited all that He ever will be, and all that He will ever yet create or develop through the expansion and propagation of creation itself.

We are the children of God, therefore we are the rightful present and future recipients of **THIS GLORIOUS INHERITANCE.**

Romans 4:13 prophesies that we will be the *heirs of the world* and that spiritually speaking we are the children of Abraham.

Titus 3:7 speaks that we are *heirs according to the hope of eternal life* and that we are justified by grace.

Hebrews 1:14 reveals that we are the *heirs of salvation* and that angels have been created to minister to our needs.

Hebrews 6:17 states that we are the *heirs of promise* and that we can have strong consolation.

Hebrews 11:7 shows that believers become *heirs of the righteousness which comes by faith* and that we can expect to be preserved in times of tribulation.

I Peter 3:7 unveils that we are *heirs together of the grace of life* and that we should give honor one to another.

But, even more glorious, James 2:5 declares that we are the *heirs of the kingdom* which God "hath promised to them that love Him."

123

This kingdom inheritance is the imperial majesty and the regal dominion that belongs to us forever . . . for we are His noble offspring, His royal seed.

The revelation of all these *inheritance-promises,* combined together and mixed with hope, provides us with — "an anchor of the soul, both sure and stedfast, and which entereth into that within the veil." (Hebrews 6:19)

Hundreds of people over the centuries have fought, argued, debated and even stooped to the extreme of murder to secure the inheritance of certain rich personalities after they died.

But the corruptible earthly inheritance that they were able to acquire is absolutely nothing, a mere pittance, compared to the heavenly, eternal riches bequested to the least of God's saints.

• We are declared to be **joint-heirs with Christ,** and without controversy, this means that Jesus has apportioned and distributed to each one of us, out of His abundance, an inheritance quite similar and parallel to His. We have been given the right of sharing in **His glorious inheritance,** therefore it has become **our glorious inheritance as well.**

Our merciful Saviour and heavenly Benefactor finds great fulfillment and deep satisfaction in generously sharing with us all that He has received from the Father.

Hebrews 1:2 declares that God has appointed His Son, Jesus — "heir of all things."

If we are joint-heirs with Christ, and we are, then we have been chosen for the privilege of sharing this portion of His birthright legacy . . . eternally.

Therefore we can reasonably assume that our inheritance will embrace everything that exists, every good thing that can be passed on to us in a final state of perfection and beauty, in realms both terrestrial and celestial.

This universal possession, yet to be manifested in the future, is of itself far beyond our capacity to fully comprehend.

But there is yet another aspect of our inheritance that transcends and surpasses even this wonderful bequest.

• We are **heirs of God** . . . not only heirs of what God has, but heirs of God Himself, for He has given us His personal presence, and poured the very essence of His being into our hearts.

The Lord is our portion.

It is certain that we have inherited His constant, loving protection and care, for we have inherited Him.

This is most assuredly the greatest of all the gifts, promises or endowments transferred to us through the New Covenant.

Colossians 1:19 and 2:9 declare that the fullness of the Godhead dwelt bodily in Jesus and that — *"It pleased the Father that in Him should all fullness dwell."*

If we are *joint-heirs with Christ,* and we are, then it has also pleased the Father to graciously grant to us this same marvellous indwelling.

Our inheritance includes everything that God is, for the fullness of the Godhead, in a certain qualified sense, now abides within every son of God. To what degree this will manifest in us eternally only God knows. But one thing we do know — this potential heritage and ability will surely reach its maximum manifestation at the resurrection.

We will then come forth precisely in the likeness of our Elder Brother.

This is God's determination for us, for we are — "the called according to His purpose." (Romans 8:28)

• Moreover — "whom He did foreknow, He also did predestinate to be conformed to the image of His Son, that He might be THE FIRST-BORN AMONG **MANY BRETHREN.**" (Romans 8:29)

How wonderful it is to know that we are actually brothers to Jesus . . . brothers to the Lord of glory Himself, His co-heirs!

But, what is even more amazing . . . Hebrews 2:11 pulls back the covering and lets us know that He is not ashamed to call us *brethren,* for we are — "all of one."

We may have been ashamed of ourselves at one time or another, but if we are presently striving to the utmost to walk with God in sincerity and truth, He is not ashamed of us, for we are "all of one."

We are all of one origin.

We are all of one source.

We are all of one similar burden and purpose in this world. We are all of one similar destiny . . . in time and in eternity.

We are one in being hated by the world.

We are one in being the target of satanic attacks.

But we are also one in being the main object of the Father's attention, devotion and desire . . . chosen recipients of His love and infinite instruments of His divine expression.

We share one common earthly goal with the firstborn Son — the burden of Calvary. And we share one common vision of ultimate triumph — the glory of the resurrection!

Surely if we were to take a full inventory of all the detailed facets of this portion of our heritage (our oneness with Jesus) an entire book would need to be written on this subject alone.

We can sum it up by simply repeating and joyously declaring . . . we are *joint-heirs with Christ,* we are *His many brethren!* He is not ashamed of us and we are certainly not ashamed of Him!

These facts of eternal life have been confirmed from heaven; so we have purposed that they be deep-rooted and deep-seated in our hearts, enthroned in the inner man.

As we meditate on these truths day and night, surely they will awaken us to our rightful place of *heirship*. This is all the more possible because we have been given the inner witness of the Spirit, testifying continually to us what we can legally claim in order to be viable, fruitful and successful — effective and mature sons of God.

AWAKE TO OUR BIRTHRIGHT

Jesus was fully awake to His spiritual birthright.

He proclaimed — *"All things that the Father hath are Mine."* (John 16:15)

Of course, a bold assertation like this is easy for us to accept coming from Him, since it was spoken from the lips of Truth incarnate concerning Himself.

But Jesus dared to go one step further.

• He assured His offspring that when the Comforter comes that — *"He shall take of Mine, and shall shew it unto you."* (John 16:15)

Why would the Holy Spirit show us these abundant spiritual riches, these treasures of wisdom and knowledge and power contained in the firstborn Son? The answer is obvious. This revelation of the character of Jesus comes in order for us to appropriate and activate what belongs to us also as His co-heirs.

It is a solid and dependable fact that the more we see Jesus, the more we become like Him . . . for His gifts, His talents, His wisdom, His personality, and His oneness with the Father are all, to a certain limited degree, imparted to us.

To partake of His divine nature this way is surely the greatest honor that we, as human beings, could ever receive.

Peter told us that this is an incorruptible and undefiled inheritance — *"that fadeth not away"* — reserved in heaven for God's chosen and elect. We are convinced that it is also a present possession.

We are called to manifest His love, His authority, and His abilities right now . . . winning the lost, healing the sick, casting out devils, proclaiming the gospel, and manifesting the supernatural, in cooperation with the will of His Spirit. By doing so we become living replicas of the Forerunner Himself.

And it must be said that this is not an option, it is a command given to all who count themselves to be His disciples, for He said — "freely ye have received, FREELY GIVE." (Matthew 10:8)

Jesus said — "Verily, verily, I say unto you, He that believeth on Me, the works that I do shall he do also; and greater works than these shall he do; because I go unto My Father." (John 14:12)

Perpetuating the work of the Lord in this world and the world to come is a principle part of God's plan for us.

This is our *birthright* and this is the blessing of the Most High God resting upon us now!

• Jesus counted it such an important thing for us to receive this birthright that He left His followers behind in the realm of time, and ascended up to the Father that this spiritual transfer might take place.

If it was that important to Him, then we consider it to be just as important to us!

We have been awakened!

We have discovered who we are, what we can be, and what we can have!

Because we are heirs of God, we now have the responsibility of sharing with others what God has shared with us.

This is our ordination from God . . . a major portion of the total true inheritance of the believer.

The very thing that brought deep satisfaction to Jesus, our Elder Brother, now brings deep satisfaction to us.

Not only have we inherited His abilities, we have also inherited His responsibilities, with respect to the needs of the human race.

What a discovery! What a life-transforming revelation this is . . . teaching us how vitally important we are to God!

• No wonder the Psalmist wrote — "BLESSED IS THE NATION WHOSE GOD IS THE LORD; AND THE PEOPLE WHOM HE HATH CHOSEN FOR **HIS OWN INHERITANCE.**" (Psalm 33:12)

And incidentally, this very scripture carries us into an even higher dimension of revelation concerning our inheritance status, for by it we perceive the following wondrous truth.

• Not only have we, as heirs of God, received an inheritance from the Lord. We have actually become an inheritance to the Lord as well.

Not only is He our supreme, sublime, living legacy; we are His!

Not only is He our most prized possession, we are His!

We have inherited His abiding presence.

He is forevermore our joy and the rejoicing of our hearts, and we certainly are the same to Him.

We have truly inherited *all that God has,* but this means little compared to the thrilling privilege of inheriting *all that He is.*

In like manner, because we have been bought with a price, Jesus has now become the rightful recipient and heir, inheriting and possessing all that we have.

But this means little or almost nothing to Him compared to the joy of winning our hearts . . . thus inheriting and eternally possessing all that we are, and all that we ever will be.

•• "FOR **THE LORD'S PORTION** IS HIS PEOPLE; JACOB IS **THE LOT OF HIS INHERITANCE.**" (Deuteronomy 32:9)

We are of supreme worth now, though at one time, admittedly, we were only worthless and wretched.

We know that, through His death and vicarious sufferings, Jesus obtained *by inheritance* a name better than the angels . . . *"a more excellent name"* according to Hebrews 1:4.

We presently share in this exalted inheritance portion as well, for the whole family of God in heaven and in earth has been named with His matchless name.

The name of Jesus in essence means *Jehovah-Saviour or Jehovah-God manifested in the flesh, and revealed as Saviour.*

It is clear that through the passion of Calvary, Jesus inherited or won the right to be called by this divine name which is truly above every name . . . lofty, exalted, and infinite.

But the firstborn Son of God also inherited a people, a godly seed, who are all the more devoted to Him because of the amazing display of love He unveiled on the cross.

So we joyously conclude: not only have we been greatly enriched by this spiritual interchange and relationship — God has been greatly enriched as well.

•• THEREFORE, THE MOST GLORIOUS PART OF **OUR GLORIOUS INHERITANCE** IS THE MOST GLORIOUS FACT THAT WE HAVE BECOME, IN THE EYES OF THE MOST HIGH GOD, **A GLORIOUS INHERITANCE FOR HIM AS WELL.**

We are God's treasure and God's trophy . . . forever and ever.

HE HAS MADE US WORTHY

As we reflect upon the statements that have been made thus far, we must admit that we almost stagger at the enormity of such a far-reaching declaration.

Yet we should never be backward in sounding out these great and precious promises . . . for they are statements of fact, settled forever in God's forever-settled Word!

We feel unworthy to receive such a magnificent gift from the Lord of creation. Yet, at the same time, faith compels us to acknowledge that, according to His Word, He has made us worthy!

Colossians 1:12 says — "Giving thanks unto the Father, which hath made us meet to be partakers of the inheritance of the saints in light."

Yes, God has *"made us meet"* — in other words, He has made us fit, worthy, suitable and qualified to receive such an exceeding great inheritance and such a supernatural destiny.

Therefore, we are worthy . . . made worthy by a supernatural act of deity.

We are worthy to be blessed.

We are worthy to be healed.

We are worthy to be received in the presence of God.

We are worthy to receive glory and power from heaven.

We are worthy to be used of God.

We are worthy to represent Him in this world.

We are worthy to be included in God's wonderful and eternal family . . . for the blood has made us worthy!

In describing the devoted, self-denying saints of God the Bible declared in Hebrews 11:38 that they were individuals — *"of whom the world was not worthy."*

Therefore God's true saints should never claim unworthiness — the world should instead consider itself unworthy of having God's saints as its inhabitants.

The grass should consider itself unworthy of being trodden upon by those whose feet have been shod with the preparation of the gospel of peace.

The sun should consider itself unworthy to shine upon those who will one day shine like the sun in the kingdom of their Father.

The flowers should consider themselves unworthy to blossom in the presence of those who are destined to blossom eternally in the semblance of the Lord Himself.

Yes, we have been made *"meet"* to be partakers.

We are justified by faith, therefore we are blameless in His sight, worthy of His fellowship.

"We have peace with God through our Lord Jesus Christ" . . . therefore we have been brought into a harmonious relationship with Him.

We are preserved in this worthiness, and kept in this position of being deserving of His fellowship, solely because we have access by faith into a heavenly storeroom full of a precious commodity called *grace.* (Romans 5:1-2)

This is part of our inheritance as new creatures, new creations, in Christ Jesus.

The Bible says that our inheritance is "in Him." (Ephesians 1:11)

We have a new position . . . an inherited standing of righteousness and power, the same position occupied by the resurrected Son of God, for we are "in Him."

But we will never enjoy the benefits of this bountiful heavenly deposit laid up for us unless we first believe, and then reach out by faith to receive.

OUR NEW TESTAMENT HERITAGE

•• It is important for us to understand the following:

We are heirs of the New Testament.

A **testament,** according to dictionary references, is . . . *a solemn covenant or a will.*

Jesus is spoken of as the Mediator of the New Testament, and also . . . the Testator. (Hebrews 9)

A **testator** is . . . *a person who leaves a will or testament to his heirs, to be enforced at his death.*

Once the testator dies, nothing can change the will. It is settled forever.

Jesus died on the cross and arose leaving a will (the New Covenant) full of *yea and amen promises* that can never be changed, altered, reversed or thwarted. But it is our responsibility to search out, discover and live in these blessed promises . . . promises of strength, deliverance, restoration and power.

If we fail to pursue these things diligently, we will simply grovel in the dust of the Adam-nature and wallow in the mire of human misery, permanent slaves to circumstance and sin.

•• The Bible warns that "the *heir,* as long as he is a child, differeth nothing from a servant, though he be *lord of all."* (Galatians 4:1)

We could certainly be categorized as children spiritually if we are self-seeking, rebellious, or lukewarm in our attitudes toward the Lord.

Then God would surely have to deal with us on the level of a Master-servant fear relationship, marked by frequent chastisements and judgments to bring us in line with His will. Or we could be labeled as children spiritually if we are just ignorant concerning our Word-rights.

Of course, it is not the will of God that either of these spiritual traps ensnare a true-born child of God.

We have not been called to servitude.

We have been called to sonship and heirship. We have been given the power to emerge as **lords** *(masters)* over the flesh and over every situation we face in life.

• Galatians 4:7 emphatically declares — ". . . thou art no more a servant, but a son; and if a son, THEN AN **HEIR OF GOD** THROUGH CHRIST."

We must trust in this scriptural fact more than we trust in our emotions or our feelings.

We are steadfast in believing that if God had only given us His Word to cling to, these promises that we have received as heirs of the New Testament are sufficient of themselves to propel us to perpetual triumph.

But, thank God — our heavenly Testator has given us much more than just His Word to convince us of the security and dependability of this New Will.

THE SEAL OF THE HOLY SPIRIT
THE EARNEST OF OUR INHERITANCE

•• We have also been **sealed** with the Holy Spirit of promise — which is **the earnest of our inheritance!** (Ephesians 1:13-14)

We know that this outpouring of the Spirit is God's stamp of approval on the life of a believer.

But in order to fully appreciate the depth of what God has done for us in this area, we must bring to light the full meaning of some of the words that God has employed to communicate His ideas, for these are spiritual words, authored by the Holy Ghost.

• First, a **seal** can be . . . *a mark, symbol or emblem that proves the authenticity of an item, or it can be a tight and perfect closure that prevents leakage or corruption.*

Surely being sealed with the Holy Ghost has produced this dual result in us. It proves that we are authentic sons of God, for by receiving the Spirit we inherit the potential of becoming everything that God intends His sons to be, and it prevents us from being corrupted, for it keeps us from the world.

Next, this seal of the Holy Spirit is also called **the earnest of our inheritance.**

• An **earnest** is defined as . . . *a pledge or a downpayment.*

We know that when any person places a downpayment on some item, it is taken for granted that he fully intends to return and pay off the rest of the purchase price — in order to take full possession of that particular piece of merchandise.

This is true with men and this is true with God also.

• Granting us His indwelling Spirit, the promise of the Father, was Jehovah's way of pledging that the inheritance-work He has started in us, He will also finish and bring to perfection.

Jesus will soon return and in a sense — "pay off the rest of the purchase price" — redeeming us from the power of the grave.

We are adamant in asserting that this mortal must put on immortality for our God has given us His solemn spiritual pledge, by the Word and by the Spirit.

We are strong in believing that we will soon be — "clothed upon with our house which is from heaven" . . . for "He that hath **wrought** us for the selfsame thing is God, who also hath given unto us **the earnest** of the Spirit." (II Corinthians 5:2-5)

• This word — **wrought** — is also quite important.

It means — *to be worked into shape by artistry or effort, to be carefully fashioned or formed.*

It can also mean — *to be elaborately embellished and expertly ornamented.*

Truly, our hearts overflow with thankfulness and worship as we realize that these really are perfect descriptions and definitions of what God is doing in us, and for us, right now.

We are being tenderly and carefully "worked into shape" . . . decorated and beautified by this heavenly artist, who daily colors our lives with the gentle brush-strokes of His mercy and grace.

• The high priest who daily ministered in the Temple wore a robe *embellished* with bells and pomegranates, personally designed by the Almighty God.

In like manner, as we daily minister to the Lord, we wear white robes of the righteousness of God, elaborately embellished and expertly ornamented with gifts and fruits of the Spirit (bells and pomegranates).

We have been excellently adorned.

We are clothed with garments of praise as we journey through time on our way to infinite perfection and everlasting glorification!

This is God's delight! This is God's great joy!

This is God's design for us!

We have not chosen this heritage for ourselves . . . He has chosen us and *wrought* us for this God-shaped destiny and predetermined purpose.

We have not elected ourselves into this eternal office.

We have been elected of God to receive this unspeakable gift of eternal life.

• Once we fully appreciate and understand that this is God's ordained plan for us, then — *"We are always confident."* (II Corinthians 5:6)

We are confident in the valley.

We are confident on the mountain.

We are confident in times of tribulation.

We are confident in times of blessing.

When we succeed, we remain confident in God.

When we fail, we remain confident in God.

When the enemy comes in like a flood, we still stand in utter confidence, knowing that He who has begun a good work in us shall perform it and continue it until the day of Jesus Christ. (Philippians 1:6)

God has not given us a spirit of fear.

Confidence in our inheritance is a part of the legacy that Jesus left behind.

We have much more than just a promise from God composed of words, we have His faithful, abiding, and manifest presence . . . continually persuading us that if God does something, He does it forever!

Our eyes have been opened by the spirit of wisdom and revelation.

We realize that we are **HEIRS OF GOD** and **JOINT-HEIRS WITH CHRIST** right now . . . but we also realize that our full inheritance is yet to be brought forth in infinite excellence.

We know that a downpayment (an *earnest)* is almost always a much smaller amount than the final price paid.

In similar fashion this *earnest of our inheritance* that we presently possess is just the "tip of the iceberg," spiritually speaking that is, compared to that which is hidden deep within our hearts, awaiting the day of manifestation.

We are thankful for our inheritance now, this foretaste of glory divine, but we long for our future state.

We refuse to sell our birthright, as Esau did, in order to temporarily gratify the flesh.

Instead, we intend to fully commit ourselves in holiness and righteousness before the Lord, that we might fully receive what rightfully belongs to us as sons of God.

This future glory is the Father's divine appointment for us, therefore we can rest in God and rejoice in hope, never wavering.

• We fully believe that if God "spared not His own Son, but delivered Him up for us all, how shall He not with Him also freely give us all things." (Romans 8:32)

And God definitely did say — ALL THINGS!

Surely God meant what He said . . . and God said what He meant!

KINGS

LORDS

PRINCES

THE KINGS OF THE EARTH

A ROYAL HOUSE

"And he hath on His vesture and on His thigh a name written, King of KINGS, and Lord of LORDS."
(Revelation 19:16)

"Behold a king shall reign in righteousness, and PRINCES shall rule in judgment." (Isaiah 32:1)

KINGS
LORDS
PRINCES
THE KINGS OF THE EARTH
A ROYAL HOUSE

*"And he hath on His vesture and on His thigh a name written, King of **KINGS**, and Lord of **LORDS.**"* (Revelation 19:16)

*"Behold, a king shall reign in righteousness, and **PRINCES** shall rule in judgment."* (Isaiah 32:1)

It has been said that certain rulers and emperors of the Byzantine empire gave a unique title to all of their offspring.
• They were called *porphyrogenitos* . . . which means *"born in the purple."*

The reason for this peculiar appellation is quite simple.

All royal babies were brought into this world in a special Purple Room set aside for that very purpose in the huge palace at Constantinople.

The walls of this unique room were covered with slabs of an expensive, purple marble called *porphyry.*

Apparently everything else in that royal deliverance chamber was also purple in color . . . purple tile, purple bedspreads, purple tapestries, decorative ornaments of every related shade and hue, and of course, attendants and midwives clothed in garments appropriately colored with that unique and rich mixture of red and blue that represents imperial honor and majesty.

This strange decor was a symbolic way of declaring to all the subjects of that empire that these were no ordinary children . . . they were of the royal seed, inheritors of regal authority, and potential heirs to the throne.

At the precise moment that they came forth from the womb they must have been wrapped in violet-purple swaddling clothes, for even with their first breath they were considered, and labeled, royal in every respect.

They did nothing to earn such an exalted position and status, neither were they consciously aware at once of their importance and greatness in the kingdom. Regal glory was simply their birthright.

They were *porphyrogenitos* . . . born in the purple.

They never chose such a lofty inheritance for themselves . . . they were birthed into it, at the express will of each one of their fathers.

From the start, great attention was shown to every detailed facet of their development.

They had to be extraordinary offspring.

Their personality had to be of such fine quality, polished to such a high degree of luster, that multitudes would respect and obey their slightest decree.

Every step that they took in life, forward or backward, would be under the scrutiny of multiplied thousands of observing eyes.

Therefore, every stage in their growth was of the utmost importance, for they were being trained potentially to assume the reins of the kingdom. Surely, this was both burden and blessing, for their lives were never their own.

From the beginning they were the product and possession of a certain blueprint, blue-blood plan . . . brought into being at the pleasure of their fathers, that great riches might be preserved and shared, that the Byzantine domain might be kept secure, and that the royal families of that kingdom might be perpetuated.

GOD'S PORPHYROGENITOS

In many respects, every child of God can claim a similar kind of heritage spiritually, yet far greater, of course, in magnificence and magnitude.

Jeremiah unveiled God's predetermined purpose concerning His eternal progeny when he prophesied that — *"a glorious high throne from the beginning is the place of our sanctuary."* (Jeremiah 17:12)

We are God's seed, inheritors of His authority and heirs destined to share His throne.

The vast majority of God's sons and daughters have never made their entrance into this world by passing through the portal of a royal bedchamber, yet in a certain sense we can all claim to have been *"born in the purple"* — for we have been supernaturally birthed into a spiritual kingdom and a regal glory far surpassing anything the Byzantine emperors could have provided for their posterity.

• The precise moment that we were born again, we were created royal in every respect, immersed in the regal nature of the High and Lofty One who is called the King of glory, the Prince of the kings of the earth.

We now dwell in heavenly places in Him.

King Jesus lives in us and manifests His personality through us.

We are learning to talk like kings . . . decreeing in His stead.

We are learning to walk like kings in this world, just as He did, with great confidence, courage, self-possession and aplomb.

We are being educated to assume the reins of authority in God's vast, limitless universe.

Jesus will always be the Supreme Monarch of all creation — the King of kings and the Lord of lords — but we are those subordinate *kings* and *lords* who are destined to reign with Him for ever and ever.

We never chose such a lofty position for ourselves.

John 1:13 declared that we were born — "not of blood, nor of the will of the flesh, nor of the will of man, but of God."

We are the purpose of God revealed.

We are the product and possession of a certain blueprint blood-bought plan formed in the heart of the Creator from the very beginning.

Regal glory is simply our birthright!

Because of this, great attention is being shown to every detail of our development . . . for we are extremely important to the kingdom of God.

We are under heaven's constant scrutiny . . . God tests our attitudes every moment and angels bear us up in their hands lest we at any time dash our feet against a stone.

We are far more than merely fortunate.

We are elected and ordained.

We are chosen; we are grateful.

• We can easily echo the sentiments expressed by Hannah who said, concerning the Most High — "He raiseth up the poor out of the dust, and lifteth up the beggar from the dunghill, to set them among *princes,* and to make them *inherit the throne of glory . . ."* (I Samuel 2:8)

• John said — *"Unto Him that loved us, and washed us from our sins in His own blood, and **hath made us kings** and priests unto God . . . to Him be glory and dominion for ever and ever. Amen."* (Revelation 1:5-6)

Notice that the author of Revelation did not place this inheritance-promise only as a part of the future glorified state.

• He stated unequivocally that we have already been made kings and priests . . . **"a royal house"** as the New English Bible puts it.

This will be the perfectly manifest wealth of the **GLORIOUS IN-HERITANCE** that awaits us in the resurrection, yet this is also our present status in the Spirit, in the inner man.

It behooves us therefore to search out and discover what God would have us to "rule over" in the Spirit, for every king must have a kingdom.

Surely, there are certain negative circumstances that can be rectified, broken lives that can be mended and satanic powers that can be successfully defeated, if we will dare to walk in the spiritual authority that God has given us as His *vice-regents.*

• It is logical to conclude, therefore, that the very people and events that we could potentially bring under the canopy of our spiritual influence actually make up *the individual spiritual kingdom* over which we are presently responsible.

This earthly, spiritual governorship, the kingdom responsibility, given to every child of God, will differ with each individual, varying greatly in nature and in size.

We may be primarily accountable for the care of only one family, or a number of individuals, or maybe a single neighborhood or community, or a body of believers, a church, or possibly an entire city, or in some rare cases, even nations as a whole.

God gives different men and women different degrees of the anointing (the specific unction of His Spirit poured out on yielded vessels to perform specific tasks).

Of course, some of these anointings will cover similar spiritual territory, and thus, at times, kingdom responsibilities in certain areas are shared by several individuals.

This could be referred to as an *overlap of spiritual authority.*

In considering these spiritual truths, we must also realize that the kingdom of God does not work in the same fashion that earthly kingdoms do.

Jesus said — "whosoever will be great among you, let him be your minister; and whosoever will be chief among you, let him be your servant." (Matthew 20:26-27)

We are not called to dominate men or bring them under the bondage of a dictatorial rule, as some earthly rulers do.

We are called to rather rule by example, leading sanctified and devoted lives, and thus rule by serving others.

We are called to reign with Christ in the realm of time by walking the faith-walk, and thus becoming channels of His deliverance power.

We are called to dominate the negative by manifesting joy in a world full of depression, and peace in a world full of despair.

We are called to rule by fearlessly promoting and declaring the authority of the Word . . . yet at the same time . . . "in meekness instructing those who oppose themselves."

We are called to rule by making intercession for others, taking authority over sin, sickness and satanic powers . . . in the spirit of prayer.

Finally, we are called to rule as kings among men by becoming vessels of the great compassion of God, for true spiritual authority is always rooted and grounded in love and humility.

This is "the royal law" *(the law of spiritual kings).*

• James said — "If ye fulfill *the royal law* according to the Scripture [the law of spiritual kings] *thou shalt love thy neighbor as thyself."* (James 2:8)

•• **This is how Jesus reigned among men.**

He came into a pride-filled world and conquered it with meekness.

He came into an unbelieving world and conquered it with faith.

He walked amid the shallow, the critical, the condemning and hate-filled offspring of Adam, and He conquered their hearts with His evident compassion.

And He did it all with such humility, taking upon Himself the form of a servant, so willing to give His life for the lowest, the last, the least and the lost.

Zechariah foresaw this noble facet of Jesus' character and prophesied:

> *"Rejoice greatly, O daughter of Zion; shout,*
> *O daughter of Jerusalem: behold **thy King** com-*
> *eth unto thee: He is just, and having salvation;*
> *lowly, and riding upon an ass, and upon a colt*
> *the foal of an ass."*　　　　(Zechariah 9:9)

O, how we must emulate the gentleness, meekness and love that our Lord displayed, if we are to truly help in His effort to bring the kingdom of God into this woeful world.

DOMINION

God revealed His primary plan and His dual motive in creating the first man, Adam, by making two foundational statements.

First, He said — "Let us make man in our image, after our likeness."

Surely, this was God's deepest desire.

• But next He declared — *"Let them have dominion."*

This was the second most important thing that God ordained man to receive and fulfill.

• It is important to note that the word **dominion** means . . . *rule, lordship, supreme authority, or sovereign power.*

Initially this Adamic lordship extended over only the earth and all creatures contained in the earth, especially the Garden of Eden.

But it is clear that the future inheritance of the regenerated sons of Adam will embrace far more.

The Psalmist David wrote:

> *"What is man, that Thou art mindful of him?*
> *and the son of man, that Thou visitest him?*
> *For Thou hast made him a little lower than*
> *the angels, and hast crowned him with glory and*

141

honour.
Thou madest him to have dominion over the
works of Thy hands.'' (Psalm 8:4-6)

This will surely include more than the beasts and the birds, the mountains, the valleys, the continents, and the oceans that make up this world.

• In confirming, enhancing and augmenting the Psalm promise, Jesus went far beyond the atmospheric border, and even the natural cosmos, when He pledged — "HE THAT OVERCOMETH SHALL INHERIT ALL THINGS." (Revelations 21:7)

This God-given gift of dominion will eventually and most assuredly involve and include the highest celestial realms above, in the New Creation to come.

But as we journey toward that blessed and absolute goal, God is taking us step by step.

We know that spiritual authority shifted dramatically (180 degrees) — the very moment that we experienced salvation.

We were nothing but sin-slaves, under the miserable yoke and dominion of Satan, until that blessed moment when the Father — "delivered us from the power of darkness and . . . translated us into the kingdom of His dear Son." (Colossians 1:13)

• The word — **translated** — means . . . *to be totally removed, transferred or conveyed from one spiritual state to another.*

We can definitely claim this as an integral part of the transcendental legacy with which we have been enriched.

• We were trapped under the horrible, oppressive, and even despotic rule of the fallen Adam nature, helpless captives in the dungeon of sin, but then God graciously lifted us to an eminent position of significant and prominent power where *"sin shall no longer have **dominion**"* over us. (Romans 6:14)

We now either live above all iniquity, which is of course God's expectation toward us and our foremost desire, or if by chance sin surfaces, the precious blood of Jesus blots it out, when we humbly repent and believe.

Therefore, it is impossible for sin to gain the mastery over us any longer, if we know our intrinsic rights as sons and daughters of God.

Jesus won this victory for us.

• The Bible also declared that because He conquered the grave once, now — *"death hath no more **dominion** over Him."* (Romans 6:9)

By receiving Jesus into our hearts, we presently share in His supreme triumph over this archenemy of the human race (and thus we become partakers and heirs of His sovereign authority in all things).

In this respect, we are reigning with Him as kings right now!

Death no longer has dominion over us, for we are linked eternally to the Sun of Righteousness who has arisen over us with healing in His wings.

He honors our words, our daily profession of faith, with sent-forth virtue from above — healing us of doubts, fears, and feelings of inadequacy.

Therefore, when death seeks to overtake us and overwhelm us (mentally, emotionally, spiritually, or even physically) we dare to decree the miraculous and the supernatural, for we know our inheritance-rights.

We know that we are kings, and we also know that — *"Where the word of a king is, there is power."* (Ecclesiastes 8:4)*[1]

Even if our appointed time comes and we have to shed this fleshly carcass, though we temporarily succumb to its control over our flesh, death does not really have any lasting dominion over us.

The Word-promise, living in us, will eventually bring us out of the pit into newness of life.

We know the resurrected Saviour who pledged — "he that believeth in Me, though he were dead, yet shall he live." (John 11:25)

• And no wonder Paul protested — "For if by one man's offence death *reigned* by one; much more they which receive abundance of grace and of the gift of righteousness shall *reign in life* by one Jesus Christ." (Romans 5:17)

• We reign as kings right now by living victoriously in the life-giving promises of Jesus Christ!

The law of the Spirit of life in Christ Jesus has made us free from the law of sin and death.

The renewing, redeeming, restoring, and refreshing life of the Word and the Spirit now makes us more than conquerors in every situation.

God has restored to us the very dominion that Adam lost in the beginning.

Of course, we recognize that this regal authority is only in partial manifestation now, but the potential for full restoration is definitely in seed form, planted deep and firm in the heart of every son of God.

• The closer we get to God, the more this dominion manifests, for righteousness begets authority.

Psalm 49:14 proclaims that — *"The upright shall have dominion."*

Job 22:23-28 reveals that — "Thou shalt also decree a thing, and it shall be established unto thee" — but only if — "thou shalt put away iniquity far from thy tabernacles."

Jesus was even more explicit in developing this revelation when He made the following bold assertation:

"To him that overcometh will I grant to sit with Me in My throne, even as I also overcame, and am set down with My Father in His throne." (Revelation 3:21)

The power to decree with authority rests in the throne.

Proverbs 16:10 declares that — "a divine sentence is in the lips of a king."

But it is clear that only overcomers, who overcome sin, Satan and self, see this kind of commanding influence and spiritual sway stirred up in the inner man.

It is an irrefutable fact that we are presently, spiritually, seated with Christ in heavenly places.

Therefore divinely-imparted authority, rooted in divinity, is potentially a present as well as a future possession.

But the measure of manifestation is totally dependent on, and directly proportionate to, the measure of consecration in our lives.

Right now, we have been given the commission to preach the Word, win the lost, pray for the sick, cast out devils and manifest the gifts of the Spirit as we cooperate with the express will of God.

We are convinced though that these gifts and manifestations of the Holy Spirit are not an end in themselves.

They are but elementary spiritual exercises designed by deity to meet the present need, while simultaneously preparing us for something far greater — an illustrious position of oracular power and viceroyship in the New Creation to come!

We are learning now to yield our hands, our minds, our bodies and our voices to the creative power and authority of God.

Every conflict, every problem, every mountain of opposition is just another opportunity for us to learn how to successfully rule in our God-given domain (the spiritual territory over which God has made us responsible).

• The Bible declared though that — "the heir, as long as he is a child, differeth nothing from a servant, though He be **lord of all.**" (Galatians 4:1)

To use this *title* in reference to a son or daughter of God almost sounds blasphemous, but it is definitely acceptable (for the definition of the word **lord** can be — *one who has achieved mastery, or exercises leadership or great power in certain areas).*

God's plan for all His offspring is that they emerge as *lords,* in time and eternity.

Therefore, this scripture plainly reveals that we can definitely be *masters* or *lords* over all the circumstances of our lives . . . even our greatest defeats.

We can *achieve mastery* in spiritual things.

We can *exercise power* over all the power of the enemy.

We have received a vicarship from Jehovah.

We are His representatives, His administrative deputies.

Dominion is very much a part of our new spiritual wardrobe (the royal regalia with which we are now clothed).

No wonder the prophet challenged the church saying — "Awake, awake, put on thy strength, O Zion; put on thy beautiful garments . . ." (Isaiah 52:1)

THRONES AND CROWNS

It is a prophetic fact, that when Jesus comes again, He will set up the kingdom of God in this world *(heaven on earth for a thousand years)*.

John the Beloved related to us, in the book of the Revelation, the governmental structure of this future theocracy.

• He said — "I saw *thrones,* and they sat upon them, and judgment was given unto them, [those who refused to be corrupted by the anti-Christ spirit of this world] . . . and they lived and *reigned* with Christ a thousand years." (Revelation 20:4)

•• Paul added to this revelation when he said — *"Do ye not know that the saints shall judge the world and . . . know ye not that we shall judge angels."* (I Corinthians 6:2-3)

In His parable of the pounds (Luke 19:12-27) Jesus indicated that those who are faithful to God in small things in this life will be made rulers over differing numbers of cities during the Kingdom Age to come.

According to the prophet Ezekiel, King David will be a prince over all the earth (Ezekiel 34:23-24; 37:25) apparently serving as the chief executive or prime minister, second in command to the King of all kings.*[2]

Jesus also promised His twelve apostles that — "in the regeneration when the Son of man shall sit in the throne of His glory, ye shall also sit upon twelve thrones, judging the twelve tribes of Israel, and every one that hath forsaken houses, or brethren, or sisters, or father, or mother, or wife, or children, or lands, for My name's sake, shall receive an hundredfold, and shall inherit everlasting life." (Matthew 19:28-29)

At the last supper, Jesus repeated the pledge that He made to His twelve disciples saying — "Ye are they which have continued with Me in My temptations. And I appoint unto you a kingdom, as My Father hath appointed unto Me; that ye may eat and drink at My table in My kingdom, and sit on thrones judging the twelve tribes of Israel." (Luke 22:28-30)

On that day, all of the redeemed, both Jew and Gentile, will be a part of Israel and thus be included in the above promises.

• The name **Israel** means *prince of God* so it is quite believable that all those who are eternally included in this great chosen nation will ultimately reign as princes in this world, over the natural people that will repopulate the earth.

The Scripture conclusively reveals that there will be both natural offspring of Adam and supernatural glorified saints of God cohabiting this terrestrial realm during the thousand year kingdom. (Isaiah 61:5-6; 65:17-25, Zechariah 14:16)

• But in reference to the glorified saints of this era Jesus promised — "He that overcometh, and keepeth My works to the end, to him will I give power over the nations: and he shall rule them with a rod of iron." (Revelation 2:26-27)

Zechariah declared that in that day — "living waters shall go out from Jerusalem . . . and the Lord shall be King over all the earth . . . there shall be one Lord, and His name one." (Zechariah 14:8-9)

Isaiah rejoiced to foretell that — "the government shall be upon His shoulder: and His name shall be called Wonderful, Counsellor, the mighty God, the everlasting Father, the Prince of Peace." (Isaiah 9:6)

Ezekiel prophesied that Jerusalem will be the capital city and the joy of the whole earth, and will be called *Jehovah-Shammah* which means . . . *"the Lord is there."* (Ezekiel 48:35)

Daniel predicted that — "The kingdom and dominion, and the greatness of the kingdom under the whole heaven, shall be given to the people of the saints of the Most High, whose kingdom is an everlasting kingdom, and all dominions shall serve and obey Him." (Daniel 7:27)

So we see that all of the prophets agree together, declaring as if with one voice the prophetic message of the coming of the government of God on this earth.

Surely, there are no words that can sufficiently describe the future heavenly grandeur of the royal court in Jerusalem, nor the ethereal beauty that will fill this realm as the glory of God's Shekinah presence goes forth to — "gather together in one all things in Christ." (Ephesians 1:10)

Praise to God will abound everywhere. Mighty angels will walk in the midst of men. The great love of God will overflow all living things.

God will wipe away all tears from our eyes, immerse us in His unspeakable bliss and exalt us by His mighty power.

We know that these blessed promises must come to pass, therefore we anticipate the day of resurrection with great joy and great expectations . . . for certainly it will be our coronation day!

*   *   *   *   *   *

Not only has God promised certain throne-positions to His royal offspring; He has also pledged to *crown* us, in various and glorious ways.

Psalm 8:5 announces that He will *crown us with honor* (the honor of inheriting all things and being brought forth in the likeness of the Lord).

Psalm 21:3 reveals that He will bestow on us a *crown of pure gold* (which speaks of infinity and divinity . . . infinite, divine life).

Psalm 103:4 declares that our God will *crown us with loving-kindness*

146

and tender mercies.

Proverbs 14:18 states that — "the prudent are *crowned with knowledge.*"

James 1:12 says — "Blessed is the man that endureth temptation: for when he is tried, he shall receive the *crown of life,* which the Lord hath promised to them that love Him."

I Peter 5:4 unveils that — "when the chief Shepherd shall appear, ye shall receive a *crown of glory* that fadeth not away."

In II Timothy 4:8, Paul declared, after fighting a good fight of faith and finishing his course, that — "Henceforth there is laid up for me a *crown of righteousness,* which the Lord, the righteous judge, shall give me at that day: and not to me only, but unto all them that love His appearing."

Paul said also concerning His converts — "What is our hope, or joy, or *crown of rejoicing?* Are not even ye in the presence of our Lord Jesus Christ at His coming?" (I Thessalonians 2:19)

• Of course, all these *crowns* speak of the perfect spiritual adornment of the glorified state.

We will be excellently and honorably clothed in the perfection of God's righteousness.

We will be nobly endued with the radiance of His glory.

We will be honorably draped with the perfection of His infinite divine life, and majestically arrayed with the perfection of His mercy and loving-kindness.

WE WILL BE CROWNED WITH SUPREME WORTH IN THE SIGHT OF ALL THE HEAVENLY HOST, AND ENRICHED FOREVER WITH ROYAL HEAVENLY REWARDS.

On that day, the works that we have done in the name of Jesus and the treasures that we have laid up on high will be unto us a *crown of rejoicing* (a source of great ecstasy).

• In light of all these truths, we conclude that it is literally impossible to satisfactorily describe in words the absolute glory and beauty of the eternal state.

What unspeakable joy it is though to meditate on this, our future destiny, for now and then the spirit of revelation falls on us and grants a fleeting momentary glimpse into the coronation splendor for which we have been ordained of God.

To reach for, and obtain, this final kingly heritage is presently our deep yearning and our constant longing.

It will be the maximum manifestation of the inner man, and the final fulfillment of that great God-birthed passion that daily grips our hearts.

We wait for this, our everlasting trophy, filled with the greatest of expectation.

147

And yet . . . we feel certain . . . that once we finally attain the heights of glory and the spectacular delights of the celestial world, we will then realize, all the more, how very gracious and merciful our God has been to us and how utterly dependent we were on the precious blood of the Lamb to make us worthy of receiving such a blessed inheritance.

We conclude, therefore, that in the ages to come it will be absolutely impossible for us to glory in our own achievements or lay any credit to our own name.

When time merges into eternity, surely every member of God's **ROYAL HOUSE** will join the twenty-four elders in casting all our crowns before the feet of His majesty, the King of kings and Lord of lords. We will return all the credit and all the praise to Jesus — "THE PRINCE OF **THE KINGS OF THE EARTH.**" (Revelation 1:5)

We will rejoice to proclaim — "Thou art worthy, O Lord, to receive glory and honour and power: for Thou hast . . . made us unto our God *kings* and priests: and we shall *reign* on the earth." (Revelations 4:11, 5:10)

We are convinced.
We are definitely elected to be *KINGS.*
We are definitely chosen to be *LORDS.*
We are definitely called to be *PRINCES.*

But, above all, we are ordained of God to be true worshippers of the very One who has lovingly chosen to bring us forth in His own regal image.

We know that Jesus came forth out of the House of David, and we know that the House of David was a part of the tribe of JUDAH.

So, because we are descendants of the Messiah, in a spiritual sense, every born again child of God could well claim to be a part of Judah (that royal king-producing tribe of Israel whose very name means *praise).*

Therefore we are called of God to be *eternal vessels of praise* . . . pure praise, pleasant praise and powerful praise forevermore.

This is the greatest privilege of our royal calling, and this is our ultimate crown!!

---

*[1]Jesus gave us a prime example of how to take authority over Satan with our words during His temptation in the wilderness. He never begged the Father to deliver Him from the wicked one; instead He commanded — "Get thee behind me, Satan," or "Get thee hence, Satan" and then He quoted the Word. We, as spiritual kings reigning with Christ, should dare to follow Jesus' example and use the same method. (Luke 4:8, Matthew 4:10)

*[2]Most Bible scholars consider these Davidic prophecies to be Messianic (symbolic prophecies referring to the Messiah). Because the name **David** means *beloved,* it speaks of the *beloved* Son of God who was also a Shepherd/King. It is possible, though, that these prophetic statements will also be literally fulfilled in the ultimate destiny of this Old Testament king.

THE MEEK

THE GENTLE

THE MEEK OF THE EARTH

―――――――――――――

*"Blessed are **THE MEEK:** for they shall inherit the earth."* (Matthew 5:5)

*"But with righteousness shall He judge the poor, and reprove with equity for **THE MEEK OF THE EARTH.**"*
(Isaiah 11:4)

THE MEEK
THE GENTLE
THE MEEK OF THE EARTH

"Blessed are THE MEEK: for they shall inherit the earth."   (Matthew 5:5)

Usually a **meek** person is defined as being *one who possesses a mild, gentle or soothing disposition or . . . one who is able to endure injury with patience and without resentment.*

But the present-day connotation of this term has become somewhat negative, implying a person deficient in spirit or courage, submissive to the point of being a coward, unresisting and even fearful and cringing in the face of opposition.

This is definitely not the interpretation of the word — *meek* — as used in the heart-warming, beatitude promise given above. (Gr. — *praus* or *praos)*

W.E. Vine suggests the following in explaining the related word *meekness* (so translated from the Greek word *prautes* or *praotes).*

> "In its use in Scripture . . . it consists not in a person's outward behavior only, nor yet in his relations to his fellow-men . . . **Rather it is an inwrought grace of the soul; and the exercises of it are first and chiefly towards God.** It is that temper of spirit in which we accept His dealings with us as good, and therefore without disputing or resisting; it is closely linked with the word . . . humility.
>
> . . . It must be clearly understood . . . that the meekness manifested by the Lord and commanded to the believer is the fruit of power. The common assumption is that when a man is meek it is because he cannot help himself; but the Lord was 'meek' because He had the infinite resources of God at His command. **Described negatively, meekness is the opposite of self-assertiveness and self-interest; it is equanimity of spirit [a balanced disposition, evenness of mind] that is neither elated nor cast down, simply because it is not occupied with self at all."***[1]

• The very last statement in the above quote (concerning the selflessness of meekness) unveils the mystery of this *title-revelation*.

• For God has purposed that the earth be ruled eventually by selfless and unassuming men and women who have sought more for *meekness* than greatness, and who have striven far more to be *servants* than to be masters.

This is the beauty of the kingdom of God, and the key to obtaining His favor, for God has already promised — "he that humbleth himself shall be exalted." (Luke 14:11)

On the contrary, though, we can look back through history and see a great number of individuals who have sought to "exalt themselves" and thereby "inherit the earth" by the force and brutality of military conquest.

When we inspect their character and motives, without fail, we discover towering egos, hearts bloated with selfishness and pride, and spirits seething with covetousness and greed. All of these, of course, are quite evidently the opposite of *meekness*.

And also quite evident is the truth that their short-lived successes, built on self-will, never healed the world of its woes and fractious divisions, and their kingdoms, acquired by violence, always eventually crumbled.

•• But then Jesus came and stood in the midst of this war-torn, strife-filled world, stretching out His arms with the gracious invitation:

> *"Come unto Me, all ye that labour and are*
> *heavy laden, and I will give you rest.*
> *Take My yoke upon you and learn of Me; for*
> *I am meek and lowly of heart: and ye shall find*
> *rest unto your souls."*   (Matthew 11:28-29)

What an amazing contrast this is . . . divinity condescending to humanity, clothed with the garment of humility and all to feel our infirmity!

The thunderclap voice that birthed a multitude of swirling galaxies, rushing through endless, timeless expanses, now softly and compassionately beckons, saying . . . *"Come unto Me."*

The boundless God who has never known any limitation, now, in a purposeful display of *meekness,* imposes upon Himself the boundaries and limitations of Adam-flesh:

He is born in poverty, in a lowly manger.

He grows as an ordinary child, developing in wisdom and knowledge.

He submits to earthly parents.

He is tempted by Satan in the wilderness.

He hungers and searches for fruit on a barren fig tree.

He tires from His journey and sits on the edge of a well in Samaria.

He sleeps in the hinderpart of a ship being tossed on Galilee waves.

He stands at a gravesite and weeps.

He is "despised of men; a man of sorrows, and acquainted with grief." (Isaiah 53:3)

He sweats blood in desperateness of prayer, but then He submits unresistingly, saying — *"Not My will."*

He is crucified.

He is altogether a man.

Yet He is Very God.

• The King who was celestially crowned, in eternity past, with the spectacular Shekinah glory of absolute oneness with the Father now wears a crown of thorns on His bleeding brow and cries — *"My God, My God, why hast Thou forsaken Me?"*

• The very Creator who clothed Himself with light as with a garment now watches brute, beastly men gamble over His vesture as they execute Him on a cross . . . yet He still compassionately pleads — *"Father, forgive them; for they know not what they do."*

• The Holy One who created the angels with just the breath of His mouth now takes each breath with agony as He "walks the wood." When He cries *"I thirst"* . . . a sponge full of vinegar is placed on His lips.

So easily . . . He could summon an army of angels.

So effortlessly . . . He could call down fire out of heaven.

But instead He allows Himself to be led as a lamb to the slaughter . . . and returns love for hate, blessing for cursing.

He dies, hanging between two common criminals.

He is buried like any other man.

But in the garden of Joseph of Arimathea . . . near the tomb . . . in the gentle wind caressing the mourning hillside . . . there is faintly heard (at least for those who have ears to hear) the echoing whisper of heartfelt, character-revealing words, spoken long before . . .

*"I am **meek** and lowly of heart."*

Our eyes mist over.

Our hearts are stilled with awe.

But then we hear that call from the "deep" that brings us to our knees.

For the soothing, echoing voice reaches all the way down into the deepest depth of us all, opening up a wellspring of hope and desire with the wooing words . . . *"Come and follow Me"*.

THE RELATION OF MEEKNESS TO GENTLENESS
MOSES — THE MEEKEST MAN

It must be reemphasized that *meekness* is definitely not weakness; it is not the sign of a limp-willed person.

Rather, it is the obvious absence of certain carnal qualities such as haughtiness, pride, rebellion, hostility and hard-heartedness.

• *A meek heart* is a melted heart that burns always with fervency toward God and compassion toward man.

• *A meek spirit* is one quick to repent and quick to forgive.

• *A meek-hearted* person is always a gentle-hearted individual as well . . . *one who is kind, amiable and free from harsh or violent attitudes.*

In fact, the New American Standard translation rendered our *title-scripture* — "Blessed are **THE GENTLE,** for they shall inherit the earth." (Matthew 5:5)

And Titus 3:2 (KJV) links the two words together, showing their kinship, commanding that believers be *"gentle, shewing all meekness* to all men." (See also II Corinthians 10:1)

Those who truly follow the Lord, becoming like Him, always exhibit these related qualities of character.

•• It is noteworthy to see that even though Moses had to often deal with the people of Israel in a stern way, still he was spoken of as being *"very meek above all the men which are upon the face of the earth."*

But this great deliverer was certainly not so mild that he was unable to make a strong stand for truth, or so intimidated by opposition that he cowered before those who resisted his authority. (Numbers 12:3)

Quite the contrary, he was just as immovable and just as undefiable as fiery Mt. Sinai in his prophetic office.

But his meek and compassionate heart would often rend in intercession over Israel to the extent that once he even prayed to Jehovah — "Yet now, if Thou wilt forgive their sin -----; and if not, blot me, I pray Thee, out of Thy book which Thou hast written." (Exodus 32:32)

Such selflessness is almost beyond human comprehension and speaks deeply and even prophetically of the *meek* Messiah to come who, in a similar manner, would show Himself willing to die in our stead.

The exemplary evidence of both the type (Moses) and the antitype (Jesus) provides every New Covenant believer with a stimulating and convicting challenge to Christlikeness. For in beholding this precious character quality we are often aroused to lay hold on the same . . . in all of our actions and in all of our reactions.

This is our desire, our deep desire . . . for we have learned (and it has been said many times). . . .

"There is nothing so strong
As gentleness,
And there is nothing so gentle
As real strength."

PLEDGES GIVEN TO "THE MEEK"

There are many vitally important, scriptural pledges made to those whom God has entitled *the meek* or *the gentle*.

In grasping these blessed promises it is essential that we first realize . . . This is not an inheritance reserved to only a select few in the body of Christ!

All believers begin occupying this challenging and God-pleasing *title-position* the moment they are born again, for *meekness* in surrender and *meekness* in repentance always necessarily precede and accompany a true salvation experience.

• But it also stands to reason that the more we deepen in this particular character trait, the more we will also be able to successfully appropriate the blessings and rewards that follow such an acquisition.

Therefore, may we ever strive for an humble, meek and unassuming posture — so careful, to "mind not high things, but condescend to men of low estate" (men who are free from haughtiness and conceit). (Romans 12:16)

May we be consistent in yielding to this noble facet of Jesus' personality and thereby "ride" triumphantly, as He did, into the blessedness and fullness of **OUR GLORIOUS INHERITANCE.** (Zechariah 9:9, Matthew 21:1-11)

May we show our works with "meekness of wisdom" and may we accept every trial of opposition as a God-ordained opportunity to develop this precious fruit of the Spirit! (James 3:13)

Finally . . . May we ever be diligent to write the following promises on the tables of our hearts, embracing them with fresh faith at the dawning of each new day!

THE PROMISES, BLESSINGS, AND REWARDS
(Corresponding points are in italic print)

*"**The meek** shall eat and be satisfied: they*
shall praise the Lord that seek Him: your heart
shall live forever."   (Psalm 22:26)

•• Because Psalm 22, in entirety, deals prophetically with Jesus' death and its ultimate effect, the reference to *eating* in the verse above (taken

155

out of Psalm 22) speaks specifically of believers being able to *"eat"* of the fruit of Calvary (partaking of the abundant mercy, grace and righteousness available there). O, how *satisfying* to the soul it is to *eat of* Jesus' flesh (to digest His Word into our inner being)! How nourishing it is to the heart to *drink* of His blood (to drink in His life-giving, soul-cleansing Spirit)! And how filled with *praise* we become in seeking the Lord, especially when we realize that His promise is *life forevermore!*

*   *   *   *   *   *

"The meek will He guide in judgment: and the meek will He teach His way."

(Psalm 25:9)

••   If God discovers yieldedness and *meekness* in the hearts of His offspring, then He will certainly *guide* them into making the right *judgments* (the right choices) in their daily walk with Him (what to believe, how to interpret the Scripture, perception of the will of God, how to deal correctly with different persons and situations, etc.). This is divine guidance, divine inspiration, and should be evident in the walk of every sincere believer.

Our Saviour and Guide sends the Holy Ghost, the Comforter, into our hearts and lives: *to teach us* all things, to bring all things to our remembrance, to lead us and *guide us* into all truth, to search out the deep things of God, and to glorify and testify of the Son, revealing all that He has inherited from the Father and subsequently passed on to us. Being led into all of these things sums up a great portion of the reward of *meekness* and should be greatly desired and fully expected!

*   *   *   *   *   *

"But the meek shall inherit the earth; and delight themselves in the abundance of peace."

(Psalm 37:11)

••   One of the most blessed gifts accompanying true salvation is the gift of peace (tranquility of mind, calmness of spirit and quietness of heart). How significant it is to see, though, that those who are entitled *the meek* do not merely possess a peace that comes *from God,* they have the peace *of God!* Jesus indicated this when He said, *"My peace,* I give unto you."

This is a supernatural reality that goes far beyond the emotional feeling of peace that a natural man can experience. This is a divine essence born in the celestial long before it is experienced in the terrestrial (in these earthen vessels of ours).

Yet even more notable and wonderful is the fact that New Covenant sons and daughters can also rightfully claim *peace with God,* for

156

we have been "made nigh" by the blood of the Lamb! We have been brought into harmony with the Most High. The sin-barrier has been lifted and the breach repaired. We can boldly claim restored oneness with the King of all creation. No wonder we possess peace *from God* and the peace *of God,* for we have obtained peace *with God.*

This is *abundant* life and *abundant* peace and a grand portion of the rich reward that has been bestowed on *the meek!* (John 14:27, Romans 5:1, Ephesians 2:14)

*　　　　*　　　　*　　　　*　　　　*　　　　*

> *"The Lord lifteth up **the meek:** he casteth the wicked down to the ground."*　　　(Psalm 147:6)

> *"But with righteousness shall He judge the poor, and reprove with equity for **the meek of the earth.**"*　　　(Isaiah 11:4)

•• Yes, we can be sure that God will fight our battles and reprove our enemies for us. Therefore, like the firstborn Son, we too can return love for hate and blessing for cursing. We can react to injustice and unwarranted persecution with *meekness,* expecting God to intervene in our behalf, for we know He judges with *equity* — *impartiality* and *fairness* — and those that trust in Him are never ashamed!

He is a God of recompense. Whatever is sown must eventually be reaped! We should therefore — "avenge not [ourselves] but rather give place unto wrath"; and if we are reviled, we should revile not again, nor threaten, but like the firstborn Son, commit ourselves to Him "who judgeth righteously." (Romans 12:19, I Peter 2:23) The mighty God defended righteous David when he was persecuted unnecessarily by Saul. He will still defend and lift up those who react to opposition with meekness . . . and all for His name's sake! This is our confidence!

*　　　　*　　　　*　　　　*　　　　*　　　　*

> *"For the Lord taketh pleasure in His people: He will beautify **the meek** with salvation."*
> (Psalm 149:4)

> *"When God arose to judgment, to save all **the meek of the earth.**"*　　　(Psalm 76:9)

•• One of the most *beautifying* things that heaven could ever bestow on any human being is *the gift of salvation.* This very term — *salvation* — means *deliverance from the penalty, power and presence of sin.* This is a continuing process. We *have been saved* from the penalty of sin; we *are being saved* from the power of sin; we will *yet be saved* from

157

the presence of sin. When Jesus came out of the grave, He *"arose to judgment"* — bringing judgment on sin, Satan, death, hell and the grave — that our *salvation* might be manifested in absolute perfection.

We, *the meek,* who surrender to His saving power, have the *beauty* of God's imparted righteousness, clothing us like a garment even now. We will yet be *beautified* as glorified saints forevermore!

This is all undoubtedly God's *pleasure* and can therefore be our continual source of rejoicing!!

*　　　　*　　　　*　　　　*　　　　*　　　　*

> *"**The meek** also shall increase their joy in the Lord."* (Isaiah 29:19)

•• Yes, meekly submitting to God's demands always brings the *joy* of the Lord, which is our strength. For by surrendering to His authority, we abide in the vine and the life-sap of His Spirit flows through us, welling up from within. This is termed *"joy unspeakable"* — for it is an intense, spiritual joy that cannot be described with mere words. It must be experienced to be understood. (I Peter 1:8)

Of course, the more that we surrender in *meekness* to the Lord, the more this supernatural joy will *increase.* This is definitely God's purpose and plan for His own. After presenting the demand of "abiding in Him", in the Vine-chapter of the gospel of John, Jesus affirmed — "These things have I spoken unto you that My *joy* might remain in you, and that your *joy* might be full." (John 15:11)

THE GRAND OPPORTUNITY

Most of the passages of Scripture we have quoted thus far were given under the Old Covenant to the people of the Old Will.

We are under the New Covenant now . . . spoken of as being "a better covenant . . . established upon better promises". (Hebrews 8:6)

But though God's covenants have changed, all of these promises are still very relevant . . . for the demand that *meekness* be resident in the heart of the covenant/recipient is still the same!

•• Isaiah even specified prophetically that when the Messiah would come to this world, He would be anointed to declare *"good tidings to the meek"* . . . for only *the meek* can receive and effectually claim what Jesus came to give. (Isaiah 61:1)

In an echo of the same prophecy, Luke depicted the Christ announcing that the Father had anointed Him to — *"preach the gospel to the poor"* . . . a reference not only to those who are *poor materially,* but those who are *poor in spirit,* meek before the Lord. (Luke 4:18)

•• It is significant to see that the word *gospel* means *glad tidings or good news.* Originally, it came from the Anglo-Saxon *god-spel* meaning *a good message* (so rendered from the Greek — *euaggelion).*

There are quite a few combinations of the word *gospel,* with other phrases or words, that together shed much light on what this *good news* really is. Some of these variations are: *the gospel of the kingdom* (Matt. 4:23) *the gospel of the grace of God* (Acts 20:24) *the gospel of God* (Rom. 1:1) *the gospel of His Son* (Rom. 1:9) *the gospel of Christ* (Rom. 1:16) *the gospel of peace* (Eph. 6:15) *the glorious gospel* (I Tim. 1:11) and *the everlasting gospel* (Rev. 14:6).

All of these are interrelated and basically somewhat synonymous, with only slight changes in meaning, according to the portion of *the good news* singled out for emphasis.

• The *gospel of the kingdom* is primarily the *good news* that God is going to set up His kingdom right here in this world. (This has been happening spiritually and subtly ever since God began dealing with fallen man. It happened powerfully and manifestly on the day of Pentecost and thereafter. It will happen gloriously and fully at the coming of the Lord). This *gospel of the kingdom* was the primary message of John the Baptist (Matt. 3:2) Jesus (Matt. 4:17) and the early disciples (Matt. 10:7). It is *the good news* that Satan's dominion will ultimately be totally broken and the celestial will once again blend with the terrestrial. This kingdom message, revealed in detail by the incarnate Son of God, was initially rejected and thereby delayed. It will finally be fulfilled and brought forth in exceeding beauty at the end of this age.

• The *gospel of the grace of God* involves the entirety of the grand work of salvation that grace performs in a believer's life. The emphasis is the unmerited favor of God.

• The *gospel of peace* rather focuses on the triune possession of peace that results from *the glad tidings* of the death, burial and resurrection of Jesus Christ (as already mentioned: peace *from* God, the peace *of* God, and peace *with* God).

• The *everlasting gospel* centers on the *everlasting* unchangeableness of the Word (in a changing and unpredictable world) and the *everlasting* inheritance that comes when the gospel is received (for Jesus brought "life and immortality to light through *the gospel").* (II Timothy 1:10)

The *gospel* was originally preached to Abraham, the Jews in the wilderness, and to one degree or another, all others chosen under the Old Will. (Galatians 3:8, Hebrews 4:2)
• God gave them *the glad tidings,* the dual-promise, that Abraham and his seed would eventually inherit the world and that in him (Abraham) and in his seed, all nations of the world would be blessed. (Galatians 3:8)
In so many cases, though, such a revelation proved to be tragically

ineffective . . . for it was not "mixed with faith in them that heard it" and it was not received with meekness (for the fallen Adam nature hindered men to such a great degree . . . constantly hardening their hearts against God).

●● But we have received the *gospel.*

●● We have received *the good news* in all its many facets.

And because we, the sons and daughters of God, have been given a new nature (a "new creation nature") meekness mingled with faith has become for us . . . *"an inwrought grace of the soul".*

By this inward transformation we have become, spiritually speaking, *the children of Abraham* — children of that great patriarch who, in great meekness, submitted to the great demands God placed on his life!

It is only logical to assume, therefore, that if we are considered and called *the children of Abraham* then we are also his heirs — *"heirs according to the promise".*

Therefore, the promise of *the gospel* is now ours.

●● **We can be bold in asserting that we will one day inherit the earth.** We will actually reign as kings and priests unto God.

In us, and through us, all nations will be blessed . . . for in us, and through us, the kingdom of God will be established in this world . . . at the second coming of Jesus Christ.

In the light of these wonderful truths, it is fully comprehensible why Jesus described *the meek* as being *blessed* . . . for the greatest *blessings* that could ever come from God, and the greatest *blessedness* that could ever be realized in God, hath both become a major part of **OUR GLORIOUS INHERITANCE.**

THE DEVELOPMENT OF MEEKNESS AND GENTLENESS A CHALLENGE TO EVERY BELIEVER

In conclusion, it must be said that the New Testament is filled with commands that sons of God develop the kindred character-qualities of *meekness* and *gentleness* (which incidentally are both listed among the nine fruits of the Spirit). (Galatians 5:22-23)

● Ephesians 4:1-3 presents the divinely authored mandate that we "walk worthy of the vocation wherewith [we] are called. With all lowliness and *meekness,* with longsuffering, forbearing one another in love; Endeavoring to keep the unity of the Spirit in the bond of peace."

● Galatians 6:1 also exhorts that if a man be overtaken in a fault, those who are spiritual should "restore such an one in the spirit of *meekness"* considering themselves.

● II Timothy 2:24 reminds us that — "the servant of the Lord must not strive; but be *gentle* unto all men, apt to teach, patient, in *meekness* instructing those that oppose themselves . . ."

• James 1:21 tells us to — "lay apart all filthiness and superfluity of naughtiness, and receive with *meekness* the engrafted word, which is able to save [our] souls."

• I Peter 3:4 even warns against becoming overly concerned with outward dress, exhorting that "the ornament of a *meek* and quiet spirit . . . is in the sight of God of great price."

Other passages are quite valuable as well such as: Colossians 3:12, I Timothy 6:11, and II Corinthians 10:1.

In all of these scriptures and more, God is clearly revealing that one of the most needful ways of emulating the firstborn Son, and one of the most effective ways of capturing the Father's heart, is to mature in these two beautiful outgrowths of the love of God.

No wonder Zephaniah encouraged the *meek* to ever strive toward even greater depths of *meekness,* saying:

> *"Seek ye the Lord, all ye **meek of the earth,** which have wrought His judgment: seek righteousness, **seek meekness:** it may be that ye shall be hid in the day of the Lord's anger."*
> (Zephaniah 2:3)

This prophecy is quite possibly more applicable than ever . . . for this generation is surely nearing the threshold of "the day of the Lord's anger."

Therefore, let us pray . . . let us pray without ceasing . . . that we may, be "accounted worthy to escape all these things that shall come to pass and to stand before the Son of Man." (Luke 21:36)

For if we please the Lord . . . by filling up this dual *title-position* of **THE MEEK** and **THE GENTLE** . . . then the gracious promise He gave will be our possession.

We will be "hid" — hid with Christ in God — hid in the Lord of love Himself — who pledged to give us "rest unto our souls."

This is far more than any *rest* an ordinary human being can experience.

This is an everlasting and divine *rest* that will know no bounds . . . the very rest of God . . . the ultimate reward of meekness met, acquired and manifested.

But more than anything else, this blessed and promised "rest" will be the becalming influence of finally gazing, with all love and devotion, into the gentle, loving eyes of the meek and lowly One who washed us in His own blood.

We will share eternity with Him.

We will finally blend together.
We will be "made perfect in one." (John 17:23)
We will fully inherit His likeness.
And it must be said . . . .

●● This is far more valuable, far more desirable, and a far greater privilege, than to one day inherit the earth.

We stand amazed that God would even enlighten our minds to the reality of such precious, eternal truth.

---

*¹W.E. Vine, *Vine's Expository Dictionary of Old and New Testament Words,* under *Meek, Meekness,* pp. 55-56. Definition in brackets placed by author.

*²This word — *blessed* — has multiple shades of meaning including: *fortunate, very happy, supremely blest, enriched with blessings, well spoken of, worthy of praise, and that which possesses the quality of what God considers to be the highest good.* Of course, all of these meanings are not always implied in every use of the word in Scripture. This term will be fully discussed in Volume Three of *Our Glorious Inheritance* in that chapter entitled *The Blessed.*

ORACLES OF GOD

*"If any man speak, let him speak as the **ORACLES OF GOD.**"*

(I Peter 4:11)

ORACLES OF GOD

"If any man speak, let him speak as the
ORACLES OF GOD."   (I Peter 4:11)

The Greek word *logion* means *utterance of God,* and it is translated four times in the New Testament as the word — *oracles.* (Acts 7:38, Romans 3:2, Hebrews 5:12, and I Peter 4:11)

• Any communication of God is considered to be an *oracle,* regardless of what method or means God may use.

It may come in a face to face encounter, as it did with Abraham in the plains of Mamre, or an audible voice, as it did with Moses, from the midst of a burning bush.

It may come in a dream, as it did with Jacob, who saw a ladder reaching from earth to heaven, or a vision, as it did with Ezekiel, who saw a wheel in the middle of a wheel.

It may come in a sign, as it did with Gideon, who felt of the fleece that was wet though the ground was dry, or in a token, as it did with Noah, who had the joy of beholding the first rainbow in the sky.

It may come in an angelic visitation, as it did with Mary, the mother of Jesus, or a word of prophecy, as it did through Elisha to Naaman, the leprous Syrian.

It came to the high priest at certain times in the Old Testament through those mysterious objects called the Urim and Thummim.

• But we are quick to say that we presently possess the greatest *oracles* ever given — the Old and New Testaments — for every word, every line and every verse in all sixty-six books is a *logion,* an *utterance of God.*

We might mention also that during the preaching of the Word under the true anointing, sometimes God will quicken our hearts in response to a certain statement and we know that it is coming directly from Him at that moment. In an instance such as this, the *oracle* is doubly manifest and doubly sure.

• Jesus is the eternal *logos (the Word)* but when He speaks, what He utters is a *logion (an utterance of God . . . an oracle).*

In our present-day terminology the word *oracle* can also mean the very channel through which the message or divine communication proceeds.

The inspired message is referred to as an *oracle of God,* but also, at the same time, the messenger can be referred to as an *oracle of God.*

The message and the messenger are one.

In fact, any person, place or thing, through which the voice of God manifests, can normally come under this categorical description, especially in our modern usage of the word.

Therefore, basically, when Peter exhorted Christians to speak *"as the oracles of God"* he was saying that we should always speak as if God is speaking out of us.

We know that in actuality this experience, in its greatest depth of manifestation, only takes place on rare occasions, though far more often possibly for those involved in ministry.

•   But on a lesser level of fulfillment, the potential of *inspiration,* and responsibility of being yielded, should be the constant awareness, the daily experience, and the deep, prayerful desire of every child of God.

This vitally important concept is something that must be explored now, from several different angles.

JESUS — THE EXEMPLARY ORACLE

We repeat again — an *oracle of God* is a channel of the expressed thoughts and feelings of the Most High God.

A true oracle will neither add nor take away anything from the inspired message.

He will not go beyond the word of the Lord to say less or more.

A true oracle is dead to his own will and his own way of reacting to circumstances; mere logic and reason do not control his actions, nor dictate his attitudes.

•   He is alive only to the expressed will of God — *(the rhema) the living Word* for that moment.

Jesus was the embodiment of the written Word, but He was filled with the fullness of the Holy Spirit, and thus, His words became Spirit and life: inspired Spirit-filled words.

Because of this, He is also called the living Word.

He is forevermore the sum total of all the words and ways in which God has or will express Himself, so He is the inspiration and the expression of the perfect will of God in every circumstance.

When Jesus walked the earth He never missed this perfect purpose of God. Jesus never erred in yielding to the *rhema* (the living Word) because He was the living Word.

Jesus never interjected His own thoughts.

Jesus said — "the words that I speak unto you I speak not of Myself: but the Father that dwelleth in Me . . ." (John 14:10)

Jesus did not do anything except He saw the Father do it first.

Because of this, Jesus was totally successful.

His words always brought results.

Jesus is our example. We as believers are called to walk in His footsteps, walking in sensitivity to the will of the Spirit, and thus, become His *oracles* — channels of the living Word.

If we have been begotten of the Word and born of the Spirit we definitely have this potential . . . but there is a great price to pay in order for it to be fulfilled in us.

THE HOLY OF HOLIES

•• **It is important to note that the holy of holies, the inner sanctuary in the tabernacle, was called the** *oracle of God.* (I Kings 6)

This was the location of the ark of God and the mercy seat, where God most often communed with man in the days of the Mosaic Covenant.

Therefore, when believers speak as *oracles* of God, they are, in a spiritual sense, standing in this holy place.

In the Old Covenant, the high priest alone could enter this blessed place only one time a year, with the sacrificial blood of a lamb.

In the New Covenant, this is radically changed.

We as believers, washed in the blood of the true Lamb of God, are now commanded to do our utmost to live constantly in this chamber, this sacred place of intimate communion with God.

•• In fact, as Christians we are called to actually become this holy of holies, this *oracle*, in which God abides, out of which God speaks, and through which God extends mercy, redemption, and the revelation of truth to the world.

To fulfill this should be one of the only reasons that we, as disciples of Jesus, exist in this world.

So we echo the question out of Psalm 24:

> *"Who shall ascend into the hill of the Lord?*
> *Or who shall stand in His holy place?*
> *He that hath clean hands, and a pure heart;*
> *who hath not lifted up his soul unto vanity, nor*
> *sworn deceitfully.*
> *He shall receive the blessing from the Lord."*

This *blessing,* in one sense of interpretation, is the privilege of being used as a channel of the voice of the Almighty, and it is given to those who sanctify their lives and dare to purge their conversation of frivolous attitudes and all superfluity of naughtiness.

This *oracleship* calling is one of the highest callings given to men, therefore it should become one of the greatest goals of our lives.

The words that *we* speak, decree, claim and confess will not always necessarily come to pass.

But when God gets in our words — God will watch over His Word, in us, to perform it.

The living Word in us will never fail to come to pass.

Therefore the more we yield to the living Word, and the more we manifestly become his holy of holies, the more of a success we will be in the things of the Spirit of God.

SPEAKING WITH AUTHORITY

Remember this next statement.

• The authority of God in us is limited by the amount of authority we dare to take in His name.

If we are timid in spirit and take only a small amount of authority, we will receive only small results.

But if we are bold under the anointing, God is more likely to get in our words, for we offer Him a suitable channel to work through.

The Spirit will not work through words that are infected with fear, doubt or timidity.

Jesus never spoke in an overly cautious or apprehensive way in dealing with Satan, sickness or sin.

He spoke with all authority.

He spoke with all boldness.

He commanded. He did not plead or beg.

He rebuked sickness. He rebuked the powers of hell. He rebuked sin.

He could act in this manner because He knew who He was.

He knew that He was the Son of God.

He knew that He was the original voice of God (the original *oracle of God).*

He cast out spirits with His word.

He commanded the leper — *"Be thou cleansed."*
He commanded the blind — *"Receive thy sight."*
He commanded the deaf ears — *"Be opened."*
He commanded the dead — *"Come forth."*

Even the winds and the sea obeyed His voice when He said *"Peace be still."*

Jesus always took charge of any situation.

He knew that He was qualified by the Father to do what He did . . . so when authority was necessary He always spoke in a commanding way.

He spoke forthrightly and forcefully as an *oracle of God.*

This was not arrogance.

This was confidence.

• Now He has commanded us to take charge and command in His stead.

He promised — "He that believeth on Me, the works that I do shall He do also." (John 14:12)

If we are commissioned to do the same works, then surely we should use the same methods.

To do this successfully, we must first recognize who we are in the plan of God.

We are the temples of God in this present world and in the world to come — ordained from the womb of the morning, to be His ambassadors — *His deputy administrators.*

When we preach or pray or testify, we must do so in a confident manner with all authority!

This is faith!

This is pleasing to God.

Life and death are in the power of the tongue, but this power can only be released in a confession that is packed with authority! (Proverbs 18:21)

No one has ever raised the dead or delivered a demon-possessed person by speaking timidly.

We must approach every situation with the knowledge that salvation, healing and deliverance have all been provided for in the atonement. So, potentially, any sinner can expect to be saved, any bound person can expect to be delivered, and any sick person can expect to be healed, if they fulfill God's requirements.

If we know this, we can boldly take authority in His name!

Jesus said that whatever we bind on earth is bound in heaven and whatever we loose on earth is loosed in heaven. (Matthew 18:18)

This action of binding on earth does not take place by just simply repeating a formula, using the words, "I bind you" — but by *praying through* until there is a release of faith, a release of power and the work is done. It is then established in heaven.

• Jesus said — "whosoever shall say unto this mountain, Be thou removed, and be thou cast into the sea; and shall not doubt in his heart, but shall believe that those things which He saith shall come to pass; he shall have *whatsoever he saith."* (Mark 11:23)

Of course, normally, we interpret this passage in a metaphorical sense, moving mountainous obstacles out of our lives by faith, but it is apparent that Jesus was also speaking quite literally.

This was His startling way of showing us the great power of faith and the great power of the spoken word, when activated unto perfection.

• Listen to the potential power of perfect faith in yet another scripture.

Jesus said — "If ye abide in Me, and My words abide in you, ye shall ask what ye will, and it shall be done unto you." (John 15:7)

• Now the key thought in this scripture is **abiding in Him** . . . and, without controversy, abiding in Him involves absolute submission to the living Word. Having His words abiding in us involves total surrender to the written Word, all His commands and promises.

When this spiritual merger fully takes place, then His will and our will become one and the same.

We know that this level of divine authority will never be completely realized or unveiled until the glorification of the saints takes place.

169

But, knowing this, we cannot just sit back and wait for the resurrection.

Our consuming passion in this life must be to come as close as we can now to a full manifestation of our inheritance-rights!

We must learn the power of confession, then activate and implement this spiritual concept daily, as we deal with the adversity that will surely come our way.

We refuse to speak words poisoned with unbelief.

We refuse to speak words contaminated with a spirit of defeat.

We speak victory! We speak success!

We can do this boldly, for we are only acting as echoes of the voice of God — dauntlessly declaring the truth that He has already spoken, truth that has already been laid down as a solid and unshakeable foundation.

•• Hebrews 13:5-6 proclaims that — *"**He hath said**, I will never leave thee, nor forsake thee. **So that we may boldly say**, the Lord is my helper, and I will not fear what man shall do unto me."*

This passage communicates a simple, yet valuable and beautiful revelation.

If we know that God has settled an issue by giving us an immutable promise in His unchangeable Word, then we can boldly repeat that promise as oracles of God ("He hath said . . . that we may boldly say").

We can be daring in our attempt to quote the Word just as authoritatively as the Lord would Himself.

We know that — "God is not a man, that He should lie; neither the son of man, that He should repent: hath He said, and shall He not do it? or hath He spoken, and shall He not make it good?" (Numbers 23:19)

We know that God will stand behind His Word.

We know that He will "make it good". He will keep His promises.

We also know that knowing this makes us quite powerful in confessing the Word.

All existing things were brought into being by the power of the spoken word, therefore it is reasonable to assume that all existing things are still in subjection to the Word of God now, regardless of what channel it flows through.

• According to Hebrews 1:3, Jesus is presently — *"upholding all things by the word of His power."*

• Another translation of this same passage says that He is — *"upholding, and maintaining, and guiding and propelling the universe by His mighty word of power."* (AMP)

We conclude therefore, that there is something much stronger than just natural laws, such as gravity and inertia, holding the universe intact.

Apparently there is a continual stream of words, living words, flowing from the very throne of the Almighty God into all of creation, fulfilling and maintaining His dictates.

Now this brings us to a strong conclusion.

• If Jesus can actually uphold the entire world by the spoken word, though this world is temporarily locked inside of death and besieged by an onslaught of satanic forces out of hell, then surely we will be upheld and preserved spiritually, if we dare to imitate him and speak the Word over the circumstances of our lives.

And if Jesus, by *the word of faith,* can actually propel the entire universe to its ultimate goal (the resurrected perfection of the New Creation) then certainly *the word of faith in us* will also propel us to ultimate victory . . . in this present world and in the world that is yet to come!

Romans 10:8-10 challenges us to believe that this word of faith is nigh unto us — even in our hearts, and in our mouths.

The words are there, resting in the womb of the heart, waiting to be born in the speech.

The mountains of opposition are before us, waiting to be moved.

The power of the Holy Spirit is there, ready to manifest in our behalf.

We know that God is able to do exceedingly, abundantly above all that we could ask or think, but it is — *"according to the power that worketh in us."*

Much of the responsibility for walking in spiritual prosperity and success rests on us. We must dare to speak as oracles of God, uttering faith-filled, God-filled words under the anointing of the Spirit.

• The darkness must flee when we truly speak words impregnated with devotion to God and **faith in Him** (and not just faith in the words that are spoken).

Jesus told us — "It is not ye that speak, but the spirit of your Father which speaketh in you." (Matthew 10:20)

Of course, this does not mean that God will always be evidently and manifestly in our words, but it does mean that we should strive to always speak as if God would choose to do this very thing!

By doing so, we provide Him with the proper vehicle of expression and consequently there will be definite times in which His voice is married to ours . . . producing phenomenal results!

This certainly does not mean that we will have one hundred percent success in the practice of the spoken word, neither does this mean that we can indiscriminately confess anything we want to confess and then expect it to happen.

But this does mean that if we dare to speak and confess the word with all confidence (as *oracles of God*) our rate of success will surely soar upward.

We are not God; we cannot usurp His authority, nor even attempt to control Him (for "who is he that saith, and it cometh to pass, when the Lord commandeth it not"). (Lamentations 3:37).

But we have been commanded by God to take authority over sin, sickness and Satan in His Name!

We accept this holy charge, as the representatives of the Son of God. He is with us.

He honors our words.

•   The Lord was with Samuel and, because of this, the Bible declared that God — *"did let none of His words fall to the ground."* (I Samuel 3:19)

So it should be with us, for the same Lord of glory abides with us as well.

Our faith-confessions are not futile.

They are not spoken in vain.

They will not fall to the ground.

They will rise like incense before the throne of God.

They can surely produce the miraculous, according to the measure of our faith, and according to our consecration.

Therefore we must — "hold fast the profession of our faith without wavering; (for He is faithful that promised)." (Hebrews 10:23)

•   O, how powerful and forcible these invisible objects called *words* really are!

David's slung-out words struck Goliath and sealed his defeat, long before the shepherd boy's slung-out stone ever penetrated the giant's skull.

David was daring enough to rush toward his enemy shouting — *"This day will the Lord deliver thee into mine hand and I will smite thee."* (I Samuel 17:46)

His words were more powerful than his rocks.*[1]

He spoke as an *oracle* of God . . . prophetically!

Can we not dare to do the same?

Can we not "sling out" the spoken word at our enemy, Satan, and fully expect to bring him down?

If God did it once, can He not do it again?

•   With one united shout the children of Israel brought the walls of Jericho crashing to the ground. (Joshua 6)

God got in their shout, and invisible sound waves, packed with the presence of God, became more powerful than battering rams ever could have been against the huge, brick, mortar and stone barrier that was twelve feet wide and thirty feet high. (UBD)

Again we dare to ask — can Jehovah-God not work in a similar fashion for us?

Can we not joyously speak the Word and shout the Word under the anointing and see spiritual walls of opposition fall before us?

If God did it once, can He not do it again?

• In battling the Canaanites, Joshua took a bold step of faith, in the sight of all of Israel, and actually commanded the sun to stand still.

It miraculously happened!

The Bible said that — *"there was no day like that before it or after it, that the Lord hearkened unto the voice of a man."* (Joshua 10:12-14)

Joshua spoke as an oracle of God and even the natural laws of the universe were held in check and brought under subjection to His voice.

How utterly amazing!

Of course, we know there were contributing factors involved that made such an awesome feat possible that day, but still — we wonder what evil principalities and powers will finally be brought under subjection and what negative circumstances will finally be held in check when we, in like manner, dare to lift our voices and **command through the Spirit.**

O, how the world will surely be shaken when the Lord raises up an army of believers who have total confidence in this area of our inheritance and calling!

O, how the nations will be stirred when the sons and daughters of God rise up *en masse* as soul-impassioned, faith-filled oracles whose lips have been sanctified with a fiery, living coal from off the altar in heaven!

How glorious it will be when we die such a death to self that God can effectively move through us this way!

• AND HOW MUCH MORE GLORIOUS IT WILL BE WHEN THIS CALLING IS PERFECTED IN US AT THE RESURRECTION . . . WHEN WE BECOME THE VOICES OF GOD IN THE UNIVERSE FOREVER — ETERNAL ORACLES!

Surely everything we speak will then be oracular in nature.

In fact, this is, to a certain degree, the authority and power of the *original Oracle* being passed on to us.

This is a breathtaking thought!

This is an unspeakable infinite gift!

This is more than mere human speculation.

• This is divinely inspired revelation, the final product of New Testament salvation, the infinite beauty of the New Creation, and the exceeding joy and glory of the restoration!!

THE CONVICTING EXAMPLE

Although the preceding section carried us into the joyous heights of the heavenly state and the utter bliss of our paradise inheritance, it is needful that we "come back down to earth" and search out a somewhat different brand of *oracle* that the world and the church are both desperately in need of now.

- In Numbers 25 we find the perfect scriptural example.

The men of Israel, dwelling in Shittim, began committing whoredom with the daughters of Moab and sacrificing unto their gods.

They became so steeped in rebellion that they joined themselves unto Baalpeor — *"and the anger of the Lord was kindled against Israel"*.

Judgment fell and a great plague was sent forth, ultimately bringing twenty-four thousand down to the grave.

Moses and the congregation were weeping before the door of the tabernacle, rending their hearts in repentance before the Lord, when arrogantly and brazenly Zimri (the son of a Simeonite prince) walked through their midst with Cozbi (a princess of Midian).

They were both so intent on sin that they were untouched by the cries and the tears of the righteous.

They were so possessed with lust, so callous and unfeeling, that they were quite blind to the seriousness of their transgression.

While others, paralyzed with grief, just kept weeping, Phinehas, the grandson of Aaron, angrily grabbed a javelin. He rushed into Zimri's tent, thrusting both he and Cozbi through the belly, executing them in the name of the Lord.

The awful plague was stayed, and Israel was restored to fellowship with God . . . yet it all hinged on one man's fervency of spirit and intense devotion to the laws of God.

•• Now, it is important that we take notice of the following fact; the name **Phinehas** means *oracle (of God)*.

Also, the name **Zimri** means *celebrated,* and the name **Cozbi** means *deceitful.* (YC)

• These three name-definitions contain a significant hidden message from God, for how often *celebrated* sons of God have been almost or altogether destroyed by foolishly locking arms with the *deceitfulness* of sin.

There have already been far too many instances in which certain advanced believers were suddenly overwhelmed by the seduction of Satan.

Though they were walking deep in the Spirit, and though they were celebrated *(highly favored of God and respectfully recognized by man)* still — tragically — the lust of this world took from them its terrible toll of devastation and destruction.

O, how we need men of Phinehas-caliber now, prophetic voices who will dare to take the javelin of the Word and cut to the core of men's hearts until sinners truly repent, and until sin is lanced from the soul of the body of Christ . . . lest the tragedy be repeated again and again.

We do not need men of hate, condemnation or vindictiveness, but rather men who are burning with zeal for the truth and jealousy for the holiness of God . . . men whose hearts are aflame with consecration, utterly consumed with love for purity and righteousness.

• God commended Phinehas and gave him a *covenant of peace* and the *covenant of an everlasting priesthood,* because he turned away the wrath of God from Israel by making atonement with the blood of Zimri and Cozbi.

O, how we need vessels of such ardent fervor that wrath can be diverted, in this hour, from a nation that has become quite perverted and a church that has become quite worldly.

God praised Phinehas because he was zealous for his God!
• It is significant to note that the word translated *zealous* in this passage is also translated *jealous,* elsewhere in the Bible.

These two words are somewhat synonymous and often interchangeable throughout the Scripture, yet they have different shades of meaning.

To be jealous is to be intolerant of rivalry or unfaithfulness; to be zealous is to be enthusiastic, impassioned and intense.

Without a doubt — we must have both!
God give us a generation of Phinehas-men and Phinehas-women who fill this double description.

O, we must be loving and forgiving, yes, that is true, but we must no longer tolerate blatant rebellion and unfaithfulness to the purpose of God, in our own lives or in the lives of others.

We must passionately present a standard of righteousness for all to see and for all to hear.
For it is time that men hold to both — "faith and a good conscience, which some having put away concerning faith have made shipwreck." (I Timothy 1:19)

This is the message of the hour!
This is the spiritual vacuum that must be filled!
We cannot hold our peace any longer!
We must cry aloud and spare not!

• We must blow the trumpet in Zion and proclaim the unadulterated Word of God . . . for only in sanctity will oracular faith mature unto perfection, and only then can we truly receive God's **covenant of peace** (His commitment and promise of peace when everyone else around us is sinking in despair) and His **covenant of an everlasting priesthood** (His promise to us of being always accepted in His throne room).

This is what you might call privilege in prayer, or having the ear of God, for "the eyes of the Lord are over the righteous and His ears are open to their prayers."
These are only two of the great benefits that come to those who search for this portion of the **GLORIOUS INHERITANCE** available to us.
The full list of the resulting benefits is endless, therefore we must determine to reach for, and pay the price to obtain, this elusive yet highly valued prize.

We know that only by being impassioned for holiness can we ever truly prove ourselves before heaven and thus succeed in possessing and manifesting this oracular gift.

The attainment of this oracleship status is recognizably of exceeding importance right here in this present world, but it is imperative that we realize the superlative greatness of the completely perfected, eternal gift as well.

What a destiny awaits the faithful and consecrated saints of God . . . the destiny of being His eternal mouth-pieces throughout the universe, vessels of the living Word, channels of inspired utterance, and voices of divine authority!

We will rule over all God's vast and infinite domain . . . by the perfected power of the spoken word!

•• WE WILL FOREVER BE HIS MESSENGERS, GLORIFIED, AND HIS REPRESENTATIVES, FULLY EMPOWERED . . . **ORACLES OF GOD FOREVER,** IN THE HIGHEST SENSE OF THE WORD!!

---

*¹It should be mentioned that Goliath also uttered a "positive confession" against David, but it did not aid him the least bit in winning. So we see, through this example especially, that words of themselves do not possess some mystical power, but David's consecrated life, and the anointing upon him, caused his words to carry far more authority. Neither rocks nor words could have been effective against the giant if David had attempted such a confrontation presumptuously within himself. And so it is with us. Jesus did say — "without Me ye can do nothing" (John 15:5). God is not some great computer into which just anyone can insert the right Word-formulas and always, automatically, come out with the desired answer. We degrade Him greatly if we believe such a thing! But if we truly represent Him in this world and if our hearts are truly right, then we must dare to speak with authority under His direction and for His glory. We have been commissioned to take authority over sin, sickness, and satanic powers in His name!

Peter did this at the gate Beautiful when he decreed to the crippled man — "Silver and gold have I none; but such as I have give I thee: In the name of Jesus Christ of Nazareth rise up and walk." It is a disturbing thing to imagine what would have happened that day if Peter had been warned by some overly cautious and well-meaning Christians never to use such a "self-exalting" method of confession in prayer. Would not the crippled man most likely ways so remained in a crippled condition the rest of his life? Again, in this area of our inheritance there is a great need for balance and discretion, but we dare not enter into unbelief in the process. We could well end up denying ourselves certain rights and privileges God intends us to have.

THE PEARL OF GREAT PRICE

"Again, the kingdom of heaven is like unto a merchant man, seeking goodly pearls:

*Who, when he had found one **PEARL OF GREAT PRICE:** went and sold all that he had, and bought it."*

(Matthew 13:45-46)

THE PEARL OF GREAT PRICE

*"Again, the kingdom of heaven is like unto
a merchant man, seeking goodly pearls:
Who, when he had found one PEARL OF
GREAT PRICE, went and sold all that he had,
and bought it."*   (Matthew 13:45-46)

• The bride of Christ is spoken of in this passage as *a pearl of great price* . . . a pearl so precious, so comely, that the Merchantman seeking goodly pearls was willing to sell all that he had to buy that one pearl.

Jesus is the Merchantman, and He did just that . . . He gave all He could possibly give, on Calvary, to purchase His bride . . . *His precious pearl.*

This eternal bride, this choice jewel of the ocean, is destined to be the stunningly elegant and lovely, infinite companion of the gentle yet glorious Shepherd-King of all creation!

But it is a fact equally stunning that this beautiful wife of the Lamb is metamorphically evolving from a beginning that could well be described as being far from beautiful.

• In fact — as it is with the pearl, so it is with the bride of Christ, and as it is with the bride of Christ, so it is with the pearl.

It all begins this way:
A grain of sand, a piece of foreign matter, or at times even an intruding parasite, somehow gets inside of an oyster and lodges in the folds of its flesh.

In a certain sense, the disturbed oyster will do all that it can do to rid itself of this uninvited and unwelcome guest . . . but almost always to no avail.

Exasperated and annoyed by constant failure, the frustrated ocean mollusk will abort its first "plan of attack" and strike out in another direction.

• You could well entitle this alternate route — *the next best thing!*

The oyster will then secrete, literally hundreds of times, a calcium-like, milky substance called *nacre,* that thoroughly coats the irritating intruder, smoothing over the rough edges of the sand-grain, or killing the leech-like organism.

As far as the oyster is concerned this inborn survival technique is only utilized to take care of the present need and make life more bearable and comfortable.

Yet, all the while, unknown of course to the oyster, something quite rare, precious and beautiful is being formed . . . one tedious step at a time.

Glory is gradually being born out of adversity.

Something of excellent value is slowly yet steadily being created out of that which appears initially to have no value whatsoever.

How well Romans 8:20 describes the nature of this difficult yet miraculous process, and even more so its spiritual antitype — *"For the creature was made subject to vanity [the victim of frustration] not willingly, but by reason of Him who hath subjected the same in hope."* (AV, NEB)

This blessed hope is the firm truth (the rigid and unyielding fact) that — "our light affliction, which is but for a moment, worketh for us a far more exceeding and eternal weight of glory." (II Corinthians 4:17)

• In other words (speaking on both levels now) the glory of the oyster's future inheritance far outweighs the temporary and comparatively minor hardship that it may have to endure along the way . . . and so it is with us!

If we are truly submitted to God, and if we are wise, we will recognize that in accordance with the Scripture, our light affliction is actually working *for us,* not against us.

All the details of our lives, both negative and positive, are being expertly woven together in conformity to a certain image and pattern predetermined from the very beginning, by the Master Weaver of the universe Himself.

Our faith compels us to declare unequivocally that we know, yes we really know . . . our Father has something exceedingly beautiful in store for us . . . so utterly beautiful that the end result will more than sufficiently justify, and support the necessity of, the means.

We have been fully persuaded that something quite valuable will ultimately be created out of that which at times appears to have no value at all.

Having traced the developmental path of the pearl, we now clearly see the parallel, parabolic truth, and the developmental path that we must also take.

We have all been conceived in iniquity, and born in sin.

Like an intruding grain of sand or a persistently tormenting parasite, the vile nature of the flesh latched hold of us with a seemingly unyielding and iron-handed tenacity, from the very moment that our conception took place in the womb.

How we tried . . . even desperately at times (by the power of our own will) to rid ourselves of this base carnal nature . . . but it was simply to no avail.

Paul said it so aptly:

> ". . . *for to will is present with me; but how*
> *to perform that which is good I find not.*
> *For the good that I would I do not: but the*
> *evil which I would not, that I do . . .*
> *I find then a law, that, when I would do good,*
> *evil is present with me."*
>
> (Romans 7:18-21)

This is the irksome, and sometimes even torturous, emotional, mental and spiritual turmoil that results from being "dead in trespasses and sins."

Of course, the experience of salvation brings about a drastic positive change, arousing a much stronger character, conscience and will within our inner being.

But we must admit that even after being born again this constant struggle stubbornly persists.

For the flesh still — "lusteth against the Spirit and the Spirit against the flesh: and these are contrary the one to the other: so that ye cannot do the things that ye would." (Galatians 5:17)

This does not mean that a Christian must resign himself over to living in sin, for that is heretical error; it rather means that, although God has given us the power to live above sin, we still can expect to be buffeted often by the cravings of the Adam-man and tempted with a variety of negative attitudes . . . at times even failing to one degree or another.

This is so much a part of living in this flesh, that no person will ever fully rise above it, regardless of the great depth of their faith or the high degree of their consecration.

Acknowledging this as a fact of life compels us to choose one of two possible courses of action.

We react either by receding and withdrawing into a self-imposed prison of defeat and discouragement . . . or by searching out God's eternal purpose, thereby learning how to turn what appears to be only a disappointing stumbling block into a grand and glorious steppingstone.

We have made our decision.

Since it has proved to be impossible for us to fully rid ourselves of this "irritating grain of sand" . . . this "vicious intruding parasite" . . . we have purposed in our hearts instead to fulfill God's plan by taking the "alternate route" that He has so graciously and purposefully provided.

• This "alternate route" could easily, and again quite appropriately, be called . . . *the next best thing.*

Having received the revelation of the creation of a pearl, we have determined, in like manner, to daily cover our parasitical fears and frustrations with the heart-secretion of utter faith in the Spirit and the power of this indwelling God, who floods our lives with His love.

We have determined to constantly coat our rough-edged irritations and disappointments with the unending hope that we have "in Christ."

We have purposed to wrap our battles with a thick nacre-like covering of the trust we have in God's Word.

We have made the decision to overspread our weaknesses and failures with total reliance on the precious blood of Jesus, and the wealth of grace made available to us through that blood.

• Over and over again, multiplied thousands of times, we have already covered this aggravating and troublesome enemy, this leech-like sin-nature, with the calcium-like, milky-like secretion of the exceeding great and precious promises of God.

Over and over again, multiplied thousands of times, we will surely repeat the process in the future as we journey toward perfection.

These life-giving promises flow constantly, like a regenerative river, out of the inner man, for they are very much an integral part of our spiritual makeup now.

This is God's gift to us — an inborn, survival technique that is definitely not deficient nor weak in meeting the present need.

We that have been enlightened have learned to utilize, and successfully apply, the subduing power of this inward river of life *(this spiritual nacre)* against sin, Satan and self, whenever these serpentine parasites try to penetrate our hearts.

But as we cope with the irritating, difficult and intrusive pressures of life this way, we may or may not be aware of the fact that something extremely beautiful is being born out of all this adversity.

• A lustrous and beautiful *pearlescent inheritance* is gradually being created in the heart of every son or daughter of God (lodged and hidden, as it were, in the very folds of our flesh, developing and manifesting, *one layer at a time).*

We are progressively learning certain facets of the character of God that we never could have experienced in a perfected heavenly state.

Ecclesiastes 1:13 declared that God has given "this sore travail . . . to the sons of man to be exercised therewith."

As we undergo this spiritual exercise (this intense revelation-training session) we are being made to clearly behold the wrath of God poured out on the rebellious and the great grace, mercy and redemptive power that is freely poured out upon them that believe.

This heaven-sent power easily subdues the most invincible and antagonistic foes that we could possibly face in this valley of the shadow of death.

Thus in all these things, we recognize the greatness of our God all the more . . . and the depth of what He can do and what He can be!

- **This discovery by itself is a gem of great value and extreme beauty.**

But not only are we learning the divine temperament here, we are also being *"changed into the same image."*

The great depth of the personality of deity is gradually taking us over, introducing certain precious qualities of character into our spirits that evidently could have never been advanced as perfectly within us, had we not first been plunged into this awful state of degradation and separation from God.

But by this portion of the earthly experience, and the introduction of grace into our lives, we recognize all the more our greatness and importance in the sight of God, and what He has chosen us to have and to be.

- **This revelation is also very much a part of our pearlescent, eternal inheritance . . . a gem of exceeding value and exceeding beauty.**

So we see, through these two valuable and beautiful end results, that God is not only interested in meeting the present need; He is constantly building toward a magnificent future.

THE GATES OF NEW JERUSALEM

•• In following this vein of thought, it is quite enlightening to read the Bible description of the supernatural splendor of the heavenly city to come . . . the infinite New Jerusalem.

John said — *"The twelve gates were twelve pearls; every several gate was of one pearl."* (Revelation 21:21)

How appropriate it is that the Master Architect of the entire cosmos chose a pearl-like celestial substance to form the very archway entrances into the splendid, ethereal dwelling place of His everlasting heirs!

For the very suffering that the pearl exemplifies is in reality the singular door through which we all must pass in order to successfully enter into, and possess, the fullness of our eternal God-given heritage.

All these twelve gates of pearl *(these doors of suffering)* are necessarily two-fold in nature, for they represent both the intense agony that Jesus endured in His passion on Calvary and also the great distress and suffering experienced at certain times by all those who are truly crucified with Christ.

This shared agony that we go through, in struggling to subdue the sin-nature, is definitely . . . all the while . . . carving out a pleasant portal in glory for each one of us.

BEING "BORN OF WATER"

• This divinely ordered training process is not an option; it is an absolutely necessary step.

•• Jesus Himself declared that — *"Except a man be born of water and of the Spirit, he cannot enter into the kingdom of God."* (John 3:5)

It is evident that the great Teacher and Revealer of the mysteries of God was not alluding to mere water baptism when He used the phrase — *"born of water"*.

He was rather referring to the natural birth process, in which the amniotic sac breaks, and the amniotic fluid pours out, right before a newborn child comes forth from its mother's womb.

The common present-day term for this is the "breaking of the water" or, as Jesus put it — being *"born of water!"*

He further embellished this statement, and proved its true meaning, by adding — "That which is born of the flesh is flesh; and that which is born of the Spirit is spirit."

In this passage Jesus was quite firm in making the assertation that we can only see (comprehend, understand and perceive) the kingdom of God by being born again (born of the Spirit).

But in order to be suitable candidates for this experience and its accompanying inheritance, and in order to enter into the kingdom of God now and eternally, we must first be *born of water* (born of the flesh).

• It is absolutely essential that we, as joint-heirs with Christ, learn certain preparatory lessons that can only be learned by passing through this realm.

SHARING HIS SUFFERING

•• No wonder Peter gave us the stern warning — "Forasmuch then as Christ hath suffered for us in the flesh, arm yourselves likewise with the same mind." (I Peter 4:1)

We must not be ignorant concerning God's purpose.

We must realize that it has been given to us "in the behalf of Christ, not only to believe on Him, but also to suffer for His sake." (Philippians 1:29)

Therefore, the recognition of reality demands that we gird our minds and brace our spirits for the battle, knowing that this world will never be a place of ease.

But we know that — "if we be dead with Him, we shall also live

with Him; if we suffer [with Him] we shall also reign with Him."
(II Timothy 2:11-12)

Suffering with Him is not necessarily partaking of like physical pain, but rather it involves sharing in the same kind of spiritual pain that He had to undergo.

For example . . . Jesus Himself suffered being tempted, so we His followers certainly cannot expect to be exempt from the same mode of testing.

Jesus suffered the throbbing, aching hurt of love unrequited and truth unreceived. So will we, if we truly love as He loved and stand uncompromisingly for the truth of His Word.

Jesus suffered, unto the sweating of blood, in yielding to the perfect will of the Father; so we are called as His offspring to pass through the oil-press of Gethsemane also, abandoning ourselves fully to His control, dying to the will of the flesh.

Jesus suffered the pain of presenting Himself a living sacrifice for the sake of others, for compassion gripped Him; so also we are compelled to pour out our lives for others for *"the love of Christ constraineth us."* (II Corinthians 5:14)

Jesus suffered constant inner grief for lost humanity, simply because He understood the mysteries of God and the awful destiny awaiting those who rebel. His own enlightenment made Him feel all the more distressed for those bound in the ignorance of flesh-consciousness.

At one point this *Man of sorrows* wept over Jerusalem saying — "If thou hadst known, even thou, at least in this thy day, the things which belong unto thy peace! But now they are hid from thine eyes. For the days shall come upon thee, that thine enemies . . . shall lay thee even with the ground . . . and they shall not leave in thee one stone upon another; because thou knewest not the time of thy visitation." (Luke 19:42-44)

In like manner, the more sensitive we become to eternal realities the more we will weep . . . the more we understand, the more our hearts become a fountain of tears, ceasing not day nor night — "for in much wisdom is much grief: and he that increaseth knowledge increaseth sorrow." (Ecclesiastes 1:18)

If we are bonafide members of the bride of Christ, **the Pearl of Great Price,** then we will automatically become men and women of sorrow, acquainted with grief.

We will feel the burden of the Lord overflowing into our spirits, at times overwhelming us, and always challenging us, to similarly pay that great price necessary to become a channel of the attributes and abilities of the Merchantman Himself.

• We cannot escape these spiritual responsibilities if we are true disciples of the Lamb, nor some of the other sorrows that usually accompany being a part of the human race, but we can react with faith, hope and charity, and thereby experience the miracle-working, circumstance-changing power of the Almighty God.

We can maintain the certitude that God is truly sovereign and thus experience the deep comfort of His presence even in troublous times.

Above all, we can drink in the joy of the Lord, the sweet elixir of heaven, by worshipfully lifting faith-filled eyes toward the future, as Jesus did before us.

•• If we dare to gaze beyond the veil we will assuredly behold an iridescent and infinite *mother-of-pearl* plan that has always acted, and will continue to act, as a hard shell of protection around us until that resurrection moment when in us, and through us, the welcome and blissful *pearl-product* is finally fully formed.

We will then surely understand all the more why the word *pearl* evolved originally from a Sanscrit word meaning *pure*. For it is through this *pearl-like* process of battling against impurity that something utterly pure is being produced in us . . . pleasantly pure (bringing restoration of innocence) and perpetually pure (imparting an inheritance unchanging).

This is our confidence and our expectation.

This is what turns our sorrow into joy, and our mourning into dancing!

• In that day, surely all of heaven will sense the extreme pleasure of the Master-Merchantman, who will have finally procured unto Himself His heart's desire . . . *His goodly pearl.*

That precious and lustrous jewel from out of the ocean of humanity will be forever enclosed in His hand and held to His bosom.

In that day, the wisdom of God will be justified and all of our questions will be finally, conclusively answered.

We will then quickly ascertain that the alternate route we once termed *"the next best thing"* in the end turned out to be *"the very best thing."*

This is the hope of our calling and the blessedness of being His preferred choice, **HIS PEARL OF GREAT PRICE.**

- A PECULIAR PEOPLE -

GOD'S OWN PEOPLE

A PEOPLE
BELONGING TO GOD

A SPECIAL PEOPLE

• A PECULIAR TREASURE •

HIS TREASURED POSSESSION

TREASURE HID IN A FIELD

"But ye are a chosen generation, a royal priesthood, an holy nation, A PECULIAR PEOPLE; that ye should shew forth the praises of Him who hath called you out of darkness into His marvellous light." (I Peter 2:9)

"For thou art an holy people unto the Lord, thy God: the Lord thy God hath chosen thee to be A SPECIAL PEOPLE unto Himself, above all people that are upon the face of the earth." (Deuteronomy 7:6)

"Now therefore, if ye will obey My voice indeed, and keep My covenant, then ye shall be A PECULIAR TREASURE unto Me above all people: for all the earth is Mine:" (Exodus 19:5)

"Again, the kingdom of heaven is like unto a TREASURE HID IN A FIELD. . . . " Matthew 13:44

A PECULIAR PEOPLE
A PECULIAR TREASURE
TREASURE HID IN A FIELD

"But ye are a chosen generation, a royal priesthood, an holy nation, A PECULIAR PEOPLE; that ye should shew forth the praises of Him who hath called you out of darkness into His marvellous light." (I Peter 2:9)

"Now therefore, if ye will obey My voice indeed, and keep My covenant, then ye shall be A PECULIAR TREASURE unto Me above all people: for all the earth is Mine:" (Exodus 19:5)

In our present day language, it is accepted that the word **peculiar** means . . . *something strange, odd, unusual, or something not necessarily odd, but distinguished in nature or character from others.*

This is certainly a correct description of God's people, because by the world's standards we are strange . . . for "the preaching of the cross is to them that perish foolishness" . . . therefore we who believe in the power of the cross are sometimes even considered fools.

We go by a different set of standards.

As far as the world is concerned, we just do not fit. We are classified among those who have deviated greatly from the established pattern and the accepted mode of conduct. We believe in a philosophy of life that was first birthed in heaven before it was ever birthed in our hearts, therefore we are not "of the world"!

Humanism, the world's philosophy of self, promotes and exalts the ego, and teaches us to satisfy its cravings, setting it on a pedestal.

But to be one of Jesus' *peculiar people* is to take the totally opposite point of view.

We choose rather to deny self.

We gain our lives by losing our lives.

We are exalted by humbling ourselves.

We are rapturously lifted into heavenly things by purposefully dying to earthly things.

In fact, we are bold in declaring that — *"to live is Christ and to die is gain."* (Philippians 1:21)

This concept of self-denial is an enigma to most carnal men and women who have not been regenerated — an unusual, mysterious and even ridiculous way of thinking.

189

Sincere Christians though, will make mortification of the flesh their daily goal, and thus they become easily distinguished in character and nature from the majority of others in this world . . . distinctly different . . . *His peculiar people!*

A PEOPLE BELONGING TO GOD

Now all of the foundational statements given so far are faithful and true, but it is clear that still we have not fully uncovered the correct definition of the word *peculiar,* as it is used in the Scripture.

• The Greek word that is translated **peculiar** in I Peter 2:9 is *peripoiesis* and it means . . . *an acquisition.* It is also translated in Ephesians 1:14 as *a [purchased] possession.*

Parallel to these definitions, the word *peculiar* can also mean — *that which belongs exclusively to a person or thing.*

In fact, two other translations of I Peter 2:9 render this particular *title* — **GOD'S OWN PEOPLE** — and also — **A PEOPLE BELONGING TO GOD.** (RSV, NIV)

Therefore, to be God's *peculiar people* automatically involves being His purchased possession, and because we are *a people belonging to Him,* we are also deeply cherished and exceedingly dear . . . uniquely special.

We are *His acquisition* . . . for He has acquired and obtained our eternal fellowship through much agony, much suffering.

Occupying this *title-position* also carries with it the idea of belonging exclusively to Him, bought by His blood and set apart for holy use . . . a people considered His very own, with no ensnaring worldly attachments.

Therefore if we, as believers, are truly reserved unto God and if we live only to fulfill His will, we can rightfully lay claim to this portion of **OUR GLORIOUS INHERITANCE.**

Without a doubt, the requirements are very great if we are to be included in this elite, blessed and privileged group.

After God delivered Israel from Egypt's bondage, Jehovah spoke to the Jews saying:

> *"Ye have seen what I did unto the Egyptians, and how I bare you on eagles' wings, and brought you unto Myself.*
> *Now therefore, if ye will obey My voice indeed, and keep My covenant, then ye shall be A PECULIAR TREASURE unto Me above all people: for all the earth is Mine."* (Exodus 19:4-5)

The New International Version of this same passage calls us — "**HIS TREASURED POSSESSION.**"

What an honor! What a sacred privilege . . . to be called God's *peculiar treasure!* What a blessing to be considered God's most valuable possession, highly prized and deeply cherished . . . exclusively His . . . precious and uniquely special in His sight!!

And how awe-inspiring it is to realize that it was not so much our choice to accept Him, but rather it was clearly His choice to include us!!
* Deuteronomy 7:6-7 and 14:2 both prove this to be a forever settled fact, for in these passages the Scripture declares, to both natural and spiritual Israel, that — "the Lord thy God hath *chosen* thee to be **A PECULIAR PEOPLE** unto Himself" and also "**A SPECIAL PEOPLE** above all people that are upon the face of the earth."

Moreover — "the Lord did not set His love upon you, nor choose you, because ye were more in number than any people; for ye were the fewest of all people: but because the Lord loved you."

This is eternal truth filtered down to its purest and most simple state.

God's motivation and reasoning, behind choosing us to be exclusively His own, is simply everlasting love toward us, a love that has no beginning and no ending . . . a love that is said to be *"strong as death."* (Song of Solomon 8:6)

In other words, this love of God that ordains, elects and chooses those who belong exclusively to Him, is just as inescapable as death . . . which always arrives at a predetermined, appointed and unavoidable moment in time.

Ezekiel 16:6-8 reveals how that our lives were at one time hopelessly contaminated by sin. We were nothing but castaways and rejects but God said — "when I passed by thee: and saw thee polluted in thine own blood, I said unto thee . . . live" — "now when I passed by thee, and looked upon thee, behold, *thy time was the time of love."*

Yes, we can truthfully say, we are not ordinary people, for the Almighty has set His gaze upon us. Our time is an ordained time of manifested love.

We are convinced of the strength of our ordination, and the reality of our importance to God, for we have beheld the awful price that Jesus had to pay to redeem us from the bondage of sin!
* He did not purchase us with silver or gold, great riches or wealth, but rather He . . .

> ". . . *gave Himself for us, that He might redeem us from all iniquity, and purify unto Himself A PECULIAR PEOPLE, zealous of good works."*
> (Titus 2:14)

191

Yes, He gave HIMSELF — an act of sacrifice so great it revealed a level of compassion that the world had never seen before . . . a love that surpasses knowledge . . . a totally selfless love!

To really experience this redemptive love automatically results in a response of deep, heartfelt gratitude, and He in turn becomes uniquely special and precious to us.

The Bible says — "unto you therefore which believe He is precious." (I Peter 2:7)

Yes, when Jesus becomes our peculiar treasure, automatically we become zealous to shew forth the praises of Him who has called us out of darkness into His marvellous light. (I Peter 2:9)

Automatically, in thankfulness, we become zealous of good works.

We begin to love what God loves.

We long to be righteous, for we have been given a new heart.

We want to do good.

We deeply desire to help others because we have been infused with the very qualities that motivate and activate our Father.

By His indwelling presence our motives have been purified, for His motives have been generated in us.

We are debtors to God and debtors to humanity.

His burden for the world has taken up residence in our hearts.

We are consumed with the zeal of the Lord's house, brimming with divine incentive and because we reflect His attitudes this way we have become all the more special in His sight.

To the world we may seem somewhat odd but the truth is that we are His, exclusively His! We have discovered that we are precious to the Almighty God Himself . . . and we just cannot refrain from acting in the extraordinary way that we do!!

Our lives have been illuminated with His purpose and our spirits have been permeated with His healing, soothing and everlasting grace.

We cannot keep this grace to ourselves!

PROMISES AND COMMITMENTS

•• In Deuteronomy 26:17-19 God reveals in even greater depth the promises and commitments available to those who partake of this portion of our covenant relationship with Him.

He declares:

> *"Thou hast avouched the Lord this day to be thy God, and to walk in His ways and to keep His statutes, and His commandments, and His judgments, and to hearken to His voice.*
>
> *And the Lord hath avouched thee this day to be HIS PECULIAR PEOPLE, as He hath promised thee, and that thou shouldest keep all His commandments,*

192

*And to make thee high above all nations
which He hath made, in praise, and in name, and
in honour . . .''*

*To **avouch** is to affirm as a matter of fact, to corroborate, to
avow . . . boldly, openly, bluntly and without shame.*

If we unashamedly avow, as a matter of fact, that Jesus is the Lord
of our lives, then surely He will unashamedly avow that we are
His . . . by lifting us high above, not only the nations, but also the negative circumstances and the principalities and powers that seek to rule over
us. We will be seated together, enthroned, in heavenly places in Jesus
Christ. We will inherit the authority, rest and dominion available in this
position.

God will honor us with fruitfulness in this world, and a notable status
in the kingdom to come. Our names will be exalted, for we will be named
with a new name, lovingly bestowed on us at the command of God.

• Supernaturally, He will release toward us the gentle wind of His sent-
forth *praise* out of the bosom of eternity, breathing God-like confidence
and blessed peace into our spirits, that heavenly touch that assures
us . . . *all is well.*

We can fully expect all of these blessings if we are numbered among
God's New Covenant peculiar people, for we are men and women "after
God's heart".

God intends to rejoice over us daily, and heap heavenly praise on
us . . . in various and wondrous ways.

Yes, this is far more than a servant-master relationship: this is an
ecstatic love-relationship that will continue to grow . . . throughout the
ages to come!

Even as the bride and the bridegroom, in the Song of Solomon,
ceaselessly and devotedly pour forth *praise* toward each other, so will
we eternally exchange loving compliments with our heavenly bridegroom.

Joyous *praise* will continually overflow out of our hearts toward
the Lord, welling up within us like an infinite fountain of life.

But somewhat more amazing is the fact that *praise* will constantly
radiate from the heart of the Creator toward every one of His beloved
sons and daughters.

Surely, this is the very thing that the bride pled for, in the Song of
Solomon, when she presented her request to the bridegroom — *"Let Him
kiss me with the kisses of His mouth, for Thy love is better than wine."*

The *kiss of His mouth* is His sent-forth Word, His living Word.
This living Word, these utterances of acceptance and *praise,* are personally given to *peculiar people* and graciously sent to the humble on
the wings of a dove.

When this happens we are compelled all the more to worship and
adore Him in return.

This is automatic, spontaneous and natural, for we are *in love.*

No wonder the bridegroom also spoke to the bride, saying — *"Thy lips, O my spouse, drop as the honeycomb: honey and milk are under thy tongue."*

This speaks of "the sweet communion" that we can have with this Lord of love and "the nourishment" that we impart to Him when He feeds on our words and rapturously discovers through them, the unveiling of the love we have for Him.

Again — the promise given declared that He will make us *"high above all nations, in praise . . . and in honour."*

Now, to praise someone is to express deep appreciation of their virtues, merits or attainments.

It is to recognize and to place a "stamp of approval" on that which is excellent in quality and superlative in nature.

God has done this for us over and over again . . . for He reconfirms His appreciation and desire for us every time He pours forth His Word and His Spirit, dropping down *praise* on us, like honey dripping from a celestial honeycomb.

This is Jesus' blessed way of showing His approval, His divine favor freely given.

•• We can be sure of the glory of our future heritage and the certainty of Jesus' abiding care for He has named "the saints that are in the earth . . . **THE EXCELLENT,** IN WHOM IS ALL MY DELIGHT." (Psalm 16:3)

• This title-word — EXCELLENT — is translated from the Hebrew word *addir* which also means *honorable.*

The New International Version of this same passage calls us His **"GLORIOUS ONES".**

The New American Standard Bible says that we are His — **"MAJESTIC ONES."**

• This clearly speaks of the fact that God's peculiar people are the most honored and blessed creatures in all of creation.

We are entitled HIS EXCELLENT simply because we are His most excellent attempt at expressing Himself and His most effectual means of unveiling the supernal splendor of His divinity and character.

No wonder He finds all of His delight in us.

We are His treasure, His prized possession . . . His infinite acquisition, His majestic ones, His glorious ones!

Now, all He asks is that we return to Him a similar kind of longing and love. We must consider Jesus to be our *excellent,* our most *treasured* possession (just as was discussed in the introductory chapter of this book).

•• But even as He is a treasure hid in a field to us, so we are a **TREASURE HID IN A FIELD** to Him.

This kingdom parable can easily be interpreted both ways. (Matthew 13:44)

As far as the Almighty is concerned, we are the one valuable thing that this world has ever produced.

We were *hidden* amid a human race that has always been at enmity with Him.

But He gave His *all* to purchase our fellowship. And He did it, not out of a sense of obligation, but "for the *joy* thereof."

Noteworthy also is the truth that the redemptive price paid bought the *field* that contained the *treasure,* for through Calvary this earth has become Jesus' acquisition as well.

Certainly, He longs for the day when He will drive out evil entirely and establish the kingdom of God here for a thousand years.

This is the glory of our future hope.

No wonder Jesus urged us, in His renowned sermon on the mount, to set our affection on heavenly things, not on earthly things, for He warned — *"where your treasure is, there will your heart be also."* (Matthew 6:21)

Of course, if this be true with respect to men, then it is also true with respect to God! God Himself could easily say — *"where My treasure is, there will My heart be also."*

• If we are *His peculiar treasure,* individually precious and uniquely special, then surely *His heart* pulsates toward us constantly!

We are now, and always will be, the center of His attention, the hinge of His eternal plan, and the blessed recipients of His lovingkindness and tender mercy.

It is no wonder Peter said we would show forth His praise, for surely we cannot hold it in our hearts.

The inspiration is too deep.

The revelation is too strong.

Therefore the response is too small, if it is contained within quietness, hidden in the dark, silent regions of the soul.

O, let us "shout with a loud voice"!

WE ARE GOD'S **PECULIAR PEOPLE . . . A SPECIAL PEOPLE** . . . HIS EXCEPTIONAL AND **PECULIAR TREASURE.**

LET US RETURN EXCELLENCY OF WORSHIP TO HIM FOR WE ARE HIS EXCELLENT (HIS HONORABLE) . . . HIS GLORIOUS, MAJESTIC ONES . . . HIS TREASURED POSSESSION!!

We can walk nobly and majestically through life even now by His grace-filled power, but ultimately it is sure that we will fully inherit the majesty and glory of His majesty, the King of kings.

In light of all this valuable truth, we are compelled to lift holy hands in adoration, and tear-filled eyes in worship, echoing Psalm 68:19.

*"Blessed be the Lord, who daily loadeth us
with **benefits**, even the God of our salvation."*

Yes — even as the nearness of the moon causes the swelling of high tide every day *(the gentle, responsive rising of ocean water)* so also the compassionate benevolence and nearness of our God has caused a daily, responsive swelling of praise in our hearts *(and a gentle, consistent, inward surge of thanksgiving every single hour).*

This is God's gift to us, as well as our gift to Him.

Therefore may we ever be careful to maintain an attitude of gratitude.

May we never forget His benefits.

May we always be distinctly different!

THE REDEEMED
OF THE LORD

THE PURCHASED
POSSESSION

THE REDEEMED

"And they shall call them, the holy people, **THE REDEEMED OF THE LORD.***"* (Isaiah 62:12)

". . . in whom also after that ye believed, ye were sealed with that Holy Spirit of promise,
Which is the earnest of our inheritance until the redemption of **THE PURCHASED POSSESSION** *unto the praise of His glory."* (Ephesians 1:13-14)

THE REDEEMED OF THE LORD
THE PURCHASED POSSESSION

"And they shall call them, the holy people,
THE REDEEMED OF THE LORD."
(Isaiah 62:12)

• *To be redeemed means — to be delivered, to be loosed away or to be set free . . . to be brought back and bought back from bondage by a purchase price.*

The children of Israel were the first to receive this meaningful *title*.

• After 400 years of bondage in Egypt, Jehovah declared to the Jews — *"I will redeem you with a stretched out arm, and with great judgments."* (Exodus 6:6)

The price paid for the redemption of Israel was the terrible destruction of the Egyptians.

God kept His promise and Abraham's seed miraculously escaped from Pharaoh, after the angel of death passed through the land of Egypt slaying the firstborn son of every Egyptian household.

Through a series of great signs and wonders, they passed through the wilderness of Sin, through the Jordan river, and then victoriously went in to possess and occupy the land of Canaan (the Land of Promise).

But, tragedy of tragedies, after receiving such a spectacular deliverance, they were eventually polluted with sin and idolatry by the heathen around them, the very nations that they were supposed to utterly destroy.

They hardened their hearts against the truth; they backslid horribly and they were sold into captivity again — carried away into Babylon.

But Isaiah prophesied of their deliverance saying — "Therefore *the redeemed of the Lord* shall return, and come with singing unto Zion, and everlasting joy shall be upon their head." (Isaiah 51:11)

The prophet foretold that Israel would come back to Jerusalem walking on the highway of holiness . . . nationally *redeemed* a second time by the mercy of Jehovah-God. (Isaiah 35:8-10)

Now it is quite clear that this same pattern of events has taken place in the church, and in many of our individual lives.

For, in a spiritual sense, God's New Covenant people as a whole came out of the bondage of Egypt (the bondage of sin) on the very day that Pentecost power first fell in the upper room.

But unfortunately again, following Israel's pattern, certain segments of the professing church have, through the centuries and from time to time, "fallen away" from a true, spiritual relationship with the God of Abraham into the "Babylonian bondage" of lifeless forms, worthless ceremonies, and unimportant doctrines often man-made.

But thank God, the Redeemer has come to our rescue again and again . . . sending heavenly visitations and anointed representatives to bring the true church out of spiritual darkness into the renewal of a real, valid and living relationship and walk with God.

How evident this is now as we witness the great surge of revival presently taking place in this world!

And what God has done for the church as a whole, He has also done for countless individuals in His body.

How many of God's chosen ones were gloriously saved and brought out of darkness, only to be swallowed up by sin again as the devil made his second claim.

• But through repentance, humility and faith, it was discovered that "in Him [in an ever-continuing way] we have redemption through His blood, the forgiveness of sins according to the riches of His grace." (Ephesians 1:7)

Yes, by experience we have come to the firm belief that the God of redemption will keep us in all of our trials and ultimately grant us an emancipation proclamation on the day of resurrection, joyously declaring us free from the tyrannical rule of the ruthless dictator called *time*.

We will march out of the valley of the shadow of death on this highway of holiness, fully redeemed, fully victorious, and fully convinced of our importance to God.

So we reemphasize, the whole idea of **redemption** is . . . *to buy back something that has been sold, lost or forfeited.*

The people of Israel willingly sold themselves into political captivity through their rebellion.

In like manner, we in times past willingly sold ourselves into spiritual captivity through our sins, but the same Lord that delivered them has proved Himself well able to deliver us also.

• The mighty God has similarly redeemed us "with a stretched out arm, and with **great judgments**" as He did with Israel of old.

For when Jesus "stretched out His arms" to be nailed to a tree **a great judgment fell on sin.** Through the death of the Messiah, God "condemned sin in the flesh". (Romans 8:3)

A great judgment fell on Satan as well, stripping him of his authority and dominion in this world, for when Christ went to Calvary He "spoiled principalities and powers [and] made a shew of them openly, triumphing over them in it." (Colossians 2:15)

The Redeemer also foretold that when the Comforter, the Spirit of truth, would come that He would reprove this world of judgment — "For the prince of this world is judged." (John 16:11)

In other words, when the Spirit moves in our hearts, He convicts us and convinces us that Satan has already been brought under judgment and that his ultimate destruction is inevitable, for it is already a forever-settled fact as far as God is concerned.

The wicked one even knows himself that his dark and dreadful destiny is irreversibly sealed and that truly — *"he hath but a short time."* (Revelation 12:12)

In light of this, we should all the more walk through this world with a confident gait and with everlasting joy upon our heads and in our hearts.

Jesus is our Saviour — we trust in Him without reservation.

We are His property.

We belong to Him now.

We know that His arm is still stretched out, but now to lovingly embrace those who call on His name.

Surely, He will watch over us with the utmost care and finish the work in us which He has so graciously started.

OLD TESTAMENT FORESHADOWINGS

• In paving the way for His salvation plan, God purposefully conditioned the minds of the Jews, well in advance, with THE CONCEPT OF REDEMPTION.

For instance, if a Jew became poverty stricken and had to sell his land, his material possessions, or sometimes even himself, his wife and his children, it became the responsibility of the "nearest of kin" *(the closest relative)* to redeem him *(to buy him, his family, or his property back)*.

• It is significant to note that the Hebrew word — *goel* — which is translated *redeemer* also means — *the nearest kinsman!*

• In fact, *goel* is translated eighteen times as *redeemer* — fourteen times as *kinsman* — and six times as *avenger!*

These three terms therefore — *redeemer, kinsman, and avenger* — are inseparably tied together in the Scripture, for they all spring from the same Hebrew word.

It is important to know that this *kinsman-redeemer,* this closest relative, was given by God the responsibility of being *the avenger of blood.*

This Old Covenant provision needs to be explained.

If any Jewish person was murdered, the next of kin was commissioned by the Law to pursue the murderer and slay him! By doing so he would succeed in avenging his slain relative, whose blood cried out of the ground for retribution.

In this manner, the demands of justice were met and the family was set free, redeemed, from the responsibility of administering the recompense that the Law prescribed for such a heinous crime.

These, and many more of the Old Testament rules and laws concerning redemption, prefigure and symbolize what Jesus came to do for us.

We were poverty-stricken, spiritually speaking. We sold out to sin and became servants to the flesh.

We had no power to *"buy ourselves back"* from the dominion of Satan. This prince of darkness had determined to make us his slaves forever — his objects of torture.

• But that's not all, for in a very real sense we were all murdered spiritually, in Adam, when he was first hit with sin's death-dealing blow.

(And certainly, far more than just righteous Abel have pled for vengeance from the blood-soaked soil of the earth).

The wretched souls of all men, soaked in the blood of guilt and misery, have cried out from the day of the fall onward . . . pleading for deliverance and redemption.

Then that which is more than miraculous and more than wonderful took place.

Jesus came to avenge us.

He left all the glory of heaven to come down into this slimepit of sin and fight our battles for us — battles that we never could have won on our own.

• JESUS REVEALED HIMSELF AS OUR **REDEEMER,** OUR **NEAREST KINSMAN** — (ONE WHO IS SO MUCH CLOSER TO US THAN ANY HUMAN BEING COULD EVER BE).

He purposefully came into this world to be "a friend that sticketh closer than a brother."

He powerfully and effectively filled the position of THE ETERNAL **AVENGER OF BLOOD!**

Everywhere He went, He was valiant in the behalf of those who had been "murdered" morally, mentally, emotionally or spiritually, victimized by the wicked one. . . . This heaven-sent Avenger was zealous and fervent about setting the captives free and healing them of their oppressions.

He found a blind man named Bartemaeus and *avenged* him, granting him the restoration of sight.

He found a man crippled for thirty-eight years, laying at the pool of Bethesda and *avenged* him saying, "take up thy bed and walk."

He found a daughter of Abraham, bound by a spirit of infirmity eighteen years, and *avenged* her saying — "Woman thou art loosed."

He found a hopelessly demon-infested man named Legion, living in a Gadarene cemetery and *avenged* him, sending the evil spirits into a herd of swine.

Finally, mysteriously, at Calvary He *avenged* us all, because through death, he destroyed him who had the power of death, the devil, and delivered them, who through fear of death, were all their lifetime subject to bondage.

He pursued our murderer, Lucifer, through this world, and possibly through the portals of darkness, to bring the judgment of recompence upon him that was meet.

How the devils must have shrieked and screamed as Jesus, with a strong arm, wrenched His redeemed out of Satan's evil, hellish grip, when He reclaimed the keys to death, hell and the grave!

Praise God! Jesus was more than successful in conquering our enemies; He was more than successful in buying us back. He was more than successful in avenging us.

He will continue to pursue Satan until he is fully repaid for his crime against humanity and cast into the lake of fire forever.

Thanks be unto God! In that day, it will be proven eternally that Jesus' death was not in vain. In fact, it will be evident that this glorious redemption never could have been accomplished any other way.

OUR DIVINELY APPOINTED SUBSTITUTE

Even as the firstborn son of every Jewish household had to be redeemed by the sacrifice of a lamb in order to be worthy of receiving his inheritance — so we too needed a *divinely appointed substitute* in death in order to receive our rightful inheritance.

• Galatians 4:4-5 states that — "when the time had fully come, God sent His Son, born of a woman, born under the law, to redeem those under the law that we might receive the adoption of sons" or as the New International Version puts it — *"that we might receive the full rights of sons."* (KJV, NIV)

And God was so desirous that we obtain our *full rights* as His blessed offspring that He was willing to give His all just to make it possible.

I Peter 1:18-19 says that we were not redeemed with silver and gold from our vain lifestyle — "But with the precious blood of Christ, as of a lamb without blemish and without spot."

He paid the ultimate price.

He went to the absolute extreme.

In Deuteronomy 28 we read of the curses that will come, in one way or the other, as a result of sin.

This *curse of the law,* this recompense of sin, includes sickness, pestilence, vexation, famine, drought, non-productive crops, turmoil in family relationships, defeat in battle, poverty, insanity, confusion, oppression, and finally destruction and death.

• But blessed be the Lord, we have the sure word that *"Christ hath redeemed us from the curse of the law being made a curse for us: for it is written, Cursed is everyone that hangeth on a tree."* (Galatians 3:13)

He took upon Himself more than just our infirmities.

He took upon Himself *"the curse".*

He was actually made *"a curse."*

In a Samson-like manner He tore down the "temple of sin" (the dominion of sin) and died in the process.

But also like Samson, He accomplished more in His death than He did in His life.

It seems certain that much more happened on Calvary than the outwardly evident, physical suffering of a crown of thorns on his brow and a Roman spear thrust into His side.

In a sense, He was crowned with all the mental misery of the human race, and His heart was pierced with all of our emotional anguish, misery and anguish that came as a direct result of sin.

He became one with our sicknesses in Pilate's Hall.

He became one with us in sorrow, sin and death.

Jesus assumed the total curse: like a sponge He miraculously absorbed it all, and conquered it, that we might go free!

• I Peter 2:24 declares that — "He bare our sins in His own body on the tree, that we, being dead to sins, should live unto righteousness; by whose stripes ye were healed."

We are overwhelmed with gratitude.

We are compelled to praise Him in ever-increasing ways as we realize the fullness of what He really did accomplish.

Our victory is secure, for mercy now reigns on the throne.

"As sin hath reigned unto death" even so, now grace is reigning through righteousness unto eternal life. (Romans 5:21)

Satan no longer has the upper hand.

Circumstances cannot rule us.

Sin can no longer have dominion over us. Sin is weak now (for — *"the strength of sin is the law"* and we are no longer under the law). (I Corinthians 15:56)

We have become intimately acquainted with the God who delights to restore.

Like the manna that came daily from above, redemption-mercy and abundant restoration-grace fall from heaven every morning to those who are sincere and real.

But we will never enjoy this new found freedom and spiritual mastery until we humbly submit to, and tenaciously cling to, our redemption-rights in Christ.

Otherwise our inheritance will only be a "hidden potential" instead of a "present possession."

•• No wonder Psalm 107:2 commands — *"Let **the redeemed of the Lord say so**, whom He **hath redeemed** from the hand of the enemy."*

We must be forthright and forceful in declaring that we are redeemed right now from the dominion of sin, sickness, poverty and death.

We have already been set free . . . yea, free indeed, for Jesus already *"hath redeemed"* us and the victory has already been won. But this God-

204

given freedom and victory will normally never fully manifest unless we dare to — *"say so"*.

We know that life and death are in the power of the tongue.

The difference between success and defeat often rests within the very words that we speak.

Jesus claimed that His words were spirit and life.

His words were full of creative power.

When He spoke, circumstance had to change.

When we speak in His name, under the true anointing, we expect the same thing to happen.

• Even when everything seems to be going under, we must be as adamant as Job, who lost everything but still cried aloud — *"I know my Redeemer liveth, and that He shall stand at the latter day upon the earth."* (Job 19:25)

W.E. Vine stresses that "upon the earth" should actually read "over my dust," while the footnote reference in the New International Version renders the possible translation "upon my grave."*[1]

Irregardless, the meaning is the same.

Job was clearly confessing in faith that even if the skin worms destroyed his body and brought him down to the grave in death, still, "at the latter day," the Redeemer-God, as a Nearest Kinsman, would "buy him back". He was boldly asserting that the heavenly Avenger of blood would yet stand over his dust, defying death in his behalf, and would, with awesome power, resurrect him into the splendorous form of a glorified son of God.

This brand of bold trust enabled Job to laugh at destruction knowing that God was on his side, so who and what could be against him. (Job 5:22)

And surely, it was such a God-pleasing attitude of resurrection faith that captured the heart of God constraining Him to come to Job's rescue.

An overflow of resurrection power spilled over into Job's circumstance, powerfully restoring him to his former glory.

Our prayers, bold confessions and utterances of faith can certainly have a similar effect, giving birth to miracles in our lives . . . if we dare to set our confidence on the finished work of Calvary, where the Avenger avenged us and the Nearest Kinsmen, now and forevermore, is — "made unto us wisdom, and righteousness, and sanctification, and *redemption."* (I Corinthians 1:30)

Such faith is well able to "buy us back" from the worst of situations.

Such truth is a constant source of hope and restoration grace for all who dare to believe.

THE COMPLETION OF OUR REDEMPTION

•• **It must be said in conclusion that our redemption is not yet complete.**

Hosea 13 unveils the fact that Jehovah will yet "ransom [us] from the power of the grave" and "redeem [us] from death" for He said — "O death, I will be thy plagues; O grave, I will be thy destruction."

Romans 8:23 states clearly that we are waiting for — **"the redemption of our body."**

• Ephesians 1:13-14 reveals how that we have been sealed with the Holy Spirit of Promise — "until the redemption of **THE PURCHASED POSSESSION,** unto the praise of His glory."

In line with this, Ephesians 4:30 warns us to "grieve not the Holy Spirit of God, whereby ye are sealed unto the day of redemption."

The day of resurrection and the day of redemption are one and the same — for only then will the redemptive work of Christ be brought to fullness of expression in us, when we emerge in His likeness — changed in a moment, in the twinkling of an eye.

Surely this day cannot be too far away — for Jesus listed certain signs that would precede His coming (in Luke 21) and He commanded us, when we see them coming to pass to — "look up for your redemption draweth nigh."

• God described far in advance, through the prophet Isaiah, the tragic yet wonderful hour in which we are now living — "For the day of vengeance is in Mine heart, and *the year of My redeemed* is come." (Isaiah 63:4)

This phrase *"the year of My redeemed"* is a direct reference to the year of Jubilee, a grand feast of redemption that took place every fifty years in Israel.

During this festive and jubilant year all redeemable persons or things, as of yet unredeemed, were instead graciously restored, brought back and loosed away from bondage . . . all over the land of Israel.

But what happened in the natural for the Jews of the Old Will is now happening in the spiritual for us on a far greater and grander New Covenant scale . . . for all over the world God's people are being supernaturally liberated and propelled, by the predestined plan of God, toward "the restitution and restoration of all things" (that latter day outpouring of the Holy Spirit that will doubtless restore God's offspring to the great depth possessed by the original New Testament church). (Matthew 17:11, Acts 3:21)

Yes, without question, though the world is rushing on in a wild frenzy of lust toward the terrible and final judgments of God, still this is our day . . . *a jubilee era of liberty, success, depth and fullness for God's people.*

• We must therefore — "walk circumspectly, not as fools, but as wise, *redeeming the time,* because the days are evil." (Ephesians 5:15-16)

In other words, out of deep gratitude and devotion we must purposefully, determinedly "buy back" all the hours that could potentially be wasted on vain earthly pursuits and invest our lives fully in the kingdom of the Almighty God, for the urgency of the hour and the great need of humanity constrains us to do so.

We also can turn wasted, meaningless portions of our lives into fruitful and useful experiences, when we cultivate this faith-filled redemptive attitude.

For through the hard places and the marred moments, we can learn in even deeper measure . . . the great worth of obedience, our utter dependency upon grace, and the absolute beauty of the merciful, compassionate character of our God.

By learning and accomplishing these things we wisely *"redeem the time"* — the past, the present and the future.

O, praise the name of God! We have received the God-given ability to take back from the wicked one the precious hours he has stolen from us.

What a miracle of salvation grace!

What a choice portion of **OUR GLORIOUS INHERITANCE!**

No wonder David penned the following inspired words:

> *"Bless the Lord, O my soul; and all that is within me, bless His holy name.*
> *Bless the Lord, O my soul, and forget not all His benefits:*
> *Who forgiveth all thine iniquities; who healeth all thy diseases;*
> *Who **redeemeth** thy life from destruction: who crowneth thee with lovingkindness and tender mercies."* (Psalm 103:1-4)

O, surely we should worship God with all of our hearts, for He manifested Himself to us right when we needed Him the most.

Leviticus 25 states that if any Israelite was negligent or slothful in redeeming certain items, the *time of redemption* could run out.

Jesus has not, and will not fail us this way.

He found us and saved us right on time (not a day early nor an hour too late).

He is presently our sufficiency, our all in all.

He will also return, in a magnificent display of celestial glory, to bring ultimate and absolute redemption at precisely the right moment.

Of course, this redemption will not only be for the people of God, for the earth in its entirety will be *"brought back"* into His possession having already been *"bought back"* at Calvary.

The creation itself will be redeemed, delivered out of the bondage of corruption into the glorious liberty of the sons of God.

"THE REDEEMED" will finally climax their journey on the highway of holiness reaching that realm where "sorrow and sighing shall flee away." (Isaiah 35:8-10)

• Then all of heaven will resound with a new song — *the song of the redeemed* — as twenty-four elders cast their crowns before His throne, and ten thousand times ten thousand lift their voices, saying . . . "Worthy is the Lamb to receive honour and glory for Thou hast *redeemed* us to God by Thy blood and hast made us unto our God, kings and priests, and we shall reign on the earth!"

Glory to God in the highest!!

We can boldly declare it now and will do so forevermore!

WE ARE THE REDEEMED OF THE LORD!!

**¹W.E. Vine, *Vine's Expository Dictionary,* under *Kinsman,* page 87, Old Testament words.*

• STEWARDS •

STEWARDS OF THE MYSTERIES OF GOD

STEWARDS OF THE SECRETS OF GOD

GOOD STEWARDS OF THE MANIFOLD GRACE OF GOD

FAITHFUL AND WISE STEWARDS

MINISTERS OF CHRIST

"Let a man so account of us, as of the MINISTERS OF CHRIST, and STEWARDS OF THE MYSTERIES OF GOD." (I Corinthians 4:1)

"As every man hath received the gift, even so minister the same one to another, as GOOD STEWARDS OF THE MANIFOLD GRACE OF GOD." (I Peter 4:10)

STEWARDS

STEWARDS OF THE MYSTERIES OF GOD

GOOD STEWARDS OF THE MANIFOLD GRACE OF GOD

FAITHFUL AND WISE STEWARDS

MINISTERS OF CHRIST

"Let a man so account of us, as of the MIN-ISTERS OF CHRIST, and STEWARDS OF THE MYSTERIES OF GOD."

(I Corinthians 4:1)

This scripture, quoted above, primarily refers to Paul and those who worked closely with him in the ministry, but in a very valid way it refers to all of God's New Covenant offspring . . . for we are all called to be **stewards.**

Normally, a **steward** is defined as . . . *an overseer, one who manages that which belongs to another man — a superintendent over another man's affairs or goods.*

We have been chosen of God, though, to manage and oversee, not just the affairs of a man, but rather, the very affairs of God — the affairs of the kingdom of heaven in the realm of time.

This is a heart-gripping thing — that God has delivered into our hands the revelation of His eternal plan, the secret of the ages, and given us the commission of promoting and publishing this good news in all the world!

•• We are so blessed . . . for it has been given unto us "to know *the mysteries* of the kingdom of God."

We know the *mystery* of the new birth — ("Except a man be born of water and of the Spirit, he cannot enter into the kingdom of God" John 3:5).

We know the *mystery* of the coming resurrection of the saints ("Behold I shew you a *mystery*; we shall not all sleep, but we shall all be changed" I Corinthians 15:51-52).

We know the *mystery* of our sonship inheritance — ("Even the *mystery* which hath been hid from ages and from generations . . . Christ in you the hope of glory" Colossians 1:26-27).

We know the *mystery* of our oneness with God — ("For this cause shall a man leave his father and mother, and shall be joined unto his wife, and they two shall be one flesh. This is a great *mystery*: but I speak

211

concerning Christ and the church" Ephesians 5:31-32).

We know the *mystery* of Jesus' divinity — ("and without controversy great is the *mystery* of godliness: God was manifest in the flesh, justified in the Spirit, seen of angels, preached unto the Gentiles, believed on in the world, received up into glory" I Timothy 3:16).

We know the *mystery* of the coming Antichrist — (and that "the *mystery* of iniquity doth already work." II Thessalonians 2:7)

We know the *mystery* of the false church — ("the great whore . . . *mystery*, Babylon the great, the mother of harlots and abominations of the earth." Revelation 17:1-18)

• And we also know the ultimate and climactic mystery — *("the mystery of His will . . .* that in the dispensation of the fulness of times He might gather together in one all things in Christ, both which are in heaven, and which are on earth; even in Him". Ephesians 1:9-10)

Now the acquisition and revelation of all this truth is at once both blessing and burden.

What a glorious, blessed and joyous privilege it is to know the *mysteries* of the kingdom of God! But at the same time . . . what a holy charge! What a sacred, burdensome, and dreadfully serious responsibility!

We are **stewards of the mysteries of God, stewards of the secrets of God** . . . and the world is our charge. We will surely be judged over the amount of zeal, fervency, sanctity and sincerity we have laid hold to in executing this sacred office. (I Corinthians 4:1 AV, NEB)

The destiny of millions is in our hands!

There are so many lost that will remain lost . . . so many sick that will remain sick . . . so many demon-possessed that will remain bound and so many blind that will remain in spiritual ignorance, if we fail to heed our call . . . and thus neglect our duties as channels of truth in this world of deception.

But we have purposed in our hearts that this will never be the case . . . in fact we cry, *"God forbid".*

The torch is in our hands . . . and we plead, *"God, keep it ablaze."*

The nations are waiting . . . and we groan, *"O, God, make them hungry to hear."*

We would rather die than fail God now . . . therefore we pray, *"Your strength Lord, Your might and Your power."*

THE PARABLE OF THE TALENTS

• Jesus let us know in **The Parable of the Talents** (Matthew 25:14-30) that we all have different degrees of responsibility and varying amounts of God-given abilities in kingdom matters (for one servant was given five talents, another two and another one).

But the servant *(the steward)* who received only one talent was expected to set about the task of multiplying his talent just as much as the servant who received five and fear was no excuse.

We are not all called to be prophets, apostles, evangelists, pastors or teachers (the five fold ministry), but we are all called to be *ministers.*

Listen to the inspired words of the apostle Peter:

• *"As every man hath received **the gift,** even so minister the same one to another, as **good stewards of the manifold grace of God.** "* (I Peter 4:10)

To minister is to serve.

The "gift" that Peter talked about is the specific grace of God uniquely applied to the life of every child of God who receives eternal life.

The grace of God is the activity of God in our lives — divinely imparted abilities (Paul said — "But by the grace of God, I am what I am" I Corinthians 15:10).

This grace is manifold (it manifests in many different ways).

This grace, once received, must be administered to others.

And "if any man *minister,* let him do it as of the ability which God giveth: that God in all things may be glorified. . . . "

Basically Peter is pointing out in this particular Scripture passage that we are all called to serve one another, and minister to the needs of the members of the body of Christ around us, according to the abilities and the grace that God has placed in our lives.

This call to service and ministry is the mark of a high calling in God and must be diligently pursued, but, O, how few ever really comprehend the importance of this call, especially if it involves that which is unpretentious.

Too often we look for great popularity-producing achievements and stunning, eye-catching, attention-getting attainments. Yet in the end, when the truth is filtered and refined to its purest and most golden state, we will discover that the elusive beauty, peace and fulfillment we seek can only be found in faithfully, humbly, and sincerely serving the needs of others.

Jesus revealed this truth explicitly when He washed the disciples' feet and commanded us to do likewise. (John 13)

This was one of the Saviour's last acts before going to the cross, and purposefully so. Surely He desired that this be, above all other memories, a lingering memory . . . and that this be, above all other lessons, a lasting lesson — lodged deep in the hearts of His disciples.

He said — *"If ye know these things, happy are ye if ye do them."*

Yes — this first "foot-washing service" was the Messiah's beautiful and humble way of exemplifying the attitude of unselfish service and ministry to others that must be the focal point of everything a true Christian does.

But the "ministry to the body of Christ" is only one aspect of our stewardship commission.

We have also all been commanded to minister to the needs of the entire world, for we have received *"the gift"* — the indwelling presence of God that automatically empowers us and enables us to reach out to humanity, in one capacity or another, to promote the kingdom of God in this world.

• We are all called to be *good stewards of the manifold grace of God,* and the beauty and enigma of this calling is the fact that God has given us this wonderful gift for the primary purpose of seeing us give it away to others.

Every manifestation of grace is vitally important to the successful functioning of the body of Christ — from the gift of helps to the gift of miracles — and it is all sent from God to ultimately return praise back to Him.

No ministry calling *(the calling to serve others)* is ever to be considered small or insignificant.

It matters little if the work be natural or supernatural, if it is done at the will of God and for His glory.

God is not glorified if we try to fill a position we are not called to fill. And we are not functioning as *good stewards* if we are unthankful and dissatisfied concerning our own calling, or if we try to be someone else, imitating his or her gift.

We each have our own individual portion of the Word to fulfill and unveil, and our own individual manifestation of God's Spirit to bring forth.

• We are following Jesus, who came for the purpose of giving away that which the Father had given to Him.

In John 17, He said — "Father . . . I have given unto them [My disciples] the words which thou gavest Me."

Jesus did not preach Abraham's vision, Moses' revelation, or Joshua's message (though of course He was the One who gave that vision, revelation and message to them).

Jesus had his own specific revelation to promote. He had a unique inspired message that was ordained for that precise moment in time, so powerful that it would bring to birth the dawning of a new age (the Age of Grace).

In like manner, we are called not just to echo the messages of other men and celebrate their great accomplishments in God.

We must find our own message, the particular way that God would desire to express the gospel through us, and our own particular anointing.

We must be true to the gift and calling God has given us, and do all that we can, with all of our might, while there is yet time!

We must live lives of much fasting and much prayer, lives of total consecration, in order to be sensitive to the leading of the Holy Spirit, and in order to fully blossom in *the gift* God has created us to be.

The more we "hide away" in God, the more effective we become.

Why bring forth just thirty-fold or sixty-fold when a life of complete submission and obedience would cause us to bring forth an hundred-fold? (Matthew 13:23)

This is our only reason for living!

This is what God expects of us!

This is stewardship of the Word, of the Spirit, and of our own individual anointing from God!

RELINQUISHING THE REINS OF AUTHORITY

• It is certain, that if we have surrendered our lives to the Lord, not only are we *stewards* over the things of God, but now, all that we have and all that we are belongs to Him.

For instance, if we are *stewards* . . . our time is not our own anymore to be filled with whatever activities we choose (and O, how often this precious commodity is thoughtlessly wasted on frivolous, unimportant things).

Our material possessions are no longer ours; they belong to Jesus to be kept, used or given away as He wills.

Our money is not our own anymore — we are like individual banks in which the Almighty God keeps an account. He can deposit or withdraw any amount He chooses, anytime He chooses.

Our businesses are His, to be used as He leads (we are workers together — partners).

Our future is not our own anymore — to be used as we see fit. The choices we make with respect to our careers, our marriages, and our goals in life must all be brought into perfect harmony with His divine purpose in us.

This is the foundation of true stewardship, and this is far more inclusive than many Christians would like to believe.

Jesus said — "Not everyone that saith unto Me, Lord, Lord, shall enter into the kingdom of heaven; but he that doeth the will of My Father." (Matthew 7:21)

We are expected to totally relinquish the reins of authority over all of these areas in our lives if we are to be true disciples of Christ, faithful stewards.

Any thing or any area not relinquished to God becomes an idol — and the first commandment in God's list of ten demands that we have no other gods before Him. (And it must be said that if we fail to purge the idols from our lives, God will often do it for us. If we fail to judge ourselves, we are judged and chastened of the Lord — and our idols topple — that we should not be condemned with the world.)

We must take the initiative!

215

We must undergird our lives with self-discipline.

Our voices now belong to Him, as well as our hearing, our sight, our minds, our emotions and our very souls.

Our hearts, our spirits, have now become His property.

Our bodies are His purchased possession and dwelling place, for we are the temple of God, little children.

We have received a charge from heaven as *good stewards* to keep all of these (our voices, our hearts, our bodies, etc.) sanctified and clean before the Lord so that He might have a suitable channel through which to move.

We are overseeing what now exclusively belongs to Him!!

*   *   *   *   *   *

Paul said — "Whatsoever things are true . . . honest . . . just . . . pure . . . lovely . . . of good report; if there be any virtue, and if there be any praise, think on these things." (Philippians 4:8)

When we learn to stay our minds in this manner on the Lord, the mind of Christ in us gains dominion and we become channels of His revelation-wisdom and knowledge.

This is no small achievement; it is a lifelong struggle, and a continual spiritual warfare. Every true steward-believer must forcefully, and at times even violently, pull down the strongholds *(the established, negative, carnal attitudes)* that Satan erects in the carnal mind.

We are commanded to cast down imaginations, and every high thing that exalts itself against the knowledge of God — "bringing into captivity every thought to the obedience of Christ." (II Corinthians 10:5)

This is stewardship of the mind.

*   *   *   *   *   *

Each one of us also has the responsibility as a *steward* to also keep our heart with all diligence — *"for out of it are the issues of life."* (Proverbs 4:23)

These "issues of life" are the manifestations of the Spirit of God, such as the supernatural gifts (healing, prophecy, tongues, etc. — I Corinthians 12) and the fruit of the Spirit (love, joy, peace, etc. — Galatians 5).

Every Spirit-filled child of God has the potential of manifesting these fruits and gifts, but this nature of God, these attributes of God, can only be correctly manifested out of pure channels.

Therefore, we must diligently — "cleanse ourselves from all filthiness of the **flesh** and **spirit,** perfecting holiness in the fear of God." (II Corinthians 7:1)

Our emotions must be brought under control.

Righteousness must become our passion, the foundation of all our

216

relationships and all our endeavors in life. Evil habits and sins must be conquered. Love must reign supreme in us.

Paul said — "know ye not that your body is the temple of the Holy Ghost . . . which ye have of God, and ye are not your own? For ye are bought with a price: therefore **glorify God** in your **body,** and in your **spirit,** which are God's." (I Corinthians 6:19-20)

This is stewardship of the body, the soul, and the spirit.

THE REQUIREMENT OF FAITHFULNESS

Believers must successfully prove themselves as *good stewards* of the body, mind, soul and spirit before they can receive deeper responsibilities in the kingdom of God.

•• No wonder the Bible declared that — *"It is required in stewards that a man be found faithful."* (I Corinthians 4:2)

• *To be faithful is to be constant, trustworthy and fully dependable — unswerving in commitment to a certain person, ideal or charge.*

God is continually testing us to find the level of constant devotion present in our spirits . . . the more faithfulness He finds, the more responsibility and authority in kingdom matters He gives!

God tested Moses during forty years of exile from Egypt before he ever returned to be the great deliverer that he was to the Jews.

God tested David with protecting a little flock of sheep from devouring beasts, then with Goliath, and then with the mistreatment he received from Saul, before he was ever exalted to the throne.

God tested the actions and reactions of the patriarch Joseph over and over again before he came into his full anointing and reigned over all the Egyptian empire as Pharaoh's national prime minister, his chief steward.

God tested Joseph with . . .

. . . the terrible treatment he received from his brothers who sold him into slavery.

. . . the humiliation of being a servant to the captain of the guard of Egypt.

. . . the adulterous advances of the captain's wife.

. . . the false accusations he received and his subsequent imprisonment.

In all these things and more, God was testing Joseph to see if he would *still be faithful* when situations seemed unfair and *still be faithful* when God seemed unmindful of his sacrifice. God wanted to see if his man would *still be faithful* when there was no glory, no earthly recognition and seemingly no reward from heaven.

If he was constant in his commitment when there was no glory (and he was — even in the lowest dungeon) God knew that he could be trusted when there would be an exceeding amount of glory!

Wherever God placed him — with his brethren, in the captain's home, in the dungeon, or with Pharaoh, **he was always placed in the position of a steward.**

This was his gift.

•• **The Bible declared that the Word of the Lord tried Joseph until the time of his word came!** (Psalm 105:19)

Now, centuries later, we can say with total certitude that — as it was with Joseph, so will it be with every son of God.

• This proving process is not an option.

This stage of testing and trying is required for everyone destined to be used as *a steward of the anointing.*

• For the wisdom of God has plainly revealed — "he that is *faithful* in that which is least is *faithful* also in much: and he that is unjust in the least is unjust also in much." (Luke 16:10)

If God has given us a gift, a talent, we must not hide it or neglect it or even take it for granted, but we must minister it to others in whatever capacity God has placed us in, and thus multiply it in the lives of others.

It matters little if our unique, individual gift may not seem as important or possibly as spectacular as someone else's.

We must still be absolutely dedicated to the calling and the gift God has placed in our lives.

This calling may be over natural things or even money matters in a church work, or it may be a supportive position in another person's ministry.

• But all of these callings are still of great importance for Jesus said "If therefore ye have not been *faithful* in the unrighteous mammon [material riches] who will commit to your trust the true riches. And if ye have not been *faithful* in that which is another man's, who shall give you that which is your own?"

• Any sincere Christian deeply desires the *true riches* of a valid ministry, a lasting and fruitful work for God, and we have discovered that faithfulness is the key.

We know that Elisha never would have come into his double-portion anointing had he not faithfully ministered to Elijah's needs for ten years.

And Joshua surely would have never been commissioned to lead Israel into the Promised Land, had he not faithfully stood with Moses forty years.

We must purpose in our hearts to be *"faithful unto death"* in following God's purpose for our lives . . . that we might receive that ultimate *crown of life* . . . . that perfected calling that the Lord would have us to possess in this present world. (Revelation 2:10)

THE ULTIMATE OUTCOME

In conclusion, it must be emphasized that every step in our walk with God is vitally important.

We are not just dealing with the needs of the present moment; we are determining and creating our future . . . in this life and the life to come!

Everything we do is a preparation for tomorrow and a preparation for that blessed dawning of the eternal day, when we will hear those long-sought-after words from the lips of the Lord of love:

> *"Well done, **good and faithful servant;** thou hast been faithful over a few things, **I will make thee ruler over many things:** enter thou into the joy of thy Lord."*　　　　(Matthew 25:23)

It is certain that one day we must give account of our stewardship in the realm of time.

On that day, **THE FAITHFUL AND WISE STEWARD** will be made to rule over all that God has. (Luke 12:42-48)

We will apparently be, forever and ever, **STEWARDS** of the entire universe, both natural and celestial.

We will infinitely be **"THE MINISTERS OF CHRIST"** . . . *administering* His will throughout creation and *ministering* to God fully in utter worship, filling His heart to the brim.

This is the infinite treasure, *the true riches,* that Jesus promised to impart. This is the glory of our calling, and the end result of our obedience, faithfulness and submission.

This is the stewardship of eternal life!!!

• HIS WORKMANSHIP •

HIS HANDIWORK

HIS WORK OF ART

"For we are HIS WORKMAN-SHIP, created in Christ Jesus unto good works, which God hath before ordained that we should walk in them."

(Ephesians 2:10)

HIS WORKMANSHIP
HIS HANDIWORK
HIS WORK OF ART

"For we are HIS WORKMANSHIP, created in Christ Jesus unto good works, which God hath before ordained that we should walk in them."　　　　　　　(Ephesians 2:10)

Everything else in creation was mass-produced with assembly-line speed and precision . . . brought into being suddenly by the quick and powerful spoken word.

A seemingly boundless, limitless universe, filled with swirling galaxies of magnificent size and overwhelming grandeur, was just birthed into existence, instantly . . . at the sound of His voice.

But then, in His curious way . . . the Master Craftsman of all the ages abruptly stopped the lightning-fast chain of events, in order to walk into a garden called Eden and set about the task of slowly and carefully molding and shaping that first man Adam . . . focusing greater attention than ever on the most intricate details of his makeup.

As always, He made each one of those details a *universe* in itself.

Lovingly, thoughtfully and patiently — "The Lord God formed man of the dust of the ground" and then "breathed into his nostrils the breath of life."

That was the Word, the pre-incarnate Christ, creatively shaping something beautiful out of that which was quite the opposite.

The Architect of the universe, expert in geometrical design and rigid mathematical balance, now becomes both Artist and Sculptor, apparently reaching for the aesthetic more than ever before.

The God of perfect intellect, being the epitome of rational, intelligent thought, now, in a certain sense, sets His intellectual prowess slightly to the side and allows His emotions the place of prominence.

The Lord God is quite involved in a personal way now, for the perfection and formation of the man is to be the central purpose of His plan and the greatest single event in the beginning of the drama of creation.

Both unfathomable love and unspeakable joy now find free rein of expression, as the nimble yet gentle fingers of the Almighty expertly yet tenderly form that which is destined to come forth in His image.

Surely God must have worked for hours on that first human frame, extremely involved in the most minute particulars.

But in like manner — surely this same heavenly Sculptor has been working for centuries, yes, even millenniums, shaping the spirit-nature of those who are chosen to inherit eternal life.

He constantly chisels away the unwanted, carnal attitudes that keep us from emerging in His likeness, for He sees an image in the stone.

He daily carves His character into our spirits and colors our lives with His sent-forth grace and with such great finesse.

He decorates the inner man, in each one of us, with sudden surges of heavenly joy as He lovingly paints our hearts inwardly with coat after coat of revelation knowledge.

He continually overshadows us with a rainbow display of His promises . . . promises that are compassionately given to make our lives far more beautiful and preserve us as we journey toward our heavenly home.

We know that our God has planted within us the potential of producing the same kind of *good works* that Jesus performed when He walked in the world.

In fact, there are certain *ordained works* waiting to be born within us at an appointed time according to His everlasting design.

These works must come to pass, for though they are yet unseen, they have already been conceived in the mind of God and laid out in His eternal blueprint plan for our lives.

• Again we affirm . . . the mighty Jehovah has predestined that we be — **"His workmanship,** created in Christ Jesus unto **good works,** which God hath before ordained that we should walk in . . ."** (Ephesians 2:10)

The New English Bible, in translating this same passage, declares that — "we are **His handiwork."**

But the Jerusalem Bible goes one step further, reaching yet a higher plane of descriptiveness, by proclaiming that — "we are **God's work of art."**

Just think what that kind of statement really means.

A work of art is defined as being a painting or sculpture of the highest artistic quality, or something that gives great aesthetic pleasure to the beholder or the auditor (he that sees or he that hears).

Of course, something *aesthetic* is something that appeals to the senses, or the heart, as being artistically beautiful.

Right now, we may not think that we fit this description.

We may feel like just a roughly hewn block of marble, or possibly a canvas covered with only uneven splotches of paint, but we must realize that the masterful work of deity is not yet complete.

"He hath made everything beautiful in His time." (Eccl. 3:11)

We are still in a comparatively inferior stage of development . . . yet, every day, we are getting a little closer to becoming *the eternal and sculpturesque masterpiece* that God envisioned in the foundation of all things.

• We know that — "the heavens declare the glory of the Lord" — but we show *His handiwork,* for we are, of all created things, the greatest example of *His handiwork.*

• We were handcrafted out of mere dust, in Adam, in the garden of Eden, therefore we will ultimately reveal God's expertise in creating that which is lovely, choice, exquisite and even elegant, out of that which is base, lowly and even disgustingly unclean.

We are the prime example of His extraordinary skill, for in that final masterstroke of creative genius we will be resurrected fully in His likeness and lifted up in transcendent excellence to reign with Him forever.

Reaching that final goal eternally is of absolute importance therefore every step of our journey that direction is also of absolute and equal importance.

• Having full understanding of this fact, God has purposed to involve Himself in all the complex intricacies of our lives, considering every event and decision crucial in nature and worthy of close attention.

In an attempt to unveil this sublime truth the Psalmist David wrote:

> *"O Lord, Thou hast searched me, and known me.*
> *Thou knowest my downsitting and mine uprising, Thou understandest my thought afar off.*
> *Thou compassest my path and my lying down, and art acquainted with all my ways.*
> *For there is not a word in my tongue, but, lo, O Lord, Thou knowest it altogether.*
> *Thou hast beset me behind and before, and laid thine hand upon me.*
> *Such knowledge is too wonderful for me; it is high, I cannot attain unto it.*
> *Whither shall I go from Thy Spirit? or whither shall I flee from Thy presence?*
> *If I ascend up into heaven, Thou art there: if I make my bed in hell, behold, Thou art there.*
> *. . . For Thou hast possessed my reins: Thou hast covered me in my mother's womb.*
> *I will praise Thee; for I am fearfully and wonderfully made: marvellous are Thy works; and that my soul knoweth right well.*
> *My substance was not hid from Thee, when*

> *I was made in secret, and curiously wrought in the lowest parts of the earth.*
>
> *Thine eyes did see my substance, yet being unperfect; and in Thy book all my members were written, which in continuance were fashioned, when as yet there was none of them.*
>
> *How precious also are Thy thoughts unto me, O God! how great is the sum of them!*
>
> *If I should count them, they are more in number than the sand: when I awake, I am still with Thee."*   (Psalm 139, excerpts)

Yes, we are God's handiwork!

The Psalmist David enhanced this revelation well, yet because of his writing we are compelled to ask a certain question and come to a certain conclusion.

If God so carefully watched over each one of us, when we were nothing but a partially developed fetus in the womb of an expectant mother, then how much more will He watch over us now . . . for we are at a far more important stage of development.

The Bible commands us to awaken ourselves out of the deep sleep of spiritual ignorance and recognize the greatness and the awesomeness of God's eternal purpose in us.

Paul said — *"be ye not unwise, but understanding what the will of the Lord is."* (Ephesians 5:17)

He also commanded — *"work out your own salvation with fear and trembling. For it is God which worketh in you both to will and to do of His good pleasure."* (Philippians 2:12-13)

God's deep desire toward us is that *the good pleasure of His will* take up its abode in us, and thereby recreate, transform and beautify our lives, propelling us toward that predetermined goal of fully blossoming in infinite sonship and heirship.

• We must realize that as we journey this direction we have a source of strength, perseverance and victory far greater than mere human will.

Divine will power now resides in our hearts.

That is exactly why, when we feel like quitting, there is something within us that just won't let us quit.

• The Phillips Modern English translation of the same passage says — *"It is God at work within you, giving you the will and the power to achieve His purpose."*

When Jeremiah wanted to draw back from His calling, because of the way the Israelites rejected his prophecies, God would not let him do so.

• Daily he was mocked and brought to reproach until finally he said, concerning the Lord — "I will not make mention of Him, nor speak any more in His name. But His Word was in mine heart as a burning fire shut up in my bones, and I was weary with forbearing, and I could not stay." (Jeremiah 20:9)

Jeremiah just could not quit, and neither can we, for it is God at work in us . . . molding our attitudes and shaping our character.

THE AUTHOR AND FINISHER

Jesus is continually improving, upgrading and refining His artistry . . . touching up the rough places and perfecting the finer details.

We are not self-made men and women.

We are being handcrafted by the Creator Himself to ultimately assume an eminent position of regal authority in the universe.

Our God is big enough and mighty enough to take us all the way there! If He began this work in us, then He will certainly finish it!

He is the Author and the Finisher of our faith.

• The Revised Standard Version says that He is — *"the Pioneer and Perfector of our faith."* (Hebrews 12:2)

A pioneer can be defined as a person who originates or opens up a new line of thought, or some new method of activity. It can also mean: the first person to settle in a certain territory as of yet uninhabited.

Surely both of these are fit, worthy and suitable descriptions of our Saviour concerning His dealings with us.

He was the first to really fully *pioneer* the faith walk, and by doing so, He definitely opened up for us a new way of thought, a revolutionary approach to life. Then He came and *settled,* so to speak, in the wilderness territory of our unregenerate hearts, territory that was overgrown with negative, carnal attitudes.

He cleared out the underbrush. He plowed deep with His Word.

He planted faith in our spirits.

He has since cultivated it on a daily basis.

He will bring it to perfection, for it was His determination to begin with.

He constantly challenges us inwardly to be *pioneers* also, to forge ahead into spiritual territory as of yet undiscovered, and He challenges us also to always bring our works to perfection and completion.

• We are called to be *authors and finishers,* like the Captain of our salvation, not quitters and defeated persons, givng up halfway through.

We have been begotten of the very will and spirit to persist.

This is the personality of deity compelling us to yield to its inner influence.

As authors, emerging in the likeness of the Lord, we are also filled with His creativity.

227

As we mature in Him, we become more daring about releasing this creative spirit into the activities of life that we pursue in the name of Jesus.

This is God's workmanship, not only in us, but finding a medium of expression through us.

First, He authored a faith-temperament in us, by writing circumstances into our lives that would compel us to reach for, and manifest, a believing spirit (believing in His promises and His power).

Then, He passed the pen into our hands and commanded us to perpetuate the work, and write faith in the lives of others.

This is apparently His normal way of doing things.

• When Nehemiah had determined to rebuild the walls of Jerusalem, an enemy envoy named Sanballat tried to dissuade him from persevering in His cause.

But Nehemiah, refusing to hearken, protested to the heathen — *"I am doing a great work, so that I cannot come down."* (Nehemiah 6:3)

Here we see the Author and the Finisher of faith at work in Nehemiah.

Notice that this great man of God, this anointed wall-builder, did not say — *"I won't come down"* — (which would mean *"I will not to come down")*. He rather said, *"I cannot come down."*

We can read between the lines.

In so many words, He was announcing — "O, I might come down if I did what my flesh wants, but I can't. For there is a greater power than my own human will gripping me, motivating me, and compelling me to stay on this wall and build, even when the odds seem to be against me. It is God at work in me, compelling me to stand against all opposition."

God authored unshakeable faith in Nehemiah (an act of divine craftsmanship) and then he in turn brought forth that same craftsmanship in those subordinate to him. He received from God, and developed in others, the kind of spirit that refuses to quit until the job is done.

That's the kind of picture God loves to paint . . . a *work of art* that reflects His own character . . . a kind of spiritual self-portrait.

SHARING IN GOD'S CREATIVITY

It is also a true saying that God's great joy and fulfillment is imparting His abilities to those who believe in Him and yield to His influence.

• After Jehovah gave detailed directions to Moses, concerning the construction of the tabernacle in the wilderness, God also appointed a man, a divinely anointed artificer, who could effectually fulfill His commands.

He said to Moses — "See, I have called by name *Bezaleel* . . . and I have filled him with the spirit of God, in wisdom, and in understanding, and in knowledge, and in all manner of *workmanship,* to devise cunning works, to work in gold, and in silver, and in brass . . ." (Exodus 31:2-4)

God also said that He put it in Bezaleel's heart to be an engraver, an embroiderer, a weaver, a cunning workman and a teacher of others. (Exodus 35)

• The tabernacle in the wilderness had to be more than a nicely constructed shelter for the ark of the covenant . . . it had to be *a work of art,* for it was ordained to be God's dwelling place for a season.

And without a doubt, it was the Spirit of God in Bezaleel that imparted artistic abilities to Him so that He could effectually participate in God's purpose.

• It was the anointing of God engraving, weaving, carving, molding, embroidering and devising cunning works, through Bezaleel's surrendered spirit and through his yielded hands.

It was the anointing of God also in Bezaleel that enabled him to transfer his wisdom to others.

• It is significant to note that the name *Bezaleel* means . . . *under the shadow of God.*

Surely, Bezaleel was under the shadow of the Almighty from the very womb of his mother, protected, elected and set aside for an ordained work of God yet to be accomplished.

Are we not all even as he, for we have also been filled with the Spirit of the living God?

God expresses His divine life in us and through us.

We are *His workmanship,* but we are also His cunning workmen, artistically engraving, carving, and sculpting the nature of the Word into the hearts of men, and curiously weaving and embroidering their hearts and their lives with His promises and His love.

• We are working towards the completion of a far more important **work of art** than Bezaleel — for we are preparing, not a temporary, but rather an infinite dwelling place suitable for God to inhabit.

We have been under *"the shadow of the Almighty"* all of our lives, under His creative influence — protected, elected, reserved, and set aside for this divine purpose.

Therefore, we can claim no glory for ourselves, for it is undoubtedly the presence of God within us imparting such creative talent and artistic spiritual abilities . . . overflowing into our words, our prayers, and especially into the love that pours out of our hearts to a hurting human race . . . painting a picture of hope where there was nothing but a dark and foreboding backdrop of dread despair and debilitating fear.

THE NEXT VERSE IN GOD'S POEM

Finally . . . it is quite interesting to note that the word *workmanship* was translated from the Greek word — *poiema.*

It is from this very Greek word, that we get our English word — *poem.*

We know that a poem is a composition in verse . . . creative writing that makes a grand departure from the norm, exploring the depth of beauty in words, and lifting them to a higher sphere of expression.

Poetry is birthed into the world through sensitivity and then married to emotion . . . it is the *deep calling unto the deep,* from bosom to bosom.

The poet is the pioneer of concepts who passionately reaches for the sublime.

He gropes through unexplored regions of thought to discover, and then effectually communicate, ideas of lofty and elevated quality.

He then joyously celebrates his discovery in intricately involved patterns of sound and rhythm *(beauty of expression).*

It is a true saying that any artistry of this kind of transcendent excellence can be spoken of as being poetical.

Therefore we conclude that the whole drama of redemption is highly poetical in nature.

The prophets for centuries sang their inspired song of the miraculous formation and final exaltation of the bride of Christ to her **GLORIOUS ETERNAL INHERITANCE.**

Then Jesus *(the pioneer of heavenly concepts)* joyously celebrated His everlasting wisdom by transferring His lofty and elevated ideas into our hearts through the use of parables *(highly poetical works of art, abounding in imagery and immersed in figurative speech).*

•   As we read and believe Jesus' poetical works, we become the next verse in His poem.

His living Word enters into us . . . and begins to sculpt the design of deity into our thoughts, our emotions and our actions . . . every single day.

This is the miracle of reconciliation and the beauty of salvation.

We are so thankful, for we have received the revelation of our position, rank and importance in God's great universal plan.

We have been given the absolute assurance.

WE ARE GOD'S WORKMANSHIP!

WE ARE GOD'S WORK OF ART!

We are His poem, His song, His melody in verse.

We are delightful declarations of the aesthetic side of God's personality.

We are the end result of God's most lofty attempt at vividly disclosing His true self.

We are His joy in creativity, the unveiling of His character, and the pulsation and revelation of His heart.

Any true artist literally pours himself into that which He creates.

He never ceases in His attempt to reach deeper into His own inner being . . . in order to more effectively express Himself in ever-increasing ways.

Has not the God of infinite poetical beauty done this very thing!

Has He not literally poured Himself into us!

Has He not breathed His very life and being into our spirits!

Are we not elected of God to display His creative genius in a measure that will eventually exceed and surpass all other expressions of divinity in the universe . . . animate and inanimate!

• Will not **the good works,** which God has ordained us to walk in, continue on eternally . . . ever expanding in importance and depth, passing ultimately from the lowest terrestrial plane to the highest celestial sphere!

Are we not, in a spiritual sense, ordained to be His authors, His artists, His sculptors, His composers and His cunning artificers . . . for all eternity!

Do we not become pleasant channels of His creativity even now every time we lift our hands to worship or lift our voices to proclaim the glory of His name! And can we not in much gratitude make every day a work of art — filled with His presence and offered to Him in worship?

This is our privilege, our choice opportunity, and one of the most important goals toward which our hearts should ever be fixed.

WONDERFULLY HIS

At this point truly all of our descriptive language is nearly exhausted . . . for what we see simply defies description.

But as our spirits soar on the wings of adoration, we come to rest on the very peak of God's everlasting book of inspired songs (Psalm 150).

We echo again words that once rang like the music of chimes in Solomon's temple, words that were dripping wet with the Shekinah glory of God's presence, words that are now as forever settled in the heaven as the Lord of glory Himself. . . .

> *"Praise ye the Lord. Praise God in His sanctuary: praise Him in the firmament of His power.*
> *Praise Him for His mighty acts: praise Him according to His excellent greatness.*
> *Praise Him with the sound of the trumpet: praise Him with the psaltery and harp.*

231

Praise Him with the timbrel and dance: praise
Him with the stringed instruments and organs.
Praise Him upon the loud cymbals: praise
Him upon the high sounding cymbals.
LET EVERY THING THAT HATH
BREATH PRAISE THE LORD . . ."

(Psalm 150:1-6)

Yes . . . let everything that has natural life and natural breath praise the name of the Lord.

But even more so . . . let those who have been filled with the very breath of God praise His name from this time forth and forevermore!

For we are chosen for inspiration and revelation.

We are His workmanship.

We are His handiwork.

We are His work of art,

But even more so . . .

We are His . . . simply and wonderfully His.

BIBLIOGRAPHY

The following are some of the Bible translation books used:

King James Authorized Version (AV or KJV)
Phillips Modern English (PME)
Revised Standard Version (RSV)
New International Version (NIV)
New English Bible (NEB)
The Living Bible (LB)
New American Standard (NAS)
Today's English Version (TEV)
Amplified Bible (AMP)

Other Reference Books:
Unger, Merrill F. *Unger's Bible Dictionary* (UBD). 1957, 1966. The Moody Bible Institute. Chicago, Illinois.

Vine, W.E. *Vine's Expository Dictionary* (VED). 1984. Bethany House. Minneapolis, Minnesota.

Young, G. Douglas. *Young's Concordance* (YC). 1984. Tyndale House Publishers. Wheaton, Illinois.

Strong, James. *Strong's Concordance* (SC). 1984. Thomas Nelson Publishers. Nashville, Tennessee.

Dake, Finis. *Dake's Annotated Reference Bible* (DARB). 1979. Dake Bible Sales. Lawrenceville, Georgia.

Our Glorious Inheritance Series

LIST OF AVAILABLE TAPES

OUR GLORIOUS INHERITANCE TAPE SERIES

On the following cassette tapes, Evangelist Mike Shreve preaches and teaches on various *titles* contained in this eight-volume series. You will be doubly blessed, and ministered to, by hearing these valuable revelations brought forth under the anointing in the exciting atmosphere of live crusade services. (Packages are listed according to the volume of *Our Glorious Inheritance* in which the different *titles* appear).

OGI-VI-T1   Volume One/Tape Package One...20.00
The Apple of His Eye, Believers, The Beloved, The Children of Abraham, His Dove, and The Elect of God

OGI-VI-T2   Volume One/Tape Package Two..20.00
Heirs of God, Kings, Oracles of God, The Pearl of Great Price, The Redeemed of the Lord, and Stewards of the Mysteries of God

OGI-V2-T1   Volume Two/Tape Package One.......................................20.00
Ambassadors, Branches, The Bride of Christ, Citizens of Heaven, Disciples, and An Holy Nation

OGI-V2-T2   Volume Two/Tape Package Two.......................................20.00
Israel, The Lily Among Thorns, More than Conquerors, Partakers, Servants to God, and Vessels of Mercy

OGI-V3-T1   Volume Three/Tape Package One....................................20.00
The Anointed of the Lord, The Blessed, Good Ground, Good Seed, Good Soldiers, and The Just

OGI-V3-T2   Volume Three/Tape Package Two....................................15.00
Peacemakers, The Poor in Spirit, and The Pure in Heart

OGI-V4-T1   Volume Four/Tape Package One......................................20.00
Adopted Sons, The Children of Light, Converts, The Faithful, The Great and the Strong, and Lion of God

OGI-V4-T2   Volume Four/Tape Package Two......................................20.00
One Bread, Pillars, Saints, Watchmen

We will replace any defective tape within 30 days of purchase.

DELIVERANCE FROM THE OCCULT

The Testimony of *Mike Shreve*

Mike Shreve studied under an Indian guru and taught Kundalini Yoga and Meditation at five Florida universities until his conversion to Christianity in the fall of 1970. This tape of his deliverance will instruct you concerning the dangerous deception of the **New Age Movement** that is presently sweeping our world.
Order # PE-1 $5.95

ORDER FORM

ITEM	QUANTITY	PRICE	TOTAL

SHIPPING AND HANDLING CHARGES		
ORDER TO $10.00	ADD $1.00
ORDER $10.00 - $25.00	ADD $2.00
ORDER $25.00 - $50.00	ADD $3.00
ORDER OVER $50.00	ADD 7%

Subtotal
Shipping
Total

Florida residents add 6% sales tax

☐ PLEASE SEND A LIST OF ALL TAPES AND BOOKS

NAME _____

ADDRESS _____

CITY, STATE, ZIP _____

DEEPER REVELATION BOOKS 2427 FIFESHIRE DR., WINTER PARK, FL. 32792